"THE LOST CITY OF GOLD"

From the Presidential files

A DREW WELLS ADVENTURE

By: C. T. Dowling

Copyright © 2018
Clyde Dowling

All rights reserved. No part of this book may be reproduced in any form, except for the inclusion of brief quotations in a review, without permission in writing from the author or publisher.

This is a work of fiction. Names, characters, places, and incidents are either the product of the author's imagination or are used fictitiously and any resemblance to actual persons, living or dead, businesses, companies, events, or locales is entirely coincidental.

ISBN: 978-0-692-13587-7

Printed in the United States by Morris Publishing®
3212 East Highway 30
Kearney, NE 68847
1-800-650-7888

Acknowledgements

Ms. Patty Patrick
My heartfelt thanks to the person who dotted all the I's and crossed all the T's. Without her help and encouragement Bo and Drew would still be only in my twisted mind.
Thank you Patty!

Ms. K. Holland
My tenth grade English teacher. Without her I would never have understood the beauty of our language. You wouldn't let me get away with anything!
Thanks and God bless

Mr. A. Furlong
A friend who forced me to pull the manuscript together and dragged me to the publisher kicking and screaming.
An Agent in mind and spirit.
Thanks

Prologue

Baghdad, Iraq
April 7, 2003

The sound of small arms fire still echoed in the streets as the two men crept carefully down the empty alleyway. Both were dressed from head to toe in black. To anyone who came upon them they would have appeared as Ninja warriors made popular in the movies.

But these men were not Oriental, they were Shiite Muslim. The taller man was named Ahmad and was from Damascus, Syria. The shorter wiry man was an Iranian citizen and answered to the name Mash'al. The two of them had worked together for many years and were quite good at what they did. This mission was a tricky one, but one they were skilled in performing. Tonight they would break into and rob the Baghdad Museum. The impressive building loomed up before them like a ghoulish mausoleum in the night as they ascended the stairs.

The last remnants of the Republican Guard were still holding out, but it was only a matter of time. Their fate was in the hands of the United States 3rd Army Brigade that was slowly crushing all resistance in the war torn city.

Climbing the stairs, they cautiously stayed within the shadows of the tall columns. Approaching the front door, they hesitated wondering if by chance, it could be unlocked, but a quick check told them the door was locked. Reaching in a bag slung over his shoulder, Ahmad removed several small explosives and skillfully placed them around the frame of the steel door.

Satisfied with his work, he stepped back and motioned to his partner to find cover. Hiding behind one of the tall gothic columns, they waited. In a matter of seconds, an explosion blew the door off its hinges with a resounding boom.

The two men scurried into the entrance and raced across the open area. On exhibit around the huge room were many display cases containing numerous valuable artifacts of gold and silver. However, they were not here to plunder, they were on a mission to steal one solitary object. While they were the first to enter, they would not be the last. Over the next week as the American Army stood by, hundreds, if not thousands of petty thieves would enter and exit the museum carrying out irreplaceable objects from the history of the Persian Empire. Ignoring the objects around them, the two men proceeded to the massive staircase at the rear of the room.

Reaching the stairs, they covered them two at a time as they descended into the bowels of the stately building. Reaching the bottom, they hurried along the passage as the tall man referred to a map ensuring he was in the right place. Rounding a corner, he stopped and counted doors that appeared along a wall.

Reaching the fifth one, he again removed some of the explosive from his pack and duplicated his effort of the main door, but with a smaller amount. As before, the men moved away and waited until the explosion shattered the frame. Pulling the remaining fragments of the oak door aside, they stepped into the private sanctuary.

Shining a flashlight along the wall, they stepped over and around objects in their way. Finally, the temptation was too great; Mash'al stopped abruptly and picked up a solid gold plate shoving it into his shirt.

"We have no time for that, stay focused!" Ahmad shouted.

"No one will know," grumbled Mash'al.

Picking their way through the room, they came upon a sealed chest in the very back. It was nine feet long and had handles on either side. It looked like a coffin, but was designed to carry something far more important.

"This is it, help me."

The smaller man assisted as the two men hoisted the lid and laid it on the floor. Shining the light inside, he shook his head in satisfaction as he observed the black granite stone.

"Be careful, it will be heavy. We must get it to the exit."

Replacing the top, the men grasped the handles and heaved. The box was very heavy; the object weighed at least five hundred pounds, they decided.

"We will never get it up the stairs, there must be an elevator. Go retrieve the table on wheels we saw in the hallway. Hurry, man!"

"I will get the table, but the power is off. We will not be able to use the freight elevator. I think I saw a ramp at the end of the first hallway. We must try and push it up there."

"All right, but hurry, the truck will be here soon," Ahmad ordered.

The smaller man did as he was ordered and soon returned with the table rolling it to the entrance.

Both men again grabbed the case, pulled, and pushed it to the door. Once through, they heaved and finally placed the object on the gurney. Moving down the hall, they passed the freight elevator and continued back the way they had entered. The two men shoved the wobbly table along the passage until they came to the ramp the small man had seen. With both of them behind, they began to push. It was not an easy task, but slowly and surely, the object moved up the fifteen-degree incline. It took over a half hour, but at last, they achieved the main floor.

    Crossing the display room, they stopped at the front door. Peeking out, the noise of the approaching military vehicle could be heard coming down the main road. They waited in silence and watched as a large Bradley Armored Fighting vehicle appeared out of the night and stopped in front of the museum. Flashing a spotlight on the building, it played the lights off the missing door. For one agonizing moment, the men thought the soldiers of the 3rd Infantry Division were going to investigate the break in. But, after a few seconds of inspection, the driver gunned the engine and the heavily armored vehicle pulled away and disappeared down the dark street.

    Almost immediately after the Americans departure, a small Nissan pickup truck pulled out of the alley where it had been hiding and stopped in front of the museum. Two more men dressed in black, hopped out and ran into the building.

    "Over here!" Ahmad shouted.

    All four men grabbed the handles on the casket and carried it out the front door and down the steps to the waiting truck. Loading it into the back of the pickup, the driver started the engine and squealed the tires as he raced off down the street. Turning at the first corner, the vehicle and its valuable cargo disappeared.

Chapter 1

Present Day
Northwest Florida Panhandle

"Help me!"

The words barely tumbled from his lips as he lay on the deck of the yacht. Again, he tried to call for assistance, but his strength failed and he lay gasping.

Aaron Eckenstadt was bleeding from multiple gunshot wounds and his power slowly ebbed from his body as he tried to hang onto life.

He remembered his life was supposed to flash before his eyes if he were dying. Well, if that was true, he must not be, he reasoned. Still, the pain was intense as he lapsed between consciousness and delirium. The sun was slowly rising over the water as the powerful boat sped along the coastline.

Several playful dolphins raced next to the bow of the yacht as it made its way down the coast, frolicking in the clear emerald green water, oblivious of the suffering on the deck of the boat appropriately named, 'NO Pain, No Gain'.

Aaron Eckenstadt, a collector of rare artifacts with his business in Jacksonville, far from the sand dunes of west Florida, was an unlikely candidate for murder. How had he come to be lying on the deck of this yacht near a hamlet called Blue Mountain, in the area known as the panhandle?

It had all begun with the phone call. The stranger announced he possessed an item from ancient Mesopotamia that he thought the collector would like to own. Eckenstadt immediately demanded proof of the artifact.

The grainy picture that slowly materialized on his fax machine startled the collector. It couldn't be here in the states. It had been missing since it was uncovered in 1901. Only the covenant of the Lost Ark was rarer than this stone. He must see it. It had to be a fake. Why, if it still existed it was priceless!

His mind continued to wander over the events of the last few hours as he drifted between consciousness and darkness. Finally, his body closed off his thoughts and he drifted blissfully into a deep sleep.

The yacht slowed and two men appeared from below deck, approaching Eckenstadt with indifference. Reaching the apparently lifeless form, one picked up his feet and the other lifted him from beneath his arms. Reaching the rail, they tossed him over the side as if he were the evening garbage.

They watched for a moment as the body sank and then retreated to the cabin. The large diesels raced and the big boat moved on away from the scene.

"Did you see that?"

"Yeah, looked like they threw something overboard."

"Not something, somebody," the tall man said to his fishing partner. "Come on, let's take a look."

The small fishing boat was anchored in the shallow inlet out of sight of the big boat when it suddenly appeared on the horizon. The two men paid little attention and continued fishing until they observed the unceremonious dumping of the body.

As the anglers neared the spot vacated by the departing yacht, the tall man stripped to his waist and dived over the side.

The smaller man held onto the rail of the boat and stared into the clear water. The sun was now visibly above the horizon and the glare caused him to squint. Still, he shaded his brow and stared intently into the emerald green surf.

After what seemed like several minutes, the surface was shattered with his partner breaking the calm dragging the lifeless form with him as he kicked towards the boat.

The smaller man leaned over and grabbed the inert shape holding him until his friend could climb aboard and help him lift the man onto the deck.

"Is he alive?"

Without answering, the swimmer began CPR on the lifeless object. A steady strong push on the man's chest followed by blowing down his air passage, and then the process was repeated. Moments passed before the body began convulsing and threw up a large amount of water.

"He's been shot. Get some bandages from the first aid kit, hurry!"

"Mr. Eckenstadt, can you hear me?"

The words drifted into his mind like a body tumbling down the stairs. As they struck the bottom, they bounced slightly. Again, he focused on the voice.

"Mr. Eckenstadt, are you able to speak?"

He tried to gasp out, but his throat was parched and he merely rasped an answer as his eyes slowly opened. The bright light shot through his brain and he stared at the shadows of two men, one immediately over him, and a second man standing slightly to the rear, observing the proceedings.

"Can you hand me the water glass and the straw please?" the one standing over him requested.

The man to the rear dutifully complied with the appeal and the first man proceeded to manipulate the glass and water to his mouth.

Eckenstadt took a long draw from the straw and felt the cool liquid brush his tongue as it slid down his throat.

"Thank, thank you," he forced from somewhere deep within him.

"Where am I? Who are you?" he asked as his eyes adjusted to the bright light from the fluorescents. As the men came into focus, he noticed one wore a white jacket and had a stethoscope around his neck. The other man wore a scruffy knit and khaki shorts. They did not seem to fit together in this scene.

"My name is Dr. Harrison and this is the man who brought you into ER, Mr. Wells."

Eckenstadt felt the stabbing pain in his side and winced as he spoke, "Am I going to live?"

"Yes, but you'll be in the hospital for at least a week to ten days. You were shot three times and nearly drowned," the doctor said as he leaned over his patient. He methodically checked Eckenstadt's heart and breathing with the stethoscope, before continuing.

"Your lung was pierced with one of the bullets and your shoulder received another. We'll have to operate to remove the third one. Is there anyone you'd like to notify?"

"No, no, I have no family, only business associates. I guess you could contact my administrative assistant, Ms. Lane, Bonnie Lane. Her number is in my wallet.

"I'll tend to that for you, Doctor, if you like," the observer said.

Eckenstadt again stared through the bright lights at his savior, and reassessed this stranger. The man in the knit shirt was tall and solidly built. His hair although still damp, was dark and streaked with gray. His face was chiseled like it should have been on the side of Mount Rushmore with Lincoln and Washington. He appeared to have a large dimple in the middle of his chin, but his eyes drew your attention, they were bright cobalt blue and fairly glistened in the light. A handsome man no doubt, the collector realized.

A nurse entered and the doctor conferred with her before leaning over Eckenstadt. We're going to put you under now. You'll feel much better when we finish."

The two men departed and the nurse returned with a large needle, injecting the contents into his IV. He shrugged to himself. At least he was alive; he'd decide what to do about the artifact after he recovered.

Dr. Harrison stopped in the hallway after they were out of earshot of the patient.

"Mr. Wells, you found him just in time. I'm sure he would have bled to death if you hadn't discovered him when you did."

"Not to mention drowning," commented the shorter man who had been standing in the shadows.

"Dr., this is my partner, Bo Boggs. He assisted me in pulling Mr. Eckenstadt out of the ocean and administering first aid."

"Nice to meet you, Mr. Boggs."

"Likewise," the Greek replied.

"Well, we gonna blow this joint. I assume our friend is going to make it."

"Not exactly, I promised to call his assistant and inform her of the attempt on Eckenstadt's life. I'd like to find out why anyone would want to kill a collector of rare artifacts."

Bo shifted his weight and said, "The same reason anyone is murdered. They know too much or they have something somebody else wants."

"Well, that's succinct and to the point," Drew said with a chuckle.

"Gentlemen, if you'll excuse me I have to prepare for surgery. Will you be around when I finish?"

"Yes, we'll be right out here."

Dr. Harrison walked away and as he disappeared into the operating room, Bo blurted out, "Now why are we going to get involved in this? I mean, we saved the guys life. Why can't we leave it to the local authorities?"

"I guess we could, but I was getting kinda bored waiting on our friend in Washington to find us another assignment."

"I sure wasn't. That last episode in Siberia almost froze my ass off!"

"Come on, I need to make a phone call. I'll buy you a cup of coffee while I touch base with this Ms. Bonnie Lane." Turning on his heel, Drew marched off down the hallway with Bo following close behind.

Reaching the lounge, Bo procured the steaming coffee from a dispenser while Drew pulled his new I-phone from a back pocket and found an empty table.

"Here you go, they ain't got no cream."

"That's okay, I'll rough it. Bo, I was wondering, did you get the name off that yacht?"

"Not really, I didn't pay it much attention. Did you?"

"No, well not exactly, I think I got the last part, but there were a couple more words in it that I missed. Something about

'Game or Gain'. I'm not positive, but I think the word in front of it was 'No or maybe Oh.'"

"Sorry I can't help. I was trying to bring the boat about and get to the body."

"Oh, well, it'll come to me. No Game, Ball Game. No Gain?"

Staring at the I-phone, he clicked off after ten rings and no answer.

Chapter 2
South Beach, Miami

▲▼▲▼▲▼

Bending over, he wrapped both his massive hands around the bar and squatted in preparation of the lift. Staring straight ahead, he looked at his impressive physique in the mirrored wall and smiled with pride.

Jean Paul Girard was a massive figure of a man, six-six, and two hundred seventy five pounds. The muscles in his shoulders and arms swelled as he poised for the effort. With a loud grunt, he jerked the bar weighing three hundred and fifty pounds from the floor and brought it to rest in a standing position. The rod held securely in his massive palms, he concentrated on the second part of the lift. With only a moment's hesitation, he dropped his lower body into a squatting position and at the same instant shoved the bar up over his head. Catching the weight, he slowly rose to a standing position.

At age forty-two, not many men could accomplish such a feat, but Girard was no ordinary man. Holding the bar for the count of five, he stepped back and allowed the massive weight to fall in front of him to the floor. It struck the ground with a resounding thud and bounced nearly two feet before again crashing to the padded mat and coming to rest.

Satisfied with his effort, he walked over to the bench and reached for the bottle of water. As he downed the cool liquid, he smiled as he remembered his youth in the ring.

Yes, Jean Paul Girard had been a popular wrestler in his heyday. Arriving on a boat from Marseilles as a deckhand, he had been spotted by a promoter who was on the dock trying to recruit dull witted men to wrestle for a living.

After seeing the strapping youth from France, the agent immediately approached him and with the aid of an interpreter, convinced the nineteen year old to join his troupe of touring wrestlers. That was twenty-three years ago and a lot had happened during that time. Looking around the facilities of his personal health club, he realized he had been most fortunate on that fateful day. If his arrival had been a day earlier or a day later, he would have missed the opportunity and would still be a deckhand on a cargo ship somewhere in the north Atlantic.

The young man had trained hard and learned quickly from his mentor. He rose in the ranks of the World Wrestling Union and reached the pinnacle while becoming a fan favorite. The money and women came quickly, and although he had little formal education, he was astute enough to hire people to manage his small, but growing fortune. With time and a little luck, he amassed over a hundred million dollars from his wrestling career.

When his days in the ring ended, he wisely utilized his pop star status to promote a string of health clubs from Miami to Los Angeles. With his fame and entertainers personality, he seduced young men and women to frequent these establishments with the promise of seeing other entertainers and celebrities. Enamored with Girard's name and fame, they hoped by visiting his clubs they too could rub shoulders with the rich and famous.

Although his youth was behind him, he knew the best was still ahead. His acquired interest in art and fashion kept him in the public's eye as he attended celebrity auctions building a collection of unusual and expensive artifacts.

Placing the bottle back on the bench, he turned to see her watching him.

"You're going to kill yourself one day, you know that! I'm going to come in here and find you on the floor with one of those dumbbells on your thick head. Why won't you listen to me and quit being so foolish?"

He smiled again and slowly walked in her direction. Like him, she was a magnificent physical specimen and those attributes were the first thing that had attracted him. However, after a torrid relationship touted in all the tabloids, he soon realized there was another side to her personality.

"*Cherie,* please do not fret. You know I'm perfectly capable of handling the weights."

Shaking her head, she approached him and the two met in the middle of the room. She placed her hands on his face and smoothed the long blonde hair back over his ears.

"Damn, you are a handsome man, Jean Paul. I don't know how I would ever live without you."

"You mean how you would live without my money," he said, as he patted her attractive backside.

The two were a match made in heaven, or possibly hell, as some of his archrivals would say behind his back. Girard's magnetic personality and drive, accompanied by his lover's skillful manipulation of his financial assets, had helped him become one of the mega rich.

"Come and clean up, I have much to tell you before we have dinner." Playfully she took him by his massive forearm and led him through the doors to their private dressing room. As they departed, the logo over the door of the Lion with its golden mane proclaimed to all 'Jean Paul Girard,' 'NO Pain No Gain.'

The jangling of the phone startled her as she prepared for an early dinner. Setting the plate aside, she made her way to the instrument on the wall. Removing the receiver, she tucked the phone under her ear as she checked caller id. 'Unknown Caller' glared back at her as she spoke, "Hello."

"Ms. Lane, you don't know me, my name is Drew Wells, I'm a recent acquaintance of your business associate Mr. Eckenstadt."

"Aaron?"

"Yes, I'm calling to alert you he has been injured, I don't know if you knew he was over here in the Destin area?"

"Destin, Florida? Well, yes, sort of, he told me a couple of days ago he was going to look at a piece someone was holding for him. Is he all right?"

"How well do you know Mr. Eckenstadt?"

Suspicious now of the caller, she asked, "Who did you say you were again?"

"My name is Drew Wells."

"Are you with the police, Mr. Wells?"

"Actually I'm with the Federal Government, affiliated with the Federal Bureau of Investigation."

There was a momentary pause on the other end as the woman recovered from her shock, "Are you still there, Ms Lane?"

"Yes, yes, did you say the FBI?"

"That's right, but let me start at the beginning. Mr. Eckenstadt was shot several times and then someone tried to dump his body in the Gulf. I happened to be fishing with a friend when we saw the attempt at disposing of his body."

"Mr. Wells, this sounds preposterous. I feel I must repeat myself, is Aaron all right?"

"Sorry, yes, he was operated on a couple of hours ago to remove a bullet from his spleen. Dr. Harrison at Sacred Heart Hospital is in charge. The hospital is located east of Destin."

"Shot and dumped in the ocean, are you sure this is the same Aaron Eckenstadt I know? He has never been cited for a traffic violation, and why would anybody want to shoot him?"

"I was hoping you could tell me that, Ms Lane."

"Well, I don't know any reason. Aaron has no family but we are close, I'll be over later this evening, if I can get a flight." Pausing, she then asked, "Does Destin have an airport?"

"You'll have to fly into Panama City, or the Northwest Florida Regional Airport."

"The what?"

"Better try Fort Walton Beach, it's the same thing." Looking at his watch, Drew added, "You'll never get in here tonight. They roll the concourse up with the sidewalk about nine-thirty. Everything and I mean everything, goes through Atlanta. You might as well plan on coming in early tomorrow. Mr. Eckenstadt is recovering from the operation, and won't be able to talk until then anyway. Let me know your flight number and I'll arrange to pick you up. Grab a pen I'll give you my phone, then you call me when you know the connections."

Completing his conversation, Drew hung up and looked over at Bo sitting with his feet on an ottoman. He was busily munching a sandwich and in the process of downing the remains of his Samuel Adams lager. Drew watched for a few minutes while Bo grunted his reply into the phone and argued a moot point with the person on the other end of the line.

Smiling, he headed to the small kitchen area, opened the fridge, and removed two more beers. Depositing one on the table next to Bo, he found himself a comfortable place to watch the end of the Cardinals, Mets game.

An unusual character, his partner Bo Boggs, nothing like the kind of friends Drew used to have in his earlier years. Yes, the team worked well even if the two approached their objective from different ends of the field.

Bo was a former entrepreneur and owner of a classic car restoration business. He still dabbled in the restoration process when he had time from his now full time job with the Bureau. It was unusual for either of them to have time anymore to go fishing or play golf, their new jobs kept them running from one corner of the world to the next. The team was known as the Presidential Agents, and reported directly to the Deputy Director, Doug Riley. While the Bureau was involved with domestic issues, the Presidential Agents had free reign of the entire Globe, as their assignments came only from the President of the United States.

Bo was a short and compact man, five-nine and a little over two hundred pounds. His hair was thinning and his waistline had expanded, but neither had slowed him. A rather large nose and two ears that appeared to be an afterthought of his maker accompanied brown eyes that flashed when he was angry. The entire appearance was tanned, and showed his Mediterranean heritage.

However, looks could be deceiving, as the little Greek was a powerful man. Drew had seen him handle opponents twice his size in fights, never coming out on the short end of the fray.

Hanging up the phone, the Greek said, "He ain't happy about your decision to get involved with this Eckenstadt thing. I tried to convince him we had the time and you had the interest, but he said for us to keep our noses out of it."

"Well, that's a fine attitude! What good are we sitting around on our butts fishing? Now mind you, I don't mind a little time off, but a month?"

"Yeah, I was getting bored too. Still, he said he wasn't furnishing us with any resources to go chasing around Florida."

"Well, we aren't spending any of the Bureau's limited resources right now, so let's wait and see what comes of this. I would like to chat with Eckenstadt when he is out from under the anesthesia in the morning."

Bo put the beer back on the small table and asked, "Oh, I take it you got that Bonnie babe this time, what did she have to say?"

"She acted like she didn't know anything, but seemed in an all fired hurry to get over here. I'm planning to pick her up at the airport in the morning."

Bo finished the last bite of his ham and cheese before adding, "I'll bet she's homely as hell."

"Doesn't matter, this isn't a dating service the Bureau is running for your pleasure."

"No, but it has its moments. I sort of miss that Russian dancer Tatiana. She was a real looker, and those legs!"

"Get serious, they came up to your chin."

"I know, that's why I liked them."

"Here we go again," Drew exclaimed with a shake of the head.

At that precise moment there was a knock at the door.

As Drew reached for the handle, Bo remarked, "Now who can that be at this time of night?"

Removing the latch, Drew opened the door and standing in the entrance was the imposing figure of Sheriff Fred Barrett.

"Come in, Sheriff, I was wondering when you'd show up."

Chapter 3

▲▼▲▼▲▼

He passed casually down the hallway with a certain air of indifference. Nodding to the two orderlies, he passed as though he had known them professionally for years. In his green doctor's scrubs, he possessed certain infallibility from the other hospital staff. Although they would say later they felt as if they knew him, they could not be sure why they had not questioned his sudden appearance. In truth, he had done this on three other occasions. Impersonating a doctor was only one of many talents he possessed. Pushing open the door to room 714, he moved to the patient's side and lifted the clipboard that was lying on the table at the foot of the bed.

    The brief narrative identified Aaron Eckenstadt and clearly defined the nature of his surgery as well as all drugs prescribed for the patient. The impersonator laid the file back where it had been and leaned over the patient who was breathing easily in his drug-induced sleep. The IV was attached to his left forearm and the heart monitor to his right bicep. The maze of lights and information produced by the simple attachments was truly amazing and he stopped to gaze at it as though it meant something to him. In truth, it could as well have been a slot machine in one of the casinos along the coast.

Turning, he double-checked his route of flight before taking the fateful action. Satisfied it was still clear of any suspicious hospital personnel, he deftly slipped the needle from his smock pocket and quickly and efficiently injected the clear liquid into the IV tube. Without waiting to confirm his actions, he returned the instrument of death to his pocket and made a hasty retreat from the room. As he passed down the dimly lit hallway, a nurse turned the corner on her evening rounds and came directly towards him. Without a moment's hesitation he continued past her and nodded as she smiled in his direction. Passing within five feet, the nurse's smile slowly disappeared as she came to an abrupt halt. Turning to follow the doctor's passing she realized something was amiss. Then it struck her, he did not have the proper identification badge prominently displayed. She raised her hand like a teacher about to scold a student as he turned the corner and disappeared.

"Oh, well he probably had it in his pocket, so many of the new ones couldn't get the hang of the proper procedure. Some even felt they were above such protocol."

As she stood there trying to decide what to do, the duty nurse from central station came running down the hallway in her direction.

Distracted, she said, "What is it, may I help?"

"Seven fourteen is in distress, hurry!"

Both women joined and raced down the hall to the open doorway.

Her real name was Mary Lewis, but she had discarded it years ago when she made her attempt at breaking into the entertainment industry. After graduating from high school in Olathe, Kansas, she ran away to the bright lights of L.A. to find fame and fortune as a dramatic actor.

Her motivation was more to escape her tragic home environment than fascination with the movies. As a child, her stepfather and several of his construction friends had sexually abused her for their own amusement. Her mother, an alcoholic and cocktail waitress, had paid little attention to the girl's pleas for help.

To Mary's chagrin, she found breaking into the entertainment industry required her to receive the same humiliation she had received at home. After two years of making the rounds of casting couches, she finally gave up her dream and accepted reality. During this time Mary changed her name to Marie Louise, thinking it sounded much more sophisticated. She began working at an upscale diner, and saved every penny to pay for her education. When she had saved ten thousand dollars, she entered a junior college in Orange County to study accounting. While a student, she realized her centerfold good looks were a definite asset in her pursuit of her goals.

One night while working a double shift at the diner, she noticed a handsome young man sitting at the corner table all alone. His chiseled features and cinematic good looks took her breath away. She was not sure, but she felt as though she should know him.

"Could he be in the movies," she asked herself.

After pleading with one of her peers, she was able to secure the service of the table where the handsome man was seated. Approaching the booth, she was in awe of this beautiful man with the long golden locks.

When he looked up from his menu, he smiled and immediately captured her heart. The two attractive people struck up a conversation as the meal was ordered, and continued it after it was delivered. Marie knew the attraction was mutual and when the handsome man asked her for a date, she couldn't write her number on the slip of paper fast enough.

Marie was surprised when she discovered the young man was a professional wrestler, but that did explain his familiarity. His face had been on TV promoting an upcoming championship match. He was thirty-six years old and she only twenty-one when they met. When she was with him, she had finally achieved the celebrity status she so desperately needed. His picture with hers, appeared in the papers and tabloids wherever they went.

Now six years later, they still had not married, and she realized they probably never would, but that was of no importance. She had worked her way into his life and become not only his lover, but also his business partner. Using her charm and guile, she had carefully pushed all of her competitors out of his life, now she was in complete control of his massive fortune.

Jean Paul had total confidence in her and her business-acumen. He gave her free reign over his amassed wealth and the power it wielded. If the truth were known, Jean Paul had no idea how wealthy he was.

Marie had invested well, not only in the Stock Market, but also in rare and unusual art forms. It was this market where she made some of her largest profits. Of course, she attended and participated in advertised auctions in New York and Los Angeles. But her real genius had been in the illegal markets, dealing in stolen artifacts from museums around the world.

Jean Paul never realized he had become the proverbial middleman in the buying and selling of stolen goods. Like her, he needed and enjoyed the attention he received wherever he went.

However, Marie was no fool. Just in case, she had set aside her own little nest egg in a secure account in the Caymans. Yes, she would stay with him forever and love him passionately. But if for some reason they parted, she had provided well for herself.

Slamming the door to his new Corvette, Drew clicked the key fob to be sure he had locked it as he turned and raced to the terminal. The reassuring beep of the horn notified him all was safe. Crossing the intersection of the parking lot and the passenger drop off lane, he avoided a taxi and mini van intent on running over him. Looking at his watch again, he realized he was ten minutes late. Damn, accident on the Mid Bay Bridge, tourists looking at the water and not paying attention to their driving were responsible for this at least once a week during the season. It was his bad luck to be coming the opposite direction when the two cars collided. He was detained for nearly an hour while the Florida Highway patrol cleaned up the mess. Lucky he was a prompt person and had left an hour early to be sure he was on time. Now he was late, but barely. With any kind of good luck, she would not have even reached the baggage claim area by now.

Entering the chaos of the terminal, he stopped to decide whether to check at the counter, page his party, or head directly to baggage claim. Since the description she gave him on the phone was rather generic, he decided to page. The white paging phone on the wall attracted his attention and he grabbed it. When the attendant answered, he gave her his instructions and then hung up. As he waited, he passed by the gift area and moved purposefully towards the baggage area.

"Miss Bonnie Lane, please meet your party at the baggage claim exit." The voice boomed over the loudspeaker and Drew could see several people stopping to listen. His eyes drifted around the area, but he was unable to determine if anyone was heading towards the exit as directed.

Stopping beneath the yellow and black exit sign, he again scanned the carousel area for anyone looking in his direction.

"Mr. Wells?"

The voice startled him as he turned around. Standing behind him was a tall brunette with a Florida tan and infectious smile.

"You're late," she commented again, before he could speak.

"Yes, sorry, there was an accident on the bridge. I would have been early." He defended himself, as he stared at the beautiful woman. She looked Drew straight in the eye and he was afraid to look down to see if she were wearing heels. Her skin was smooth and her eyes a softer blue than his own. She couldn't have been much over thirty, if that he thought. The only telltale age sign were the small almost unnoticeable lines around her eyes that shown when she smiled. High cheekbones and a small mouth, accented her narrow nose. Her only concession to vanity was a touch of lip-gloss highlighting her pearl white teeth, which glistened as she smiled.

"My car is right across the street. Do you have all your luggage?"

"Yes, I only brought this one overnight bag," she said, as she turned and led Drew out through the automatic doors. He dutifully followed close behind and glanced down to notice she was wearing flats. While looking he couldn't help but admire her short skirt and shapely legs. Smiling to himself, he thought Bo would approve. "Looks like the dating service is working overtime," he mused silently.

As they approached the Vette, Drew released the hatchback and was grateful he had opted out of the convertible he so coveted, for the practicality of the hatchback.

"Nice car, looks new."

"Yes, I've had it just over a month. Always wanted one but my ex never would allow it."

"You don't look like the type to let women order you around. May I call you Drew?"

"Yes, certainly Bonnie, well those were different days and different times, seems like a hundred years ago. Here, let me handle that for you," Drew offered, as he took the small black bag and deposited it in the rear. Smoothly he slipped around his guest, and opened the door to the passenger side.

The woman gracefully, and with only a small sign of discomfort, eased her long legs into the confining space of the Corvette.

Drew tried not to look, but her legs were a major distraction as he closed the door.

Leaving the parking lot, he turned north on Highway 85 and headed towards Destin.

"Tell me something about yourself, Ms Lane. How did you hook up with Mr. Eckenstadt?

She smiled as she began the conversation that was comfortable to her.

"I met Aaron at the University of Florida a few years ago while I was working on my masters. He was a guest speaker on Middle Eastern artifacts. I had finished my Liberal Arts degree and thought I wanted to go digging around the Middle East like a female Indiana Jones. Aaron was a fascinating individual; I felt an attraction right away. Not sexual, mind you, he is old enough to be my father, but one of family. We kept in touch and after I finished my graduate work, he offered me a job. The pay was staggering compared to the amounts that were available in my chosen profession. I thought, why not, I could do it for a couple of years and then dig my way through Israel and the sands of Persia after I paid off my student loans.

That was eight years ago, and I'm still doing his bidding. He is a wonderful man and has become my surrogate father. I have complete run of the business and travel all over the world on interesting searches for unusual artifacts."

"Sounds like a wonderful job, you're a lucky person."

"Yes, I think so, but enough about me. Tell me about you, Drew. I can't imagine an FBI agent that tools around in a Corvette wearing a polo shirt and golf slacks. Has the Bureau changed their dress code?"

Laughing, Drew shook his head as he spoke, "No, my partner and I have an unusual job, and like you, it's a match made in heaven. I used to be in the private sector and was money motivated. I had a life altering experience you might say that brought me into contact with the Bureau. That was about five years ago. Since then I have evolved into a special agent of sorts. But enough about me, I'd like to know."

The soft ring of his I phone cut off Drew before he could finish.

"Excuse me," he said, as he flipped the phone open," This is Drew."

He uttered not another word, but she noticed his face took on a hardened appearance before he closed the handset.

"Are we going to the hotel or the hospital first? She asked."

As he turned his full attention to the woman, she could see his eyes turn from a soft blue to the cold icy Pacific before he spoke.

"I'm afraid we're going to the hospital first. I'm sorry to be the one to tell you Bonnie, Mr. Eckenstadt is dead."

Chapter 4

▲▼▲▼▲▼

The elevator doors hissed softly as they parted and the couple exited into the hallway.

"It's down this way, around the corner." Drew motioned, as he headed off down the corridor.

Bonnie Lane followed closely alongside the tall agent as he made his way down the dimly lit passageway. As they approached the central station, Drew pulled his wallet and flashed a badge at the duty nurse. It is doubtful the nurse would have tried to stop him, but he had learned that courtesy to the staff was always proper protocol.

Approaching 714, Drew spotted Dr. Harrison standing along side the imposing figure of Sheriff Barret.

"Well, I see you don't follow instructions very good, Mr. Wells. Thought I asked you the other night at your place to not meddle in our affairs. I don't believe this is a federal case."

"Sorry, Sheriff, but I have a personal interest seeing as how I pulled Mr. Eckenstadt out of the Gulf. Oh, sorry didn't mean to be rude," Drew added, as he noticed all eyes were on the woman standing beside him.

"This is Ms. Bonnie Lane, Mr. Eckenstadt's associate. Mentioned her last evening to you and I picked her up at the airport this morning. So you see, Sheriff, I have a legitimate reason to be here."

"Would somebody please tell me what happened to Aaron? I was under the impression he was going to be all right."

Dr. Harrison scanned his clipboard again before speaking, "I can't say with total authority. All I know for sure is his heart stopped beating and it appears to be a textbook heart attack. We won't know for sure until the autopsy is completed. The duty nurse found him early this morning after his monitor alerted her. She and another nurse tried to revive him. The emergency team on hand did their best, but he didn't respond. He was pronounced dead at four thirty-three AM."

Now it was Drew's turn to ask the questions, "I was here yesterday and both of us spoke to him before the operation. He seemed fit and obviously had some kind of workout regimen, not an excess pound of fat on him."

"I can attest to his exercise routine. When he was at home, he ran three nights a week, at least three to five miles. I know his health club membership was at one of the new spas and he worked out at least four times a week there in the early AM."

"How old was Mr. Eckenstadt?" Sheriff Barrett asked.

"He was sixty two and looked like a man of forty."

"Yes, I'd agree with that," Drew said.

"Was the operation considered a success?"

"Yes, Sheriff, It was simple and straight forward. Dr. Laurel assisted and the whole procedure was wrapped up in forty-five minutes. I was confident he would recover; there was no doubt in my mind of any lingering after effects. There is one thing though that the nurse mentioned that bothers me."

The two men stared at the Doctor in anticipation before the Sheriff finally asked, "Yes, what might that be?"

"Well, the duty nurse said she saw an unfamiliar doctor on the floor just before the alarms warned her of the patient's distress. She didn't make much of it, except he didn't look familiar to her and he wasn't displaying his badge properly. Probably nothing, there are always new doctors passing through these halls."

Drew stared at the Sheriff and was about to speak when the door to 714 opened and the gurney carrying the body of Aaron Eckenstadt appeared being pushed by two orderlies. One of the Sheriff's deputies exited with the body and stopped to place yellow tape across the door.

"Is that necessary? We have deaths in the hospital on a regular occasion, so why are you closing the room off?"

"I'll have to consider this a crime scene, Doctor, until we can determine the exact cause of Eckenstadt's death. Sorry, I know bed space is at a premium here, but it shouldn't be more than 48 hours."

Noticing the deputy still standing by quietly, the Sheriff turned and asked, "What is it, McDonald? Is there something else?"

"Only this, Sheriff, it's probably nothing, I found it on the floor with this pen. Mr. Eckenstadt may have dropped it."

Handing Barrett the yellow sticky pad, the deputy quickly departed following the gurney down the hall.

"What is it, Sheriff, what does it say?"

Shaking his head in confusion, as if he had been handed Egyptian hieroglyphics, he replied, "No pain."

"That's it, No pain?" You suppose he was commenting on how he felt before he died?"

"I have no idea, Wells. Your guess is as good as mine. We don't know for sure he even wrote this note, and if he did, when he might have written it."

At that precise moment, Bo Boggs appeared, turning the corner heading straight for the small gathering. Staring at the sheriff, the doctor, and his partner accompanied by the attractive woman, he said, "Did I miss anything?"

The Hampton Inn located at the intersection of old Hwy 98 and the bypass was not a luxury hotel by any stretch of the imagination. However, at the peak of the summer season it was all that Drew could find on such short notice.

Bonnie Lane placed her overnight on the rack to unpack, but after the scene at the hospital, her heart wasn't in it.

Drew and Bo stood watching and realized the woman was struggling with her emotions. It was obvious she had a genuine affection for her mentor.

"Bo and I won't hang around, I know you'd like to get unpacked and have some time to yourself. Why don't we meet later for an early dinner, there's a restaurant across the highway called the Back Porch. It's kinda touristy, but decent, if you like fried food," Drew added, with an attempt at humor.

"No, no, please don't leave. I'd like to talk if you can stay. Have a seat and let me get a few things off my chest that are bothering me, perhaps that will help."

The two agents looked around the room for seating and spied the small desk with two chairs. Bo reached the table first and shoved a chair over for Drew. As the two men seated themselves, the tall brunette sat down on the edge of the bed and stared down at her feet. Kicking off her shoes, she began slowly, "I really don't know where to start, but I'm going to try to tell you all I know."

"That's fine, we're here to listen and help. Mr. Eckenstadt seemed like a decent man, we're both sorry about his death."

"Thank you. I was surprised when Aaron told me he was coming here to Destin. I was curious, and he was somewhat mysterious. It took me quite a bit of effort to pull the story from him. He swore me to secrecy, that's why I was a little evasive on the phone yesterday."

"So," Drew said, "what's the big secret? Feel free to talk in front of Bo, he's been my partner for four years and I trust him with my life."

She looked at the little Greek and smiled, "Actually I feel more at ease with Bo than you, Drew. All right, here goes and please feel free to interrupt if you have any questions."

Bo's smile told Drew he was pleased with the compliment from the beautiful woman, and would now probably believe anything she told them.

"Have you ever heard of 'The Code of Hammurabi?'"

Drew was the first to speak, "Code of Hammurabi seems that rings a bell in my memory from my academic days. What about you, Bo, you're the scholar in the group?"

Bo scratched his head and placed the candy bar he was enjoying on the table.

"Boy, that takes me back! Let's see, Code of Hammurabi, I seem to remember from the eleventh, no tenth grade, World History with Mrs. Clark. Wasn't the code a set of laws the King of Mesopotamia drew up to guide his people? Arab, wasn't it?"

"Very good, Bo, it was Arabic and dates to around 1760 BC. King Hammurabi enacted the laws to guide his people through a particularly difficult time in history. They are compared to the Ten Commandments the Jews used to guide them. Only much more specific, they left little to the imagination.

There were 283 different laws etched in cuneiform on the stone. For example, if you stole from your neighbor, you would lose a hand. If you coveted another man's wife, you would lose your life. All of this was carved in the stone. There was no court for explanation, although preserving evidence was considered acceptable.

Hammurabi had a large stone tablet made of black granite placed in the center of Babylon for all to see. As a citizen, it was your responsibility to know the laws even though most citizens couldn't read."

"Sounds like it left little to the imagination. Wonder how many hands they cut off?" Bo mused.

"So, you're saying Eckenstadt came over here for the tablet?" Drew asked.

"I really don't know what he thought he would find. You see, the tablet was lost for centuries, and presumed destroyed. In 1901, a Dr. Élan from the Louvre Museum in Paris was searching in what is now Iran, stumbled upon a village, and there in the middle of the town, was the tablet. It was on display and had been since the Twelfth Century BC, when it was taken as plunder by an Elamite king.

Of course, he was shocked, but somehow convinced the local authorities to let him have it to take back to civilization. The stone was removed and loaded on a wagon; he planned to take it to France. From here, the story gets a little vague. Somewhere along the way he was ambushed and the tablet stolen. The museum in Paris claimed they recovered it and put it on display."

"You don't sound convinced," Drew commented.

"I'm not, and many in the field agree the stone in the Louvre is a counterfeit. Where the real stone is, no one knows. At least that is the common theory, but Aaron was different. He was convinced he knew what happened to the real stone."

"Well, Bo and I are aching to hear this, right, Bo?"

"Aaron let it be known in the community that he was interested, and would pay a premium for the stone."

"Wouldn't that have generated a number of leads as to its whereabouts?" Bo asked.

"Certainly, this wasn't the first time he had gone traipsing around the country in search of the Code. There was always someone trying to pass off a phony to him. I know he was frustrated, but he never lost hope he would find the real tablet. Of course, his efforts did not go unnoticed, the Louvre kept a close watch on his activities. They warned him on more than one occasion to cease his effort. They were convinced their stone was the original, or at least that's what they want everyone to believe."

"Do you think he believed the stone was here in North Florida?" Drew asked.

"I don't know for sure what Aaron thought. When he told me of his impending trip, I assumed he had some strong evidence. I saw the fax picture he received and it showed a large granite stone. However, it could have been a fake like all the others. Even if I could see it standing where you are, it would take some skillful study to determine its authenticity. I believe it was a ruse to get Aaron over here. I'm sure the perpetrators planned to hold him up for millions if they could. I can only surmise that he saw this imitation and called their bluff. They took exception and killed him."

"Interesting story, but there is one more question I have."

"What's that?"

"If the stone is Arabic as you say, it would seem to me in this age of political correctness; it should reside in an Arab country. Being in the Louvre would appear to be a slap in the face of the Muslim faith. I think you know who I'm talking about."

"Yes, now you see why possessing the stone is a dangerous proposition, Drew."

Chapter 5

Paris, France

The sign above the door read 'Director of Antiquities,' but he was more than that. Louis Marchant was one of those characters you meet who is bigger than life. Anyone meaning to do business with the Louvre knew they would have to deal with him, and he could be most difficult.

    Louis was a tall, rather angular man, in his mid fifties, who spoke five languages fluently. His appearance was precise and conveyed a sense of importance to anyone who met him before a word was spoken. His hair was coal black without a hint of gray, and his long aquiline nose seemed to point him in the direction he wanted to go at all times. A small pencil thin mustache was the only vanity he needed to set the desired image.

    As a young man, he enjoyed digging through the sands and dirt of time around the world, searching for history and treasure. After Marchant made a spectacular discovery in the Valley of the Kings in 1984, he came to the attention of the Louvre. Asked by his predecessor to become a junior Director and work exclusively for the famous French museum, he was flattered.

On this particular evening, the Director was at his desk, which had once belonged to Napoleon, working late. Marchant was meticulously studying a rare statue from the fifteenth century. The figure was that of an Inca warrior made of bronze and believed to be from Cuzco. The artifact had been recorded as being secured at private auction. Of course, that is the story that would be fed to the press, when and if the artifact were ever put on display. In truth, it had been stolen from a museum in Ecuador and smuggled into France by a petty thief aboard a cargo ship. Along with the statue were several pottery pieces from the same museum.

Smiling at the little warrior, he pondered how he would display it in the newly renovated section for South American civilizations.

It was quite late, but the Director was still in his office oblivious of time. His work was all he enjoyed and spending twelve to fourteen hours behind his desk was not unusual. When the phone rang, he instinctively reached for the receiver with one hand without setting the statue aside.

Glancing at the ornate Louis XIV wall clock that adorned the corner of his office, he noticed it was after midnight.

"Marchant speaking!"
The voice on the receiver was soft and feminine and Marchant had to fight to keep his composure. This one had fooled him before and she was always one-step ahead of her adversaries.

"Aah, I was wondering when I would hear from you again. I understand that our mutual friend, Eckenstadt, is no longer with us. What a pity, he was such a wonderful adversary."

Again, he paused and listened to the response, as he reached for the glass of wine that he had absent-mindedly placed on his desk several hours earlier. As he swirled the Pinot Noir, he inhaled the bouquet while listening to the woman's response. When she finished, he added, "Now that he is out of the way I assume you have the item?"

Suddenly his eyes narrowed and he put the glass down before speaking, "What do you mean, you don't have it? I thought it was only a matter of time, to use your words. When will you have it for me?"

Leaning back in the chair, he listened intently at the response before adding, "I am tired of your excuses, I gave you the retainer you asked for a month ago when you assured me it would be in my possession in a couple of weeks. The time has passed and all I am getting now are excuses. I will give you another week to have it here. Call me when it is in your possession. May I warn you that I don't like to be disappointed!"

Slamming the receiver down, he looked around the room for something else to abuse. Slowly his temper subsided and he regained composure of his emotions. He had waited this long another week would not be too much of an inconvenience. After all, the museum had waited over a hundred years to recover what was rightly theirs.

"Yes, another week was not too much to ask."

Washington DC
J. Edgar Hoover Building
935 Pennsylvania Ave. NW

As she finished removing the last of his files, she looked around the room for any missed mementos. Janet knew she had been thorough, but you could never be perfect. On top of the filing cabinet, staring back at her was a small picture she had overlooked. Rising from the boxes, she made her way across the room and lifted the small frame. Staring at the photo, she smiled as she remembered when it was taken. It was late in Clinton's administration and Director Clark had recently received another of his many promotions. She was with him then, as she had been from almost the very beginning. Returning to the boxes, she carefully wrapped the frame in paper and placed it lovingly in the top of the box. Placing the tape across the opening, she again looked around. The office was empty, except for the ten boxes stacked neatly against the wall.

    A tear slipped from her right eye and she dabbed at it with the back of her hand. Director Clark's death had been so sudden and a shock to all. Just two weeks earlier, he had a complete physical at Bethesda Naval Hospital, and was pronounced in perfect health. The heart attack had happened while he was alone in his office late one night, and his body not found until the following morning. That was late last week with the memorial service this afternoon. Tomorrow a new interim director would be taking control of the Bureau and her services would no longer be needed.

    Leaving the office, she closed the massive door and turned to return to her desk. She had not taken time to start on her on packing as of yet. Although she knew the interim director, she also knew he had a secretary that he was quite fond of and would most assuredly bring her along. Therefore, she was startled when the voice interrupted her thoughts.

    "Janet, are his personal belongings packed?"

    Looking up, she tried to smile as she said, "Director Riley, I didn't see you come in."

    The former Deputy Director stood barely inside the reception area and stared in her direction, almost apologetically.

"I don't mean to rush you, I don't need access yet, I only want to use the conference room. The Attorney General is coming by in the morning and I thought, well."

"Certainly, it's ready and I will personally see that everything is in order for your meeting. I believe his secretary said 10am, is that right?" she asked, as she fumbled for the reservation calendar.

"Yes, ten am is correct."

"Fine I'll make the arrangements and see that you have coffee and sweet rolls. I know how partial the Attorney General is to pastry," she added with a good-natured smile.

"Janet, there is another matter I'd like to discuss with you, if you have a few minutes."

"Why yes, of course, I was just now beginning to clean my desk out, and should be out of Sarah's way by tomorrow evening. I hope that is all right."

"That's what I wanted to speak to you about, mind if I sit down?"

"Oh my no, this is your office now, after all."

Taking a seat in a large overstuffed chair across from the secretary's desk, Riley crossed his legs and gave the grandmotherly figure his best smile.

Doug Riley was a tall man, six foot-two. and trim for a man of fifty-one. His daily workout regimen at the gym kept the excess pounds off and gave him the appearance of a man much younger. He was an Arizona State Graduate, where he had an outstanding collegiate career as a halfback for the Sun Devils football team. He nevertheless bypassed a chance at the NFL to begin his law enforcement career with the Sacramento Police Department. His immense talent and analytical skills soon brought him to the attention of the Bureau, where he accepted a position he had been seeking since his college days. His promotion to Special Agent was in record time, as was every promotion he received. Although he hated deskwork, his aptitude soon brought him to the attention of then Director John Clark, who made Riley his Deputy Director.

It had been two years and Riley's success in several high profile cases made him a favorite of the President, and now with Clark's death, he was assuming his mentor's job as Director. Although the appointment was on an interim basis, it was widely known in the halls of Congress his approval as permanent Director was assured.

"Janet, that's what I wanted to talk to you about, your position that is."

"You don't have to worry Mr. Director, Sarah will do a fine job for you, I've known her since she started out and she is a smart girl."

"Oh, I know that, but well, I'll need help from someone with experience. I know you might find this a little unexpected, but I'd like for you to remain in your present position."

This caught Janet unprepared, as she had fully expected to leave her position as the Director's secretary, and retire to her small farm in upstate Maryland.

"But what about Sarah, I couldn't, she rightly deserves the promotion."

"Now don't fret about Sarah, we've talked and I've taken care of her. She will remain in her present capacity until the appropriate time."

Stammering with some confusion, she said, "You want me to stay, but I thought."

"I know, I know, but Janet, no one has the experience and insight of the job like you do. I will need all the help I can get in this job, if I'm confirmed."

"Oh you will be, that's a foregone conclusion, Mr. Director."

"Thanks for your vote of confidence, but that proves my point. You know more of the members of Congress by their first names than anybody on Pennsylvania Avenue, now here's what I'm proposing. I'd like you to remain in place for two more years. By that time, I should be able to navigate the treacherous halls of congress with some degree of skill and balance. If you want to retire then, I'll grant it with reluctance, but Sarah will be standing by to fill in if you leave. Please consider this a personal request. I sincerely mean I need all the help I can get right now." The Director rose and approached her desk, placing his hand on hers, he added.

"I wouldn't ask if I didn't mean it."

The woman looked into his eyes and as tears welled up in her she whispered, "I would be honored to serve."

"Now that we have that behind us, I'd consider it an honor if you'd attend the service with me."

"Thank you, I was hoping you would include me in your party." Glancing at her watch she said, "I guess it's time, shall we go, Director Riley?"

Chapter 6

▲▼▲▼▲▼

His fingers fairly flew over the key buttons of the old Selectric typewriter like a secretary on steroids. His talent on the keyboard was remarkable; years of typing had honed this skill to a razors edge.

His name was T.C. Darling and he was an author of sorts. He had never been published, so to call him an author was being generous. Still, he knew he was only one novel away from fame and fortune. His huge desk was strewn with research material, and to the casual observer it would have seemed impossible to find anything in this corner of chaos. As his concentration intensified, a wrinkle in his brow told anyone who looked he was deep in thought.

His gray hair was neatly cut and wavy from his forehead back to his crown. It appeared as if someone had used a curling iron to place the perfect waves neatly in place. His face was chiseled with natural good looks given him by his Scottish mother. A strong chin, accompanied by pale blue eyes, were his best features. The small nose, adorned with reading glasses, completed the image of a scholar he was seeking. T.C. was well past middle age, however, when he stood, you could see his waistline was firm, and he wore his years well.

This morning, he was putting the final touches on a science fiction novel about two time travelers he had created several years ago. Their chronicles were unique and the characters fascinating. At least to T.C., he was their biggest fan and he knew if some tight-fisted publisher would ever give them a chance, he would have a blockbuster.

Removing the last sheet of no. 20 lb bond from the platen of his machine, he smiled with great satisfaction as he reread the final lines of the story. He had not decided on a title yet, but it would come to him, it always did.

Pushing back from his desk, he tried to focus his thoughts on the narrative as he meandered over to the window. Staring down on Wisconsin Ave from his antique town home, he surveyed the scene as people hustled to make the almighty dollar. Thank God, he did not have to work. Writing was hard enough, but to have to make a living was a dreadful thought.

T.C. had inherited twelve million dollars from his father, who had been an oilman the likes of T. Boone Pickens during the seventies. The senior Darling's death when T.C. was only eighteen was a shock. His mother died when he was a small boy and now at this young age he found himself alone. The townhouse was his parents and he never considered moving and making it on his on.

With a degree in journalism from Georgetown, he first took a job at the Washington Star. However, his one sided liberal slant on every story got him into trouble with his editor. Eventually he wore out his welcome, and was fired.

For a while, he was content to spend his inheritance and travel the world. It was while he was in Italy; he was robbed and could have been killed. He might very well have met his maker that day if it had not been for two young men who stepped in and saved his life.

Years later, he decided to use one of them as the model for the protagonist in his time travel novels.

After fifteen years, he had finished seven stories and chronicled their travels through time around the globe. Even though no publisher found them entertaining, he never gave up his belief in his quest.

Recently he had considered writing a different kind of novel, one of adventure and intrigue. Several months ago, while in a Georgetown bar, he overheard an intoxicated bureaucrat discussing a most interesting idea for a story. The disgruntled government employee was belittling two special agents of the FBI. His term for them was 'Presidential Agents'. The term was new to T.C. and he made a note to pursue it at a suitable time.

Looking down on the small reading table next to the old worn sofa, he noticed the newspaper carelessly thrown there this morning. How could he have failed to observe the small headline at the bottom of the page? FBI Director John Clark's memorial service was being held this very afternoon. Staring at his wristwatch, he realized he could just make it to Arlington if he hurried.

Why not start his research today, what better place than at the Directors funeral. Surely if these two men actually existed, they would be in attendance. Well, if they were, T.C. would sort them out.

Arlington Memorial Cemetery

The wind blew in from the Potomac and wound its way through the
elms of the hallowed grounds of the nations fabled Cemetery. Even though it was only a week past Labor day, the feel of fall was in the air. Several of the ladies in attendance had wisely chosen to wear shawls to fight off the chill. Black clouds loomed in the distance and rain appeared imminent. The weather channel had not forecast any inclement weather until later this evening, but they might be wrong and the group of assembled dignitaries was anxious to get the service started before it could be interrupted by weather.

    Director John Clark would not be buried here in the nation's capital, but the memorial tribute was being held here in Arlington as befitted a man of his dignity and stature. The short stocky Director would be returned to his beloved hills of Tennessee and buried overlooking the Smokey Mountains where he was born sixty-eight years ago.

    In attendance were the most important officials of the government. Beginning with the President of the United States, the Vice President, and running down from the Speaker of the House to the most junior members of Congress, all had come to pay their last respects to the little man who had made a difference. He had served two Presidents and been a fixture at the Bureau for over twelve years. His appointment was originally seen as nothing more than political payback to a faithful bureaucrat, but Clark proved to be much more than anyone expected. His analytical mind and shrewd manipulation of people made him a capable and dependable Director. Everyone on both sides of the Aisle mourned the passing of their friend, Director John Clark.

    The military band completed their pre service selections and silently waited for the tribute to begin. President Janice Mitchell stepped forward to the makeshift podium and placed her prepared remarks on the stand. The President was visibly moved and it was well known to the audience that she and the Director were close allies.

"Mr. Vice President, Mr. Speaker and all of the honorable men and women of Congress. Thank you for coming. It is with a heavy heart I stand before you today to honor our good friend and loyal servant, Director John Clark."

Drew and Bo stood in the rear behind the seated dignitaries. The two men were in a somber mood as befitted the occasion. Neither had spoken much since their arrival in the District late the previous evening. The morning had been taken up at headquarters completing the all too necessary paperwork to insure they would be reimbursed for expenses incurred outside their normal line of duty. The President spoke for nearly thirty minutes and when she finished her prepared remarks, a marine bugler began the somber notes of Taps. As the crowd waited for the service to end, Bo and Drew silently made their way in the direction of Director Doug Riley.

Riley saw them as they approached and nodded. He was standing with Senate Majority leader Art Miles and Minority Whip Angela Foster. His head movement indicated he was aware of their presence but wished them to wait before joining him. The two Agents hung back and watched as the music ended and Riley shook hands with the two members of Congress. A few more words were exchanged and they departed.

Again, the Director held up his hand as if to ask the two men to hold their position. Riley then moved towards the President and the two Agents could see a conversation of more than social significance was taking place.

"Madam President, I'm sorry to break the moment but there is important news I feel I must convey to you." Riley said.

"Yes Director what is it you feel is so important?"

Riley motioned to President Mitchell and the two walked away from the small gathering. Two Secret Service Agents trailed their movement at a discreet distance.

Riley had been wondering how he would break this news but no matter how many times he went over it in his mind, he knew he could not do it justice.

"Madam President I have some disturbing information to share with you. It was given to me this morning and I felt it imperative to get it to you immediately. Otherwise I would not have imposed on you at the service."

"Go ahead Doug this better be good."

Taking a deep breath the Director began, "The autopsy results on Director Clark were completed last night, and the results given to me this morning as I was leaving for the memorial service. I must tell you I was not expecting anything out of the ordinary, you must realize then how shocked I was to find out the Director was murdered!"

The words fell from his lips like boulders from a mountaintop. The President stopped and turned to face her new Director.

"You're telling me Clark was murdered?" She fairly spit in Riley's face.

"Yes Madam President the results show the Director was poisoned. The substance was a chemical we have encountered before. Inhalation of its vapors will cause the heart to seize appearing like a heart attack. We're not sure where he got it, at present we have sealed off his office and are going over it with a fine tooth comb."

"What about his secretary Janet?"

"She is fine, I have taken her to the emergency room at Bethesda Naval and she is being given a thorough check up. I was with her this morning and she seemed okay, but I didn't want to take any chances. I have taken the liberty of moving all activities from that floor of the building and all employees are being given a complete physical."

"That's a wise precaution!"

"I thought it prudent Madam President, and I would like to suggest we keep this quiet until we have more information. I don't want to have to explain this in the press right now."

"I agree, I want a complete report on my desk in the morning. I don't expect anyone to sleep until we clear this up. Do you have any suspects?"

"Not at the present time, but I think we must consider our friends in the middle east. Somehow, they may have figured out how to smuggle this past our security. I will pull everything together and have it in your office at ten in the morning if that's acceptable?"

"Fine I will expect you to have more answers then."

Riley bowed slightly and turned away. As he headed towards Drew and Bo, he pointed away from the departing crowd and the two men joined him as he hurried towards his limousine.

Standing next to a large Elm tree at the rear of the proceedings the slim figure of a man stood taking notes. He watched as Riley and the two men departed. Quietly without calling attention to himself, he folded the pad and placed it in his jacket pocket. Looking around, he noticed no one was paying him any attention, with a slight shrug, he walked towards the street.

Chapter 7

▲▼▲▼▲▼

The limousine doors had barely closed when the powerful Cadillac pulled away from the parking space. Bo fairly fell into his seat as Drew looked expectantly towards Riley. The three men sat quietly for a few uncomfortable moments until the new Director could compose his thoughts.

"Drew, Bo, I've got some disturbing news that I gave the President, I want you to know the situation first, because I need your service."

Drew furrowed his brow as he spoke, "Mr. Director, what's happened? I mean, the death of Director Clark, I understand, but what's going on?"

"It's still Doug, unless we're in the presence of the President, or members of Congress. Now as for what's happened, it's a shocking story. I'm afraid I don't have all the pieces yet, but here's what I know. Director Clark was murdered; either a toxic gas was used or a chemical agent was placed in his food. We suspect it's a chemical agent known as Fentanyl, capable of killing through ingestion or inhalation. We aren't sure at this time how it was smuggled into the Director's office. We're not even sure that's where he got it."

The two Agents stared blankly at the Director as Bo tried to speak, "I'm sorry, Doug, you're saying someone smuggled a chemical agent into the J. Edgar Hoover building and killed the Director of the FBI? I wouldn't think that possible with all the security."

"Yesterday I wouldn't either, but now, well I don't know. If they actually got it into our headquarters that means they can probably do it anywhere."

Drew cleared his throat, "You think that's part of the message?"

"Don't know, but yes, that's a compelling thought. After speaking to President Mitchell, I was told to put together a team to find and prosecute the murderer. As of right now, you're part of that team."

"Doug, I kinda committed us to the Eckenstadt murder in Florida," Drew said, almost apologetically.

"Well un-commit yourself, I told Bo a couple of days ago that you were to stay out of that business and let the locals handle it. It sounds like a straightforward gang slaying to me. Let Barrett earn his paycheck."

"Yeah, well maybe, but it's gotten a little more complicated since then."

"Sorry, Drew, this takes priority. I need you and Bo to take the lead since it may take us to God knows where."

"You mean?"

"I mean God knows where. It could lead to Tampa or Tehran, for all I know. When we get back to headquarters, I've called an emergency session and you'll be announced as the lead

Agents. I want complete co-operation from you with the other Agencies. Do I make myself clear?"
"Yes, Sir."
"Yes, Sir."

The conference room was packed and three agents had to stand against the wall for lack of seating. Fifteen of the Bureau's best and toughest agents sat and stood eyeing each other. Drew and Bo knew being a part of this team was a great honor, one not to be taken lightly.

When Director Riley entered the room, all of the agents stood like a military platoon. Even Drew and Bo found themselves jumping to attention when the boss entered.

"Take your seats."

The crowd of special agents complied and a shuffling of chairs ensued as they settled in for the important session.

"I've asked all of you here to hear this first hand from me. I know the rumor mill is running hot on this one and I want to put it to rest right now. Nothing I say can leave this room. If any of this winds up in the newspaper, the person or persons that leaked it will be terminated. Do I make myself clear?"

Although no one said a word, the head nodding indicated their understanding of the seriousness of the message.

"Now some of you may have deduced the reason for the meeting while some of you are still in the dark. I won't delay the message with a lot or rhetoric, so I'll come right to the point. Director Clark was murdered in his office four days ago."

The room erupted with startled expressions and several conversations between small groups broke out.

"That's enough, knock off the side talk, and pay attention. The reason you're here is of paramount importance," Riley almost shouted.

For the next hour and a half, the Director explained as much of the details as he knew. When he finished a forensic expert rose and added to Riley's comments for another half hour.

When the expert completed his explanation, he quietly took his seat in the back of the room. Riley began once again and paused before continuing.

"I think everyone in this room is acquainted, so there's no need for introductions. You're all a part of a special task force to determine the person or persons responsible for this insidious crime. Drew Wells and Bo Boggs will be lead Agents. All of you will report to them and me in various ways. A complete description of responsibilities is in this folder."

Riley raised a three-ring binder and watched as a similar notebook was handed to each agent. Waiting until they had all been received, Riley continued.

"Guard this book with your life. Now as I was saying, please note your responsibility and be prepared to communicate your findings to team leaders immediately."

For another hour, all of the agents studied the instructions and asked many pertinent questions. When Riley was satisfied they were all on board, he rose before speaking.

"I expect an answer to this attack on the Bureau and our honor; I want all of the people responsible. You will have the complete co-operation of the other agencies in this matter. That's all!"

Drew and Bo rose and turned to leave with the others; the little Greek was about to ask his partner a question when he was interrupted.

"Drew, Bo, wait up, I want you to stay."

The two men stopped and looked back at the Director. Standing next to him was a tall Raven-haired woman that had somehow mysteriously slipped into the room. Drew could have sworn she was not there previously, but where had she come from.

"I want you to meet someone."

The two men strode towards the Director and Bo laid his copy of the notebook on the table.

"Drew Wells, Bo Boggs, I want you to meet your new partner, Special Agent Doe Eys."

The tall woman reached out, and shook Drew's hand, staring at him with the deepest brown eyes he had ever seen. She stood nearly six feet and her skin was a deep mocha color. It was obvious to him she was of Latin heritage. She wore a charcoal gray pencil skirt with matching jacket and white blouse. A gold pendant around her neck accented her slender neckline. Her tailored clothes clung to her figure in a mildly provocative manner, yet she came across as all business. It was obvious to Drew that his partner was enamored with the woman's presentation.

"Doe? That's an unusual name," Bo blurted out.

Smiling with perfectly white teeth, the woman responded, "Yes, it's really Dorothy, like in the 'Wizard of Oz," but my brother shortened it when I was small and the rest of the kids picked it up. I guess I'm stuck with it."

"I think it's rather fitting," Drew interjected.

"Doug, I'm afraid I must complain. I'm sure Ms. Eys is perfectly qualified, but Bo and I have always worked alone and that's the way we like it."

"Sorry, Drew, normally I wouldn't have added to your team, but this murder hit too close to home and is far to important to quibble over turf. Agent Eys has special qualifications you don't possess and will need in this case."

Drew again stared at their new partner and considered what those special talents might be.

"Special talents?" Bo asked, almost sheepishly.

"Yes, she's a forensics expert with a background in chemical analysis. She volunteered for field duty recently and I immediately realized she'd be a valuable addition to your team. I'm sure you will find her a great asset, Drew."

Drew and Bo stared at each other with clouds of doubt in their eyes.

"Sir, with the addition of Ms. Eys to the team, well, I was wondering might I not be able to finish my commitment to the Eckenstadt murder. I'm confident I could finish my obligation in a couple of days."

"I said drop it, Drew, I have a meeting with the President in the morning. I promised her a plan to find and prosecute the perpetrators of this attack on our government. I'll need a presentation in place by that time. You've got part of it, now finish it for me."

"Yes, Sir," he replied, as he hung his shoulders in mock disgust.

Turning to the woman, he said, "Doe, why don't the three of us have a cup of coffee and get better acquainted."

"Fine, I'd love that. Bo, I understand you live in Gaithersburg, where exactly? My sister lives there, maybe you know her."

Chapter 8

▲▼▲▼▲▼

"Eys, that's an unusual name for someone who, well, it's German, isn't it?"

"Yes, quite good, Mr. Wells, as you can see I'm not German, at least not one hundred percent. My German Grandfather migrated to Spain after the war and married my grandmother. My father was a result of that marriage and I am one-fourth Spanish. However, anyone who knows my family will tell you I got my mother's Spanish blood."

"I meant no disrespect, just wondered about the name." Drew apologized.

"None taken, I get that all the time."

"Oh, and it's Drew please. Bo and I are kinda informal; we came to the agency late and in an unusual manner."

"So I've been told. Director Riley gave me a quick thumbnail and I took some time to research your backgrounds myself."

"I should have guessed, like any good agent would."

Bo continued to stare at the attractive woman and Drew realized he was more than a little infatuated. He had not said a word since they sat down and that wasn't like Bo.

"Well, now I have a Bo and a Doe, shouldn't be too hard to keep them straight." Drew mused.

Bo suddenly realized he had been staring and finally interjected, "Yeah, well I like the addition to the team. Do you think this is going to be permanent?"

"I don't know what the Director has in mind Bo, but from what I understand the two of you get all the good assignments. I'd be honored to work with you whenever I can. I asked for a transfer from the lab operation to field work. I never expected to be assigned to work with the two Presidential Agents my first opportunity."

Drew interrupted her train of thought, "its unfortunate it had to be in a case where our own Director was murdered. Enough chitchat, I'd like to get down to business. I've given this some thought and here's what I need the two of you to do," Drew stated with authority.

"First, I want you two to put together something for Riley to present in the morning. It doesn't have to be too detailed since we don't know all that much yet. Doe, I want you to take the lead on the presentation. Second, Bo, I want you to make contact with the other members of our team and give them directions on how we'll work together. Then I want you to work with Doe on the presentation to the President."

Bo looked at Drew as Doe took notes on the instructions, "What may I pray ask, are you going to do?"

"I have a little matter to clear up in Florida."

"Riley told you to stay out of that business, last I heard."

"Yeah, well this won't take long and I'm obligated. I expect you to cover my tail in the short term."

"Okay, but don't take too long, what do I tell him if he asks?"

"I don't want you to lie, but well, tell him I'm tracking down a lead that came up suddenly. Tell him I'll get in touch with him as soon as I know something and fill him in."

"Talk about stretching a point," the Greek shrugged.

"Doe, you'll now report directly to Bo and I expect complete cooperation from you, and oh yeah, one more thing."

"What's that?" She asked.

"Complete loyalty, Bo and I don't always work within the guidelines and some of the things we do is, well not to belabor a point, downright illegal. Oh yeah, this matter in Florida I'll let Bo fill you in and that is part of the loyalty. If you can't work with us on this I'll find a way to send your sweet ass back to Forensics."

The woman blushed slightly before she replied, "You don't have to worry about me; just don't get me terminated on my first real case."

Jacksonville, Florida

She had only been home for one day, and escorting the body of her former employer was not a pleasant task. Bonnie Lane was in her nightgown and robe as she entered the kitchen for the tea she'd been brewing in the kettle. As she picked up the pot and poured the steaming liquid into the cup, a light tapping on her apartment door caught her attention. Placing the cup in a saucer, she returned to the living room and crossed to the door. Never one to be afraid of the dark, she boldly opened the door and stared into the face of Drew Wells.

"Drew, is that really you?"

"Hi, Bonnie, I should have called but things are kinda hectic and I wanted to see you as soon as I got in from the airport. Hope it's not too late for a call, not social, business."

"Please come in, how in the world did you find me?"

"One of the perks of working for the Bureau, all knowing all seeing, if you know what I mean."

"I do now. Have a seat, would you like some tea? I just boiled some water and I'm having some."

"Thanks, uuh you don't have any instant coffee, do you?"

"Just happen to have a new tin. I'll make you a cup, cream or sugar?"

"A little milk if you have it."

Reentering the kitchen followed by Drew, she quickly mixed the coffee and placed it with a small pitcher of milk in front of her visitor.

The couple sat down and Bonnie looked expectantly at her guest. "Now what's so important you found it necessary to stop by after ten PM, and by the way, what are you doing in Jacksonville? I missed you after you and Bo mysteriously disappeared the other day."

"Thought you might have picked it up in the paper. The Director of the FBI died suddenly and we were required to be at the memorial service."

"Oh no, I'm sorry I didn't know. I've been so busy what with bringing Aaron back to Jacksonville and making plans for his funeral, I really haven't had time to look at a newspaper or watch CNN. How did it happen?"

"I'm not at liberty to say actually, and the truth is we're not sure, but that's not the reason I'm here."

"Well, I was wondering that myself? What is the purpose of your visit?"

"I guess I'm inexplicably involved in Eckenstadt's murder whether I want to be or not. I've been told to stay out, but I'm intrigued."

"Intrigued?" That's a new one on me. Well, the police in Okaloosa and Walton counties don't seem to have a clue. I'm glad you feel obligated. I'm sure with all your resources you'll find his murderer."

"What can I do to help?"

"First, I'd like access to Aaron's files on the 'Code of Hammurabi.' I'd like to do a little research and learn as much as I can about the stone. I think once we find it, or whatever they were trying to pass off, we'll find the killers."

"Everything is in Aaron's office I can let you see it in the morning."

Drew glanced at his watch and replied, "I was hoping you could take me there tonight."

"Tonight? What's the hurry?"

"I'm on a tight schedule and I don't have a lot of time. If you could get me in tonight and perhaps steer me through the right files it would shorten my search considerably."

Staring at the handsome Agent, she realized she couldn't turn down his offer of assistance.

"Very well, let me get out of this night gown and house coat and I'll take you over. It's only fifteen minutes from here."

Jefferson Avenue was near the east end of the old downtown waterfront and consisted mostly of unoccupied dilapidated brownstone buildings. As the Honda pulled up to the curb, Drew could see the small sign in the first floor window. 'Eckenstadt Antiquities.'

Removing the keys from the ignition, Bonnie opened her door and stepped out into the cobblestone street. Drew followed and the two of them approached the front door climbing the three steps.

"Kinda off the beaten path, aren't you?"

"Yes, I guess you could say that, but Aaron liked the area. I think he used to have family here and visited them when he was a child. He told me once this area had a rich and interesting history."

"Well, interesting maybe, but rich, I'm afraid not."

Removing a key from her purse, Bonnie placed it in the lock and opened the door. Stepping quickly inside, she moved to the wall and keyed in a security code to silence the warning buzzer.

"Follow me, Aaron's office is in the back, mine is upstairs."

Drew found himself inside what for all practical purposes could be considered a museum of sorts. In every nook and cranny, some artifact resided and stared back at him.

"I feel like I'm in Tutankhamen's tomb," Drew mused.

"I guess in some ways you are. Aaron was a funny man. I think he cared more for collecting than selling. He would part with some of these items occasionally, but I must admit reluctantly. I'm sure he didn't need the money, he was in it for the love of the chase."

The couple crossed the floor and Bonnie again produced a key and unlocked the door to Eckenstadt's office. Entering the room Drew could not help but notice the musty smell.

"Smells like a damp basement."

"Oh no, nothing like that, Aaron was quite careful to keep the office and his storage rooms dry. It's the old pieces that smell. You get used to it after a while."

"I bet!"

In the corner were five filing cabinets that stood out from everything else. They were obviously new and padlocked with a bar running down the front.

"Eckenstadt was certainly security conscious."

"Yes, he taught me to keep everything under lock and key as well."

Once more, she produced a key and opened the padlocked cabinets. Scanning the front of the drawers, she selected the third one and opened it. The drawer was crammed with manila folders and Bonnie meticulously picked her way through the assembly. Finally, she removed one and handed it to Drew.

"I think this is what you're looking for," she exclaimed.

Drew accepted the offering and looked for a place to sit down as he examined the contents. Bonnie moved across the office and turned on two more lamps.

"Use Aaron's desk."

Drew took the suggestion and seated himself at the massive wooden structure. As he opened the file, Bonnie disappeared into the main room leaving him alone with the material and his thoughts.

Drew carefully removed the typed information and spread it over the enormous desk. Going slowly from document to document, he studied the material carefully.

Time slipped by and Drew was startled when Bonnie said, "Well, did you find anything important?"

Looking up Drew replied, "Maybe, have you ever heard of a company called Girard Enterprises?"

"No, can't say as I have, but that doesn't surprise me. Aaron dealt with a lot of companies and individuals. Some were a little on the sleazy side. He had contacts everywhere."

"This letter from Girard is the only really interesting piece of information. It's an offer from them to buy the stone. Says here they would like to examine and purchase it from him."

"That seems rather straightforward I don't see anything unusual about an offer of that nature. Still, Aaron didn't have the stone, but they must have assumed he did."

"No, I guess the offer is not unusual, but something else here is."

Handing the paper over to Bonnie, he tapped the letterhead at the top of the page. "What does that say?" Drew asked.

Bonnie accepted the letter and stared at the expensive and beautifully embossed letterhead. Placing her finger over the raised ornamental design she replied, "You mean this, the logo, 'No Pain, No Gain?'"

Chapter 9

Georgetown D.C.
▲▼▲▼▲▼

He pushed open the old iron door to the trendy Georgetown restaurant with some difficulty. Adjusting his eyes to the light, he stared down the long row of bar stools where patrons were busily consuming their favorite beverage. The restaurant was known as Clyde's, and had been a favorite watering hole for regulars and tourists alike for many years. In the late seventies, a local group, known as the 'Starlight Vocal Band', composed and recorded the song 'Afternoon Delight' named for the restaurant's Sunday brunch menu. Since that time, tourists flocked to the tavern day and night. It was located on M Street near the corner of Wisconsin Avenue and was always crowded.

"Damn tourists, why don't they go home, it's after Labor Day, don't the kids ever go to school anymore?" he thought.

The man was small and some would describe him as mousy. His black hair was slicked back like a character in an old B movie. His pencil-thin moustache gave him the look of a weasel staring from behind Venetian blinds. At five-nine, he was on the short side and his slight build always caused him to be jostled in a crowded bar. Tonight was no exception.

He took a few steps and immediately excused himself after bumping into an attractive woman; she stared at him as if to say I know your kind. He paid her no mind and moved on continuing to search for his party.

Near the end of the bar in a table for two, another man with wavy gray hair raised his hand to signal him of his presence. As he moved along, he scanned the bar to see if anyone he knew from work might by chance be hiding in a corner.

His name was Lonnie Thweatt, and he was a second level bureaucrat at the Federal Bureau of Investigation where he had worked for twenty-three years. While his position was insignificant, it allowed him access to all of the pertinent information in the Bureau. With a Top Secret Clearance, Lonnie was someone who knew where the bodies were buried. However, on his salary, trendy restaurants were a luxury, not the norm. The foray into Georgetown this evening was at his friend's invitation.

The man rose and extended his hand in greeting, "Lonnie, so good to see you again."

"T.C., it's been awhile, I'm still looking for that copy of your book you promised."

Thweatt took a seat and the two men settled into a friendly exchange.

"Let me buy you a drink, Jack and coke, right?"

"You've got a good memory. Yes, that would be great."

T.C. placed the order with a waitress in a short cocktail outfit, causing him to sneak a quick glance at her long legs.

After the drink was delivered, Thweatt asked, "Well, I'm here as I promised. Now what's all the mystery, what can I do for you?"

"Lonnie, I'm trying to gather some information on a rumor I've heard about the Bureau. I know we've collaborated in the past and I was hoping you could provide me with some information, strictly confidential of course. I'm willing to pay the usual, if I use anything."

Lonnie looked at the writer and wondered how he could possibly know of the Director's murder. The entire building was abuzz and he had no idea how long they could keep it quiet. Now this writer was quizzing him about it in a local bar.

"How did you hear about it? I mean, they have the lid on so tight on Pennsylvania Avenue, none of us can breathe. If the truth gets out, it could mean my job."

Darling suddenly realized his informant knew something of paramount importance and had wrongly assumed he was inquiring about the matter. T.C. was planning to ask about the Presidential Agents he had heard rumor of but now, well, let's see what this bureaucrat knows.

"Lonnie, I know you've been sworn to secrecy, but these things always get out. I promise you complete anonymity and will pay you top dollar for the story. If I can use it, I may be willing to kick back an additional few bucks."

Thweatt again looked around the room and then whispered, "It's going to get out sooner or later. Might as well make a few dollars on it while I can. You're inquiring about the murder of the Director, I presume."

The surprised writer cleared his throat before responding, "Huuh yes, that's right." Tell me everything you know."

Thweatt leaned forward and began the lengthy narrative. The startled writer pulled out a note pad and furiously jotted down the notes as fast as he could. Occasionally Darling would ask a question to which the bureaucrat would quickly reply. It seemed Thweatt knew everything there was to know. He had even seen information typed that afternoon to be presented to the President. According to Thweatt, a Presidential Agent was in charge and reporting directly to Director Riley.

"Presidential Agent, I've never heard that term before," Darling lied.

Thweatt quickly filled the writer in on the title and names of both men assigned to the President's personal task force. T.C. could not believe his luck. This second level bureaucrat was telling him so much more than he could have ever imagined!

"Now what will I do with all the information?" he wondered.

He had left his I-phone on the nightstand and when it began chiming, he raced across the room to retrieve it. Flipping the marvelous little device over, he noticed the caller id confirmed the party was his indeed his partner, Drew Wells.

"It's about time you called, where the hell are you?"

"Jacksonville, running down a lead on the Florida murder," Drew replied.

"Well, I'd suggest you get yourself back here and help me start running down leads on the Director's murder."

"Found anything interesting yet?"

"No, nothing much has changed since you left. Doe is deeply involved with the chemical analysis of the agent we suspect killed Clark. I hope to know something new on it this afternoon."

"Keep me informed when you do, how did the presentation to President Mitchell go?"

"Not bad, even if I do say so myself. However, she ain't impressed with bureaucratic process. She wants results."

"So do I, anybody miss me?"

"Let's see, only the Director, the President, and Attorney General. Oh yeah, I guess I don't count. You owe me big time, I lied thru my teeth to save your ass."

"I told you not to do that."

"Telling and doing ain't the same thing. That flimsy excuse you gave me didn't seem very good when the President personally asked me where her boy was. I told her you were deeply involved in tracking down the source of the Fentanyl. She seemed to buy it, but told me to tell you she expected a personal report when you returned."

"Great, what do I know about Fentanyl?"

"Probably no more than me, but lucky for us Doe is on top of it. She promised to help me give your cover some credibility when you return."

"Tell her thanks, I owe her."

"I already have, and like I said, you owe me."

"Bo, I need you to do something for me. Have you got a pencil and paper?"

"Just a minute. Okay, shoot."

"I need you to find out everything you can about a company called Girard Enterprises. In addition, find out what you can about their president, a broad named Marie Louise. Got that?"

"Girard Enterprise and Marie Louise, gotcha."

"Soon as you find out something, call me. I plan to be here until I hear from you, but I may be on my way to Miami."

"Miami, what's in Miami?'

"Girard Enterprises, if I can believe their letter head."

Chapter 10

Louis Marchant's demands had been surprising to her, and yes, annoying. A man of his position and social status did not come off well making threats. Besides, what was there to gain? A simple relic from the twelfth century BC was valuable, but not worth threats. Why did he now find it so important to have the real statue? The one in the Louvre had fooled all the patrons for more than sixty years. Rumors of its legitimacy had been around for years, so why the big rush to replace it. In fact, why replace it at all.

    Marie Louise sat at her desk staring out the window wondering about the sudden change of heart in the Director of Antiquities. She had dealt with him and his kind for several years, and they were always overjoyed to secure some valuable artifact without asking questions as to how it was obtained. Her ability to seek out and procure legitimate pieces had won her a handsome income from these institutions. Girard Enterprises was known for its willingness to produce when others failed. Of course, her willingness to bend and break the law when she found it advantageous did not hurt her efforts.

Her desk was covered with pictures and narratives about the statue and she had spent the morning reviewing her file to be sure she hadn't missed something important. When she first received the request from the Louvre, she was pleased at their recognition of her talents. Her commission was agreed to quickly, almost too quickly. Then like a miracle, the information had fallen into her lap that the stone was in the US and available. Of course, the price was considerable, but her profit would be substantial.

Eckenstadt was a minor nuisance that got in her way, but she resolved that with her usual skill. Disposing of him had been simple enough, but not before the Stone disappeared. None of her agents were able to explain what happened. Somehow, Eckenstadt must have secured it, and hidden it before her people could intervene, but how and where.

Doubling her hand into a fist, she softly pounded her desk as she rose to pace the floor. She still didn't understand Marchant's attitude. Was there more to this stone than she had been told? She needed an expert, one who could fill in the blanks for her. Unfortunately, she didn't know any right off hand, except for that woman who worked for Eckenstadt, "What was her name? Oh yes, Bonnie Lane."

"That was quick."

"Yeah, well your friends at Girard Enterprises are an interesting lot. You better know shorthand if you want to take notes on them," Bo said.

"Tell me what you know, I'll be the judge of that," Drew snapped.

"Okay, well to start with, they're a fairly good size conglomerate. Their main business seems to be health clubs. They have them in almost every major city in the US and they're making inroads in Europe and Asia. To add to that, they have their own line of work out equipment and health food is another sideline."

"Interesting, go on."

"A few years ago they branched out into real estate, not residential, but commercial development. They're now in the process of building a casino in Atlantic City, like the Hard Rock, only they're using a wrestling theme."

"Wrestling theme? What the hell is that all about?"

"You remember the wrestler a few years back, Jean Paul Girard? Sort of the 'Hulk Hogan' of his day."

"That's the Girard?"

"The very one," Bo said.

"Now let me get this straight, a wrestler is interested in ancient artifacts from Persia?"

"He's known to have a large personal collection, and one branch of his conglomerate does buy and sell rare art. I'm reading from a brochure, that's how I know. Oh yeah, I failed to mention that the 'Marie Louise' you asked about is the President of Girard Enterprises and Jean Paul is the CEO. Now don't quote me on this, but our sources think Marie is the brains behind the outfit. Jean Paul is merely a figurehead, a rather large and imposing one I'll grant you, but he really isn't involved with the day-to-day running of the company.

"Now that I think of it, I remember seeing him at one of President Mitchell's fund raisers."

"Not surprised, he's a big contributor to her party and the President in particular. They're regularly invited to social gatherings. From my sources it seems the big guy even has a picture of him and the President on his desk."

"Well, this gets more interesting all the time."

"Glad you find it entertaining. Now when do you think you can make it back here to lend a hand?"

"I may drop by this evening to be seen so the boss doesn't get too suspicious."

"Don't kid yourself."

"What do you mean?" Drew asked.

"He knows what you're doing."

"Did you fess up?"

"No, you forget that next to you and me, Riley is the smartest sum bitch in this place. He stopped me in the hall an hour ago and demanded to know your whereabouts. When I started my song and dance, he cut me off. He said he knew you were in Florida and you'd better wrap that up post haste. He wants you back here and in the saddle ASAP."

The other end of the phone was silent for a moment and caused Bo to ask, "You still there?"

"Yeah, well coming back won't do me any good. I think I'll make a call on Marie Louise; I'd like you and Ms Brown Eyes to continue to manage the investigation on that end. If Riley bugs you again, tell him I'll give him a call soon."

"Soon?"

"Yeah, soon."

She had hung up the phone and was staring at the grandfather clock in the corner of her office. It was a quarter to five and time to close the doors for the day. She had sent the young man home that ran the downstairs showroom at lunch, and handled their only two visitors that afternoon herself.

Most of the day had been spent on the phone with her lawyers trying to clear up some confusing aspects of Aaron's will that would allow her to transfer ownership. It seems he had planned for every contingency, except murder.

The ringing of the door chime alerted Bonnie that she had a late visitor to handle before locking up. Descending the stairs, she noticed two men looking over various pieces of art as she approached.

"May I help you?"

Both men turned to face Bonnie and she had that funny feeling they weren't interested in the Egyptian funeral mask one had removed from the wall, right above the 'Don't touch' sign.

The first man smiled with a curious look on his face as if he had been caught with his hand in the cookie jar. He was tall and heavy. Bonnie guessed over two hundred pounds. His hair was cut in a short buzz, popular with some athletes. His nose was crooked and pressed to one side. The teeth he showed in his smile were obviously missing in two places.

"Yes, mam," he said with surprising politeness.

"I was just browsing. Are you Bonnie Lane, the expert on Middle Eastern artifacts?"

Bonnie was taken aback, "What could this lout possibly know about Middle Eastern artifacts." Nevertheless, she was willing to give him the benefit of the doubt, even if the hair on the back of her neck told her to beware.

"I am, and I have been known to possess a certain amount of knowledge in that area. What is it you're looking for?"

The smile got larger as he approached. Even though he was still five feet away, the stench from his breath assailed her lungs. She almost wanted to place her hand over her nose, but professional courtesy kept her from doing so.

Standing so close she could count the stubble from his unshaven beard, she held her breath for as long as she could before taking a step back.

"Well, I'm waiting," she postured. Although the shop was in an old run down neighborhood, she had never felt threatened before, that is, until now. She assessed her options as the second man approached. He was much smaller, but as unsavory as the first. She had taken some martial arts courses in college, but had never found a reason to use them.

"Mr. Eckenstadt and I had an interesting discussion about a certain statue that I have in my possession. I thought you might be interested."

"Statue, what statue?"

Pleased that he was now in control of the situation, the big man said, "The Code of Hammurabi."

She felt herself slump as she spoke, "You, you have that statue?"

"I do. I was expecting to conclude a deal for it with Eckenstadt in Destin. We had a meeting where he verified the piece and we discussed a price. When I told him, he laughed at me and I don't like being laughed at. Anyway, he left and said he wanted to think about it. I waited for a couple of days and then saw in the paper where he had been murdered.

I knew he had a partner, and thought I would make you the same offer. I went to a lot of trouble to get this statue. I had it removed from the Baghdad Museum and transported to the United States. That was no small feat, I assure you."

"No, no I'm sure it wasn't," Bonnie said, even though she was sure he didn't have the talent to pull off a theft like that. "Where is it now? Did I understand you to say Aaron verified it as the real thing? Of course I'd have to look at it myself."

"The statue is in a warehouse here in Jacksonville. If you like, I'll show it to you, or you can take my word for it that it's legit."

"How much do you want for it, if I find it acceptable?"

"One million bucks."

"A million dollars, why even for that item that's a ridiculous amount!"

"Maybe, but that's the price. If you ain't interested I have other people on my list who are."

"No, I'd like to see it first."

"I can arrange it." With that, the man reached in his pocket and handed Bonnie a card.

She looked at the small piece of paper and said, "I don't see your name, only a number, who are you?"

"That ain't important. Call that number in the morning and I'll pick you up and take you to the statue."

After the two men left, Bonnie locked the front door and turned off the lights to the showroom. Returning to her office, she reached for the desk phone.

"I think Drew would like to know about this," she thought to herself.

Across the street, the onlooker sitting in the black BMW watched as the two men exited the building, and disappeared into the night.

Chapter 11

"Drew, I don't know why this stone is worth a million dollars, I don't have that kind of money to invest and neither did Aaron. I can only assume he had some financial backers that would provide him with the capital."

"Is the statue worth that kind of money to the historical community, would a museum pay that for it?"

"I really don't know the actual worth. Some items are priceless, for example the 'Ark of the Covenant', but to put a value on this would be impossible for me. I'd have to collaborate with someone more knowledgeable to come up with a market value."

"Well, I think we ought to see it ourselves before we make a determination. I'll meet you at the office in the morning, say 9 AM. We can call your friends and set up a time to look at the merchandise."

"Very well, I must admit I'm curious, I'll talk with you in the morning, sweet dreams."

Hanging up the instrument, she closed her office and descended the stairs. At the bottom, she hesitated and decided to take one more look at Aaron's files. Unlocking his office, she switched on the overhead light and approached the filing cabinet.

Unlocking it again, she removed the file and returned to Aaron's desk where Drew had studied the material earlier.

Spreading the contents across the desk, she sat down and began her search, going from document to document, but the neatly typed material held no solutions to the mystery. A stack of pictures that appeared to have been snipped from encyclopedias lay neatly clipped together. She removed the clip and scanned them. Again, nothing appeared unusual to her trained eye.

Near the bottom of the stack of papers lay a yellow sheet of paper torn from a spiral binder. On it was the unmistakable scribbling of Aaron, she smiled as she remembered how difficult it always was to read anything he sent her. Another picture lay beneath the yellow paper, a black and white 8x10, wrinkled and cracked by the years. This time it showed the statue in a coffin like box with handles of braided rope. She picked up an encyclopedia picture and made a comparison. Yes, they were similar, but not identical.

Opening the top right hand drawer of her mentor's desk, she removed a magnifying glass he always kept there for just such a purpose. Placing it up to her right eye, she peered closer at the statue in the box. The top portion showed the unmistakable hieroglyphics of the ancient Babylonian Empire. However, near the very bottom, a different kind of writing appeared. Again, she looked at the encyclopedia picture; the second writing was not visible.

She moved closer and squinted at the symbols, different but somehow familiar. Leaning back, she scratched her chin unconsciously as she tried to recognize the ancient script.

Again, she scrutinized the picture, and then like a bolt from the blue it hit her, Hittite! The second text was Hittite, the fourth great kingdom of the old world. Bonnie remembered from her studies, the Egyptians were the first, the Babylonians second, the

Greeks third, and the Hittites fourth. Their kingdom was shrouded in mystery, little was known of the Hittites, except they were believed to live near the Golan Heights of modern day Syria and were considered barbarians by their contemporaries. The Pharaoh Ramses the Great called them women soldiers because they wore their hair long and braided. However, history regards them as tenacious warriors. One war with the Babylonians is said to have lasted for over a hundred years. When the war ended the Hittites were victorious, but instead of ruling their new kingdom, they merely sacked it and returned home. Only one archaeological site had ever been unearthed and confirmed as Hittite.

"What could this mean?" she asked herself, as she squinted through the glass. The writing was almost undecipherable from the picture, but one phrase leaped off at her. Near the middle of the script, she could make out the cuneiform symbols for 'Tarhut Land of Hatti.' Tarhut was the Hittite God of Thunder and it was said a solid gold statute of the God over thirty feet tall, stood in the center of Hatti.

Bonnie leaned back in her chair, her pulse racing and adrenalin pumping through her body. "It isn't possible, it really doesn't exist. Everything she had read and learned about the Hittites said the lost city was merely a tale told by their detractors. Could this really be the lost kingdom of the Hittites, and if so, why was it on a statue purportedly created by a seventeenth century king of Babylon?"

With trembling hands she reached for the yellow scrap of paper. Staring, she again tried to decipher her friend's note. Squinting, she thought it said, "Box holds the original Code of Hammurabi, the statue has been in the museum of Baghdad for over fifty years. Removed by thieves during the Iraqi invasion, stone holds the key to the missing Hittite lost city of Gold."

Bonnie felt her mouth fall open as she pieced together the words of the now dead Aaron Eckenstadt. "Lost City of Gold, it really did exist."

Bo looked up as the tapping on his office door caught his attention. Focusing on the unmistakable outline of Doe Eys, he smiled and said, "Doe, please come in, you don't have to knock. We ain't that formal around here."

The Latin beauty slipped easily into the room and found a seat across from Bo's self-assigned workspace. He stared as she coiled into the chair. Something about her movements reminded him of a stripper looking for a pole. Pushing the thought from his mind, he asked, "What's on your mind, got anything new for me, I hope."

"Yes, and no, hate to be evasive but we've finished the final tests on the chemical that killed Director Clark."

"So, what did you find?"

"Well, it's a form of Fentanyl as we originally suspected, but it has been chemically altered."

"Well, you've got my curiosity up, how so altered?" Bo asked.

"The chemical Fentanyl is an agent used by several governments to control crowds. What I mean is riots and such. The most recent and infamous use I might add, was by the Russians. Do you remember a few years ago the Chechnya rebels took over a movie theatre in Moscow and held hundreds of people hostage?"

"I do seem to remember that. They waited a few days trying to starve them out, and finally rushed the place. Some people were killed, as I recollect."

"That's right. They waited three days to be exact and when the rebels continued to posture and call attention to their plight, the

Russians used Fentanyl and gassed the place. It was supposed to render everyone unconscious, but the dosage couldn't be exact and ten women and children died as a result."

"So this is the exact same chemical that they used?"

Essentially, only this time it was meant to kill, and it did."

"How did our murderers get the gas, or are you saying it was the Russians who did it? I'd find that a little hard to believe."

"No I'm making no such accusation, even though they could have done it. Fentanyl is a chemical agent that almost all governments have. It is not banned by the Geneva Convention specifically like some other well-known nerve agents. In fact, it's easily obtainable," she said, as she handed Bo a sheet of paper.

"What's this?"

"Read it, you'll see."

Bo accepted the paper and quickly scanned the writing as he reached the bottom he looked up.

"You telling me I can buy this on the internet?"

"I'm afraid so. Of course, you can buy a lot of things on the internet that are considered against the law. It's all a matter of supply and demand."

"Wait till Drew hears this! I guess you're telling me we don't have no suspects yet."

"Sorry, I think I just made the problem bigger"

After the second attempt, Drew became concerned. He again tried the door and felt the resistance it offered when locked. Checking his watch, he noted the time at exactly 9:10 AM. He had been only a few minutes late, but it shouldn't have made any difference. She knew he was coming and the pre-arranged hour had been easy enough to remember. Once more he thought, this time he banged the door with some added authority.

A shopkeeper from a few doors away peeked out and stared at the stranger trying to gain entrance. Finally after Drew had decided he would break the door in if need be, the man spoke.

"She ain't there, can't you see that?"

Caught by surprise, Drew turned to return the stare. The sign above the man's head said Lowe's Custom Cabinets. Drew assumed this must be Mr. Lowe.

"Thanks for the information; I had an appointment this morning at 9 AM. Ms. Lane is not usually late."

"Yes, that's right; she's a most prompt person. She was here, got in around seven-thirty or so. I was opening up and she spoke to me. I saw her leave about forty-five minutes later with two men. They seemed to be in a hurry."

Drew left the porch and approached the man, "My name is Drew Wells and I'm with the FBI," he proclaimed, as he offered his badge for identification.

The man seemed unimpressed, but stared at the shiny symbol out of curiosity.

"Would you recognize these men if you saw them again?"

He hung his head to one side and said, "One of them I could, but the other was blocked from my view. I hardly noticed anyway. Bonnie is always coming and going with strangers, kinda her business thing. I heard about Eckenstadt, nice man. Sorry to hear he was murdered, that why you're involved?"

"Yes, now tell me about the man you saw."

"I'd say in his late thirties or early forties, nicely dressed in a three piece business suit, broad through the shoulders, kinda like he spent a lot of time in the gym. Had neatly cut brown hair, fair complexion. Didn't notice much else. Didn't know I was going to get quizzed about him."

"What about his car? Did you see it? What kind and color?"

"Black uuh, I think it was a Beamer."

"BMW."

"Yeah, exactly."

"Don't suppose you saw the license plate?"

Again, Mr. Lowe hesitated before speaking, "Funny I did actually, seemed a little unusual, one of those vanity plates."

"Well," Drew pressed the man.

Smiling, the shopkeeper replied with pride, "No Pain 6, ain't that a funny one?"

"Yeah funny," Drew replied, placing a business card in the man's hand he hastily beat a retreat to his rental car.

"I'll be back, if you think of anything else call me," he shouted over his shoulder.

Chapter 12

She sat at her desk reviewing maintenance authorization sheets she had requested from building security. It had been over ten years since the Bureau employed its own personnel to maintain the building's internal systems. The J. Edgar Hoover building was now over 34 years old, the usual systems were requiring regular maintenance for which local companies were retained, and the bureau outsourced its needs.

All of the service businesses had been vetted thoroughly and there seldom was a problem. Each company employed personnel free of criminal records and every worker was expected to be squeaky clean.

Nevertheless, an occasional person slipped through the cracks, but to this point, nothing of a serious nature had happened. Now, however, the Director of the FBI had been murdered and somewhere, someone knew something.

Placing the sheets in a pile, she removed the one for Eastern Shore Air Tech. The air conditioning and heating company had secured the contract for the last five years and proved to be a dependable and competent company. The service request was from a secretary on the Director's floor and said simply, 'Can't regulate cooling in conference room.'

The service personnel were in house for two days and finished just hours before Director Clarks' death. Now it would be Doe's turn to investigate. She scooped up the paper and placed it back in the folder. Placing the material in her briefcase, she dropped it off in her office on the way to the conference room, number B901, at the end of the hall near the Director's office. She found the door unlocked and the room unoccupied, filled with a table and twelve chairs aligned neatly. As she moved around the room, she looked at the vents above the table. Finally, she pulled one of the chairs out and used it as a ladder to ascend to the tabletop. With her height, she was barely able to reach the vent.

"I was looking for you, Janet told me you were in here. What'cha doing?" Bo asked, standing in the doorway.

Looking over her shoulder, she smiled and replied, "I had a hunch and thought I'd test it before I wasted your time."

"Nothing you do would be a waste of my time," he replied.

"Here, let me help you, with those heels you might bust your pretty little ass."

Bo proceeded to use the chair and joined her on the tabletop.

"This would probably look funny to someone if they just walked in, now what are we looking for?"

I checked the maintenance records and discovered this room had required service to the air conditioning ventilation two days before the Director's death. I thought that looked kind of suspicious and decided I'd check it out."

"Good thinking, so you planned to remove these vents covers and see what's in the air duct?"

"Exactly, I'm kinda surprised that hasn't been done as a matter of routine."

"Me too, well, let's see what we can find."

Standing on his tiptoes, Bo was not quite tall enough to reach the vent. Finally giving up, he got down and placed a chair on the table. Again, resuming his former position on the table, he climbed on the chair for additional height.

"Careful, this isn't the steadiest platform," Doe pleaded.

"If you remember, I'm an engineer at heart, stand back and watch."

This time Bo easily reached the vent as he hunched over to keep from banging his head on the ceiling. The cover was surprisingly loose and unscrewed easily.

"That was almost too easy."

Handing the metal apparatus to Doe, he peeked inside the duct. Nothing out of the ordinary appeared to be in the recess of the ceiling. Reaching in his pocket, he removed a small penlight flashlight.

"Never know when one of these things will come in handy."

Shining the light in the dark recess, he reached in and removed something.

"What did you find?" Doe asked.

"Just what you might expect, duct tape," he laughed at his own joke.

"Although this one has something sticking to it, probably nothing."

Bo handed the tape to Doe who stared at the brass fitting stuck to the end. Carefully she placed it on the table as Bo moved the chair over to the next vent. Again, he removed the cover and using his penlight stared inside.

"Don't see nothing in this one, what was it they were supposed to be doing?"

"According to the maintenance sheet this room would not cool and they were called to fix the problem. That's about all I know."

"Here, what are you two doing up there?" the female's voice demanded.

"Startling Bo as he was climbing down, he slipped and started to fall. Doe saw his plight and quickly grabbed the Greek by the arm and the two fell in a heap on the table.

Staring into the woman's soft brown eyes, Bo found himself wondering how she would be in the bed. Seeing he was not going to move, Doe pushed him gently away and got to her feet. Bo sat up, slid his feet off the table, and climbed down.

"Oh, Mr. Boggs, I didn't realize it was you, I hope you aren't hurt?"

"No, no, I've had bigger falls in my life," he replied as he glanced back at Doe.

"We were inspecting the vents. Are you the one that called the AC people for service? Sorry, I don't know your name."

"It's Patty, yes I did, we had a meeting scheduled and when I checked the room earlier in the week it was hot. Nothing I could do got it to cool down. I called the Air Tech people and they came right out. Unfortunately, they couldn't get it in working order in time. We were forced to move our meeting down to the seventh floor. Why, is something wrong?"

"No, that's fine, Patty, I'll let you know if we need you. Did you happen to know the air conditioning technician they sent over?"

"No, can't say as I did, but we haven't had a problem in a long time, I wouldn't expect to know them."

"Thanks again."

The woman turned and exited the room. Bo turned back to Doe who was twisting the brass fitting that had been stuck to the tape.

"Here, let me see that again," Bo requested.

Taking the fitting in his hand he turned the round end and watched as it moved around the small brass stem. Then as if struck by lightning, he said, "I'll be damned."

"What is it, do you recognize it?"

"Yeah, it's a valve stem, one that could regulate air flow or water flow. We may have found something important."

Eastern Shore Air Tech was located in Bethesda, about ten miles from the District. Bo slowed the Government Issue black Ford Sedan and parked next to the curb. Doe was excited and beat Bo out of the car onto the sidewalk. As he joined her, he said, "Calm down, I know this is all new to you, but try to act like you're an old hand at this investigating stuff."

"You're right, I'm afraid I'll make a mistake and screw things up."

"Follow my lead, I'd like you to watch and listen. Sometimes you'll pick up something I might miss. Now let me do the talking."

Following Bo through the front door of the small storefront, she waited as he approached the receptionist.

"May I help you, sir?" The matronly redhead asked.

Placing his identification on her desk, he pushed it towards her.

"We're with the Federal Bureau of Investigation. We'd like to see the owner, Mr. Wilcox, I believe."

"Yes, sir, one moment."

Placing her thumb on the intercom, she spoke without a hint of concern. "Mr. Wilcox, a Mr. Boggs and a lady are here to see you. They're with the FBI."

The reply from the small black box was immediate. "Tell them I'll be right out."

"I believe you heard his reply, he said he'd be right with you. Please have a seat, if you like," she offered, pointing to a small sitting area.

Bo shook his head in the negative and picked up a Sports Illustrated from the table. The door to the back office opened and a small round man in coveralls appeared. The name over the pocket said Charlie, and the man appeared to be in his late fifties. A little short on gray hair, but with a large infectious smile on his face, he said, "Mr. Boggs, I presume."

Bo stepped forward and shook hands with the owner. Turning to his partner he quickly added, "This is Agent Eys."

"Agent Eys, a pleasure, won't the two of you join me in my office?"

The two Agents followed the little man through the door and into a tiny office covered with paper work. After they found a seat, Mr. Wilcox settled into his chair and asked. "Now what is it I can do for the Bureau today?"

Bo pulled the service requisition from his pocket and handed it to Wilcox.

"I'd like to know who you assigned to this job early last week."

Taking the paper, the man scrutinized the request and immediately rose and crossed the room to a filing cabinet in the corner. As he went, he said, "Why, did we not complete the job? I've never had a complaint; we usually deal with the administrative personnel."

Opening the drawer, he rummaged through several files before he pulled one from the cabinet. Returning to his desk, he seated himself and waited for a comment from the Agents. When none was forthcoming, he cleared his throat before speaking.

"Is something wrong, did someone complain about the work?"

Bo reached into his pocket and removed the brass fitting he had found in the ductwork.

"Can you tell me what this might be used for?"

Wilcox reached across and accepted the piece of brass. Turning it over in his hand, he squinted before removing a pair of reading glasses from his pocket. Staring at the item for a few silent moments, he shook his head before returning it to Bo.

"Can't say as I can, is it supposed to mean something to me?"

Without answering, Bo again asked, "Who did you say the responsible technician was?"

By now Wilcox was becoming somewhat annoyed at this treatment, but he gathered his composure before replying.

"I didn't, but just a moment and I'll tell you."

Staring down at the blue copy, he ran his finger up and down the page as he mumbled to himself. "Hmmm, had to be him."

Bo leaned forward, "I didn't get that."

Again, a sudden tinge of anger filled Wilcox eyes as he returned Bo's stare. It was a calculated gamble on Bo's part. He'd found a long time ago in his own business that getting people confused or angry made them say more than they intended. He didn't know Wilcox, but he played the game just in case.

"Mr. Boggs, this is obviously more than a botched repair job, I don't know what the problem is but my reputation, and the reputation of my company is important to me. The technician you are asking about is named Edwards, Randy Edwards. Unfortunately, he is no longer employed here. I had to let him go."

"When did you terminate him, and for what reason?"

"Ordinarily that would be confidential," Wilcox replied, with a certain amount of hostility in his voice.

"I can get a search warrant and have you brought in for questioning." Bo was now beginning to like the bad cop routine he was playing. Almost as though they had rehearsed the dialogue, Doe spoke up.

"Now, Bo, I'm sure Mr. Wilcox plans to cooperate, he doesn't want to lose the contract with us and the other agencies he represents."

Seeing the woman was being reasonable, Wilcox blurted out, "No, that's right! Listen, give me a minute to think about this. I don't want any trouble from the unions either."

Bo sat silent and Doe offered the man a supportive smile as he tented his fingers in front of his face before speaking.

"I let him go for sexual harassment. He was hitting on a married secretary at a customer's office. They complained and I had to terminate him. He only worked for me for a month, but he was a damn fine employee other than that one incident."

"Can you give us his address and phone number?"

Glad the tense situation had passed Wilcox removed a pencil and paper and hastily wrote the information down for the two agents.

Stepping back out onto the sidewalk, Doe caught Bo by the sleeve. As he turned to face her, she said, "I think I'm going to like this field work."

"You did good in there, I couldn't have scripted it any better. Now I want you to take this information on Mr. Randy Edwards and run it through the Bureau's system. Wilcox said this picture was a good likeness, too bad he didn't have his fingerprints."

"I'll do it first thing when we get back to Headquarters. Again, thanks Bo for having so much confidence in me."

Chapter 13

▲▼▲▼▲▼

Bonnie's first impression was 'What have I gotten myself into now?' The two men had been insistent and even intimidating, but in the end, it was her own curiosity that made her leap into the fire.

Pulling into the parking lot of the up scale health club, Bonnie observed the comings and goings of young and middle aged people all with two things in common. They were healthy, attractive, and no doubt well healed financially.

The passenger opened the door for her, and she stepped out onto the asphalt. Waiting for the driver, the three of them strode across the lot and made their way to the front door. Upon entering, they were directed to a corridor off the workout facility. Bonnie glanced at all the beautiful bodies before they moved swiftly down the padded hallway. Passing through a door with a cipher lock, they made their way to the end of the hall and entered an executive office. The room was tastefully appointed with an antique desk and the usual trappings of a middle manager with a few minor exceptions. A large oriental rug was centered on the floor and several pieces of art deco were placed perfectly on the walls.

The pictures were not to Bonnie's taste, but not many people cared for what she found attractive. The younger of her escorts pulled a chair out and motioned for her to sit.

Again, she complied, more out of curiosity than fear. If she had refused the offer this morning, it was unclear if they would have forced her into the limousine. Still, curiosity as they say sometimes kills the cat.

She accepted the offering and gracefully sat down to wait, but not for long. Another door opened and a beautiful young woman entered with the grace of a movie star, stylishly dressed in a short navy skirt and white blouse. Around her neck was a simple gold pendant and on her wrist, a diamond encrusted Rolex watch. However, what caught Bonnie's attention was the diamond ring on her left hand. Not a wedding band, that place was still reserved for more jewelry. The stone was conservatively five carats, causing every woman who saw it to gawk with envy. Bonnie was no exception. The woman's smile showed perfect teeth and a flawless complexion, all in all the entire presentation was perfect.

"Ms. Lane, so good of you to come on such short notice. My name is Marie Louise," she said, as she extended her hand in greeting. Bonnie took it and was immediately impressed with the woman's firm grip. No doubt, a customer of her own spa, she surmised.

"Well, to be perfectly honest I wasn't sure I had a choice," Bonnie replied.

"Nonsense, Jerry and Mike are sometimes less than cordial, but you were never in any danger from them. Boys, you may go. I will call when Ms. Lane is ready to leave."

Ready to leave? Well, that answered one question; she would be able to go home.

"Ms. Louise, you have a nice place here." Nice was the only word Bonnie could cough up on short notice, but to tell the truth she found this whole set up a little unusual. After all, a health club proprietor interested in Middle Eastern artifacts. Well, she'd play her cards close to the vest and see what she could discover.

"Thank you, but Jean Paul gets all the credit. If it weren't for his name, the clientele we get would be the usual run of the mill health club members."

"Oh, this is one of Mr. Girard's clubs?"

"Yes, we opened it last week, which is the reason I am here instead of Miami. I try to make all of the openings to show the area we are enthused about the opportunity to serve. Jean Paul comes with me when he is able to get away. I was hoping to combine this opening with a visit to your Mr. Eckenstadt, but I understand the poor man died."

"Murdered, would be a more precise way to put it."

"Why, I didn't know!"

"I'm surprised; it was in all the local papers."

"As I said, I've been involved with the club opening and it takes all my time. That is tragic; do the police have anyone in custody?"

"Not so far, they're still searching for the murderers."

"Well, I wish them luck. I didn't know Mr. Eckenstadt personally, only by reputation. I communicated with him on two occasions about a Middle Eastern Artifact I was interested in obtaining."

"You mean the Code of Hammurabi!"

"Yes, that's the reason I sent for you. I was hoping you were versed in the statue. I want it for my collection, and I must admit I possibly have a buyer myself."

"The stone is supposed to be in the Louvre. You knew that, didn't you?"

"Come, come Ms. Lane, we both know that is a fake. In fact, almost everyone who collects knows, or has their suspicions."

"Yes, I've heard that rumor myself."

"Tell me, Ms. Lane, what did Aaron tell you about the stone, did he take you into his confidence? Do you know where the stone is?"

Bonnie caught the slight edge in the woman's voice when she asked the question. It was a gamble, but she decided to take a chance and lead the woman on without giving away too much.

"On the contrary, I didn't know everything Aaron was involved in all the time. He kept a number of irons in the fire. He did mention to me on one occasion he was pursuing the stone, but nothing more. I suppose I could follow up on his work and possibly come to some conclusions."

"Wonderful, I'll make you the same offer I made Eckenstadt."

"And what was that?" Bonnie asked.

"I'll pay you one point five million dollars if you can deliver the stone to me within the week."

Bonnie almost lost her breath, but she recovered in time to stammer, "That seems like a reasonable offer. How will I get in touch with you? Are you planning to remain in Jacksonville?"

"No, I'm returning to Miami tonight. Let me give you my card." The woman moved to the desk and opened a drawer. Removing a business card, she handed it to the astonished art collector.

"You may reach me at this number twenty four hours a day. Please do not hesitate to call at any time."

"Are you sure? These kinds of things tend to turn up at the oddest hours."

"I am well aware of that, Ms. Lane; as I said, any time."

"Bonnie, is that really you? Are you all right? I was about to call out the National Guard," Drew said into the phone.

"I'm fine, sorry I couldn't make our appointment, I didn't mean for you to get worried. You'll never guess who I was with an hour ago."

"Marie Louise," he answered.

"How in the world did you know that?"

"Thanks to your nosy neighbor, Mr. Lowe, I was able to track down the license plate on the black sedan you left in."

"I should have known. Well, wait until you hear the offer I was made. Why don't you meet me at a little restaurant near the office? We can have a quick lunch and I'll fill you in on all the details."

"Sounds good to me, what's the name and location of this bistro?"

Bonnie quickly answered his request and hung up the phone. Locking her door, she made her way out of the office telling the young man working the showroom to take her calls.

Thirty minutes later, she was sitting at a sidewalk table of the Italian restaurant when Drew entered the patio area. Waving in his direction, she caught his attention and he pointed to the waiter to indicate his party.

"Well, into the vino' so early?" he remarked, as he seated himself across from her.

"I have every reason to celebrate. Drew, I'm so excited, I was just offered an outrageous sum of money if I could produce the statue of Hammurabi. Guess how much they're willing to pay?"

"I have no idea, Bonnie. I'm way out of my league here, and even you said last night you needed to collaborate with another expert to set a value."

"True, but now I understand why Aaron was so involved. Drew, they offered me one point five million dollars!" she exclaimed.

Drew let out a soft whistle, "Now I understand; you can pick up the item for a million, and hand it to someone else and make a cool five hundred grand. That's a nifty handling fee. But before you get too excited, I think I need to tell you something you're not aware of."

"I thought you'd be a little more excited," she pouted. Well, what is it you want to tell me?"

"Bonnie, I don't have any proof yet, but I think the people you were with are the same ones that, well, they killed Aaron Eckenstadt."

"Drew, are you sure?" she fairly shouted, causing several patrons to stare in her direction.

"No, I said I can't be. Still, there are some compelling coincidences, like the company's name."

"What, you mean Girard Enterprises?"

"No, it's the logo, 'No Pain, No Gain.'"

"Drew, you're making no sense at all."

"Let me start at the beginning. Remember I told you Bo and I were fishing when this boat appeared, well."

Drew continued until he had finished his narrative, then picking up the wine the waiter had delivered, he sampled his selection.

Bonnie leaned back taking everything in that had been said and then replied, "I see, I guess that could be a possible answer to some of the complications. But, but why didn't they simply grab me and force me to help?" she asked.

"I don't know for sure, but I suspect they killed Aaron in a rush to judgment. They must have assumed he had the statue and they were going to take it without paying him. I think that's the kind of people we're dealing with here. What do you think would happen if you called this Marie Louise and said you had the real statue? Did you ever consider she might send Larry and Moe over to take you out without honoring the one point five commitment?"

Bonnie looked a little confused as she absorbed the facts Drew had presented.

"I see," she said. "Hmmm, Drew, since we talked last night I've found out something that possibly makes the statue worth the one point five million. I was going to tell you right off, but you interrupted."

"Go ahead, what's that?"

"Have you ever heard of the 'Lost City of Gold?'"

Chapter 14

"The Lost City of Gold, is that anything like King Solomon's Mines?"

"Not exactly," Bonnie said with a smile.

"Then why don't you tell me? I'd never guess in a million years."

"The Lost City of Gold is a story everyone in our business has heard, but most dismiss as pure bunk. You can find similar stories in every passage of history. There is supposed to be one in South America the Inca built and hid in the jungles and Egyptian stories of hidden cities in the deserts of Africa. However, the only one with any credibility is the one the Hittites are supposed to have created."

"The Hittites, that's the fourth great dynasty you told me about the other night?" Drew asked.

"Precisely, but most of us wrote it off as an old wives tale like all of the others. You see, Drew, everyone needs a golden city to believe in. It's the kind of thing that kept the Conquistadors searching Mexico and South America."

"Are you telling me you know where a Lost City of Gold is located? What has that got to do with the Code of Hammurabi?"

"Both are good questions. I can't answer either right now, but I believe if we find the stone those two men claim to have, we should be able to sort this out. You see, I was able to ascertain from Aaron's notes last night that the real stone may have directions to the lost city. In Aaron's files was an old picture of the stone with more than just Arab laws written upon it. There was also Hittite cuneiform writing at the bottom referencing the lost city. I couldn't read it all and I can't explain why it's there, but anyone in my profession would be excited to make such a discovery. Now I understand why someone is willing to pay a small fortune for the stone. I wonder if the two men who offered it to me really have it, or are they trying to get me to pay for another fake."

"The scruffy characters we were supposed to meet this morning?" Drew commented.

"Yes, in fact I called them before I went to see Marie Louise. I told them it would be this afternoon before I'd be able to go with them. They assured me the statue is nearby. I said I had a distinguished Doctor of Archaeology from the University of Florida who would be coming with me."

"Really, how did you find him?"

"I'm surprised you don't know him, Dr. Wells."

"Dr. Wells? You mean me? Oh no, I'll never pull that off."

"Oh yes you will, I'll tell you what to say. These two men are not that sophisticated, Drew. I needed a reason to bring you anyway, and that's the best I could come up with on such short notice. I couldn't tell them I wanted to bring my friendly FBI agent. I suspect they would have hung up on me."

"Do I get to wear a hat like Indiana Jones?"

"Don't be ridiculous, just slick your hair down and put on a bowtie."

"What time did you tell them?"

Looking at her watch to confirm the present hour, she frowned as she said, "I told them about two o'clock, that will give us enough time to get back. I have a couple of phone calls to make that should help me confirm the authenticity of the stone when we see it."

"Good, I need to make a call to my boss too. He's probably about to send agents to pick me up if he doesn't hear from me soon. I'll get lunch. Why don't we meet back at your studio at a quarter to two? If there's a problem call me."

Dropping several bills on the table, Drew patted Bonnie on the hand as he rose and made his departure. She watched him as he left and wondered if there might be more to this relationship in the future.

Nevertheless, right now she was excited about finding the stone, and helping solve Aaron's murder.

Looking up from his desk, Bo waved Doe to a chair as she entered the office.

"Well, what have you got on Randy Edwards? I hope it's something I can give Riley. He's in a foul mood right now, what with the Director's death, Drew missing in action, and all the Congressional hearings making demands on his time."

As she settled in, a small smile greeted Bo before she spoke, "Yes, Randy Edwards appears to be what he claims, an air conditioning technician. However, he goes by a couple of aliases sometimes, aka, Eddie Richards and Randy Sanders. He's never been considered anything more than a minor con man in the past. He has no record to speak of, that's how he slipped through the cracks. He's got a certificate in air conditioning maintenance from a community college in Omaha, and graduated from high school, in Scottsbluff, Nebraska. He's been mostly a drifter and has had numerous jobs along the way, all of them in a technical capacity. He's never been arrested for anything, not even loitering. The reason we got a hit on him is his service record. He was in the Army eight years ago. Since his discharge, he's been squeaky clean."

"Yes?" Bo asked.

"Yes what? That's it, there's nothing else on Mr. Edwards?"

"I don't like it, there's something here that doesn't meet the eye. Our Mr. Edwards is conveniently terminated just when we want to question him about his recent visit. By the way did you find out anything on the air nozzle?"

"Oh, almost forgot, I picked this up on the way back from the lab. Eddie handed it to me with his report. I haven't had time to read it yet."

Bo accepted the envelope with what he assumed was the nozzle inside, and the neatly typed report.

"Give me a minute and let me read this."

Scanning the document, Bo consumed the three-page report in a matter of moments. Looking up, he stared at Doe, "Just as we figured, the nozzle was used to regulate the chemical Fentanyl. Traces of the chemical were found on the nozzle and stem. It apparently broke off when it was removed and stuck to the piece of tape. Whoever used it must have installed it and then had the balls to return and remove it. I guess he assumed that we wouldn't suspect the chemical agent. They were almost right. It got past us for three days before the autopsy. If the Director hadn't had a complete physical within the month it might not have caused the extra effort."

Placing the report on his desk, Bo said, "Get that Patty woman. I want to question her again. There might have been more to this that she can remember. Then you and I are going to make another call on our friend Mr. Wilcox."

"Who are you calling now?"

"I'm going to have a couple of agents check the address we have on Edwards. I'm sure it's bogus but it never hurts to check. Now hurry up, we've got a lot to do."

"Hello, Janet, is the boss in?"

"Drew, is that really you? The Director is fit to be tied. I hope you have a good explanation for your whereabouts."

"I do, don't warn him, let me surprise him."

"You know I can't do that, hold on, I'll get him on the line."

Several seconds passed and Drew placed the phone under his chin as he put the final touches on his disguise. He had taken Bonnie's advice and used some hand lotion to slick his hair back on the sides. A new crisply pressed cotton shirt, and striped tie, added to the scholarly look he was seeking. Next, he placed a pair of clear wire rimmed glasses on his nose. The glasses were his idea and he was sure they made him look more academic.   As he admired the finished product, the obviously distressed voice of Doug Riley came on the line.

"Wells, you SOB I told you to get your ass back here two days ago. Where the hell are you now?"

"Right where I was two days ago, Jacksonville, Florida."

"Look, Drew, I know you think whatever it is you're doing is important, but nothing is more important than Clark's murder."

"Doug, I understand your concern, but you've got your best man, Bo, and that assistant forensics gal, Doe, on it. What's more, you got another dozen of the best and brightest in the Bureau. I doubt I could add much to that list of experts. Listen, before you go off the deep end and elevate your blood pressure, let me tell you what I'm doing. I think you'll find this not only interesting but something you will move up the priority list."

Pushing back in his chair, Riley paused before he spoke, "All right, I owe you the right to an explanation for your insubordination. What's so damn important about that art collector's murder?"

"Thanks for the vote of confidence. I won't get into all of the details, it would take an hour to do it justice, I'll only touch on the high points.

Doug, I'm sure what I've stumbled on here is of national importance. It appears that Aaron Eckenstadt was murdered over a valuable art relic that was stolen from the National Museum in Iraq. The statue is the historically important 'Code of Hammurabi.' I don't have to tell you, it's worth a small fortune. Now if that's all there were to it that would be enough. However, there's more, a lot more."

"Go on, Drew, you've got my attention now."

"According to a Middle East expert, the stone appears to have directions to the ancient Hittite, Lost City of Gold."

Pausing for effect, Drew waited for what he knew would be the inevitable rebuke.

"Now wait a minute, Drew. I thought I'd heard everything, but a lost city that's made of Gold?"

"I'm not making this up; I have it on good authority we're on the trail of the Lost City of Gold. I hope to have my hands on this statue within the next two hours. Of course, I'll keep you apprised of the situation."

"See that you do," Riley fairly shouted into his receiver.

"Now before I'm completely sidetracked with this story of

gold, I must remind you of the importance this statue may be to certain Middle Eastern countries. I'm talking about Iran and Syria. If it can be retrieved and returned to its proper owners, we may have a major diplomatic coup."

"I see where you're coming from. This is rather perplexing, can't you leave it to someone else to find? What if I assigned the local Special Agent in the area to the case?"

"No doubt, I could use all the help I can get, but I want to see this through."

Then to change the subject, he asked," Has Bo come up with anything that would point to the killer of Director Clark?"

"Bo and Doe have made some progress; they left my office an hour ago with a lead they were running down. I'd like to tell you the team I put in place is working well, but they really have nothing to report. So you see, I wanted my best agent on the case. I have met twice with the President and she's giving me all the rope I need. Still, I don't know how much longer we can keep this out of the media."

"I promise I'll be back within the week. I'm convinced I know who the killer of Eckenstadt is, and if the statue is recovered, I'd consider my job done."

"No chasing around after lost cities of gold?" Riley asked.

"Well, I'm not making any promises yet, there's a lot to accomplish before I make that commitment. However, you have my word I'll be back in Washington as soon as I'm able."

"I know you, Wells, that's a pretty weak promise."

Chapter 15

Bonnie hung up the phone and looked over at Drew where he sat lounging on the sofa.

"Well, what did they have to say?"

"They said for us to meet them at the location where the Statue is being kept."

"And where might that be?"

"Let's see, the address is 12 North Adams. I've got a map here in my desk. I think it's the old warehouse district."

Reaching in her top drawer, she pulled out a neatly folded piece of paper and began to spread it on her desk. Drew rose and strode over to the desk bending down to look with her.

"Yes, here it is. He said it was near the water and he's right, it's on the water!" she exclaimed, stabbing her finger at the exact spot.

"Well, are we ready, or have they changed the time too?"

"No, he said he'd be waiting when we arrived. It should take about a half hour in mid-day traffic. I'm ready if you are, let's go."

Smiling coquettishly as she stared at Drew caused him to ask self-consciously, "What, what is it? Did I forget something?"

"Did I tell you I think the glasses are a nice touch?" she remarked as she reached up and brushed his cheek with her palm.

"Here, let me fix that," she said, as she straightened his tie. "You know, you remind me a lot of my father. He was a little absent minded and his tie was always crooked."

Finishing her self-imposed task, she again smiled coyly and then almost as an afterthought, leaned forward and placed a warm kiss softly on his partially open mouth. Satisfied, she released the surprised Agent and stared back into his cobalt eyes.

"What was that all about?" he stammered.

"Thought I'd like to do that," she replied.

"Well, did you?"

"Yes, how about you?"

Drew said nothing. For the first time since she had met him, he was speechless.

Pretending to pout, she shook her head and turned away, muttering under her breath, "Men."

The drive across town was largely uneventful and the small talk was kept to a minimum. When they arrived at 12 North Adams, Bonnie pulled the Honda over and parked against the curb. The entire area was deserted except for a blue sedan parked a half block away. When the two exited the auto, the lights on the distant car flashed catching their attention.

"I think that means wait here," Drew said.

The car pulled away from the curb and approached the couple standing on the sidewalk. Making an illegal u-turn, it pulled behind Bonnie's Honda and parked. The two men she had seen from the previous evening exited and approached the couple.

"Ms. Lane, I'm glad you had no trouble in finding us," the tall man remarked.

Turning to Drew, Bonnie began, "This is Doctor Wells, I mentioned on the phone. He'll assist me in authenticating the statue."

"As you wish, but I'm telling you it's authentic. Come on, follow me."

Drew followed closely behind Bonnie as the two men led them through an unlocked gate and across an empty parking lot covered with weeds.

"Nice fellow, guess introductions weren't necessary for them," Drew whispered.

Retrieving a key from his pocket, the tall man placed it in the padlocked door and removed the security device from its resting place. Taking hold of the large aircraft-like doors, the two men shoved it open and motioned for Drew and Bonnie to enter.

A light switch on the wall illuminated the vast hangar and the four people walked across the bay towards another door in the rear. After passing through the second entrance, they were greeted with a musty smelling room filled with large crates. The smaller man continued to the corner and began to pry open a crate.

Drew watched patiently and as the final boards came off, he approached.

Bonnie was right behind him. When the top was removed, a basket-like coffin was inside the box. The man reached across, grabbed two rope handles, and removed the lid from the casket. As the light struck the statue, a small gasp escaped Bonnie's lips. There, lying on its back was a large black stone. At the top was a bas-relief of the God Marduk, and the King Hammurabi with his hand over his mouth showing respect.

Bonnie leaned over the casket and studied the writing that to her was unmistakable cuneiform script of the Babylon era.

Drew stood alongside and waited for Bonnie to speak. However, she was self-absorbed in the ancient artifact.

Tracing her finger along the script, she finally arrived at the bottom and there she noticed the change in language from the ancient Babylonian to the more European like Hittite scratching. With trembling hands, she quickly scanned the information as it was presented to her. Rising to look at Drew, her face told the story without her having to utter a word. Now it was Drew's turn to intervene.

"Please stand back, Ms Lane. Without the help of a carbon dating device, I must give this the field test."

Bonnie stepped away not understanding what Drew had in mind, but she played along as though he knew what he was doing. Drew removed his glasses and wiped them with a handkerchief. Placing them back on his nose, he bent over the stone. The two men watched curiously from behind as Drew brushed his face against the stone and then placed his tongue on the side of the statue. He held it there for a moment and then rose shaking his head.

By now, Bonnie was beside herself as she said, "What did you find, what do you think?"

"I think the stone is a fake."

"Fake!" the large man shouted, as he approached Drew.

"Yes, my good man that is what I said. It is a fake. Ms. Lane, I wouldn't give them a single dollar for this attempt at highway robbery."

The big man flushed with anger as he flailed his arms and shouted, "I paid good money for this and I know where it came from. It's authentic!"

"My dear boy, you were had," Drew interjected through the tirade.

As the argument continued, in the background unnoticed by the four people, several visitors silently entered the room.

Bonnie pushed Drew away from the side of the casket and quietly said to the enraged man.

"I only have Dr. Wells' opinion that the stone is not authentic. However, I am still interested in purchasing it from you."

The big man calmed as Bonnie's words began to slowly sink in.

"Well, I should hope so. This two bit doctor don't know nothing."

Drew puffed out his chest and was about to interject another comment when Bonnie said, "Of course, I'll have to reduce my offer."

"Reduce your offer, whadda you mean?"

"While I cannot be assured the statue is authentic, I will still give you three hundred thousand."

"Why that's ridiculous! I tell you what, I'll take nine hundred and fifty thousand."

"No, I'm sure I can pass it off as legitimate and make a few dollars, but a million is way out of the question. No, three hundred is more than fair."

"Okay, I'll take eight hundred thousand, and that's final."

"No, I'm sorry, you'll have to fool someone else. Doctor, if you're ready, I'll get you back to your hotel.

The couple nodded to each other and began to leave.

"Wait, what is the most you'll offer?" the big man interjected.

Bonnie stopped and stared back at him with more nerve than Drew thought she could muster.

Pausing as though to reconsider her offer, she finally said, "On second thought, I'll give you two hundred and fifty thousand and that's my last offer."

The smaller man looked at the bigger one as if to say let's take it. Finally, after an agonizing moment, the big man said.

"Okay, you got a deal."

"That's all I wanted to hear," Drew replied.

The visitors in the back of the dark room emerged from their place of observation and moved towards the engrossed negotiations. Two of the men were in police uniforms and two were plain clothes. Drew turned to the group and said, "Officers, please take these two gentlemen into custody and see that you offer them a nice cell in the city jail. I'll be down shortly to assist in placing charges."

The police detectives nodded and without a word, displayed their badges to the two men as the uniform officers placed cuffs on the surprised con men.

As the two men were led out the door, Bonnie turned to Drew, "What in the world were you doing kissing that statue?"

"I wasn't kissing it, if you knew as much as you think you'd have known I was giving it the field test."

"The field test?"

"Yes, I read where you should always put your tongue to ancient artifacts that are being passed off as legitimate. If they taste of salt, they have a better chance of being the real thing. If not, it's probably been made to look ancient, and is a fake."

"I'm impressed, even though that's bunk. What did it taste like?"

Drew smiled one of his all-knowing smiles and said, "I lied, it tasted of salt."

"I'm glad to hear that, now where on earth did you read that garbage?" Bonnie asked.

"Well, it wasn't in Playboy magazine, Miss Smart Ass, it was in National Geographic. Now what do you think of that?"

"Come to think of it, I'll bet you can't even spell Geographic. Knowing you, it probably was Playboy." Having said that, she turned on her heel and walked away, leaving Drew standing alone with the casket containing the statue.

"Hey, aren't we going to take this back to your office?"

"I'll call and make arrangements to have it picked up. I use a moving company; they know how to handle such items," she said over her shoulder.

"Besides, I have what I came for."

Drew hurried to catch up as she passed through the outer door.

"What did you learn, what did it say?"

Stopping, she smiled again before she spoke, "The Lost City is not where anyone would ever think to look, I can't believe what I read, but if it's true, we're on our way to Africa, Dr. Wells."

"Uuh, I don't think I have time to go to Africa right now," he pleaded, as she walked away.

Chapter 16

▲▼▲▼▲▼

'Those fingers in my hair,
That sly come-hither stare,
That strips my conscience bare,
It's Witchcraft'

He had been humming the strains to that old Sinatra classic all afternoon. No matter how hard he tried, it wouldn't go away. Well it was obvious he was smitten by the intriguing Bonnie Lane.

She wasn't the most beautiful woman he had known, after all his ex was a drop dead center fold runway model. No, and certainly not the most challenging, she had begun the pursuit of him that very afternoon. So, what was the fascination? As hard as he tried, he couldn't figure it out.

They returned from the warehouse about three and true to her prediction, Bonnie's personal movers had the statue in her possession by five. When it arrived, Drew sat with Bonnie again to stare at the mysterious writing someone had scratched into the stone over three thousand years before.

However, after a brief time, his interest waned and he left her to work on the project alone. She was still at it as he looked at his watch and noticed it was now a little after ten pm.

During his free time, he had made two phone calls, the first to Director Riley filling him in on the results of their early afternoon activities. Next, he called Sheriff Barrett in Okaloosa County to see if they had any success on Eckenstadt's murder. Barrett told him they still had no one in custody, but were pursuing the mysterious doctor the nurse had seen. Drew thanked him and asked to be posted if anything new turned up.

Around six, he went down to the local precinct and filed formal charges against the two men who were in possession of the stolen artifact from the Baghdad museum. Of course, they now insisted they were mere pawns and the big fish was some mullah in Iran. Drew shrugged it off and bail was set at a million dollars each. It would be interesting to see if anyone wanted to post that amount for Stan and Ollie, as Drew had begun to call them.

When he returned he couldn't be sure, but he suspected Bonnie had not left the statue alone for ten minutes since it had been delivered. He doubted she even knew he had been away for two hours.

Occasionally she would mumble something incoherent or shout out a key word or phrase. Still, he had grown tired and was thinking of taking a nap when she closed her notebook and laid the pen aside.

"How about a glass of wine?" He offered.

"That sounds wonderful, I'm going to wash my hands, the Chardonnay is in the fridge, and a bottle of Shiraz is on the counter." She said as she left the study.

Drew rose and since she had not stipulated her preference, he assumed either would be acceptable. Finding a couple of glasses in the cabinet, he poured a healthy portion of the Shiraz for both of them.

She accepted the wine and thanked him as she sat down on the sofa and curled her legs beneath her.

Drew reseated himself in a chair next to her and asked, "Interesting reading?"

"Drew, I know this must be terribly boring for you, but I feel as though I've discovered Noah's ark. I mean the stone is more than I could have ever imagined. Hammurabi's laws are so specific and the punishment so final. I can't imagine having to live under such harsh judgment."

"As a woman, you were not expected to be punished, after all you were a man's property. I still can't figure out how we ever got talked out of that." Drew said with a chuckle.

"Drew, if that was all that was on the stone, it would be enough, but the Hittite writing makes the mystery even more intriguing."

"Yeah, so you said, tell me more."

"I will but first help me decide on what I'm going to do about Ms. Louise and her muscle bound boy friend, Jean Paul."

"I wish I had some new information on them but I'm afraid I don't. I talked to the sheriff over in the panhandle while you were absorbed in your work. He has nothing to tie them to Eckenstadt's murder. All I have is a suspicion the boat that dumped Aaron was theirs. Still, I can't prove it, and nothing has turned up with the mysterious physician. It seems pretty apparent to me he's the one who murdered Eckenstadt."

"But what do I tell them about this stone, I can't let them know I have it."

"I understand, and my suggestion is you simply tell them your information was incorrect and you don't have it.

Bonnie wiped a tear from her eye that had appeared at the mention of Aaron's name and quickly composed herself before speaking.

"I had almost shut my mind to Aaron's death; I guess I'm still in shock. I had forgotten with all the excitement about the memorial tomorrow, you are still planning to come aren't you?"

"Yes, I'll be there, it might be interesting to see if anyone else shows up uninvited. Now are you going to tell me what's new that you found or will I have to shake it out of you?"

Bonnie took a sip of the wine and then said, "I was wrong about Africa, although I'm sure there are cities strewn throughout the desert that will never be found. The Hittite were a close-knit group, I think I mentioned before they were thought to be a lost European tribe. Their fair complexion and long hair were Scandinavian in nature. When they disappeared, they literally slipped off the pages of history. With only the one city in Syria, most historians assumed their nation lived in and around the Golan Heights. You could get a good argument from experts on that, but, other than hundreds of stone tablets, and the foundation of a few buildings, nothing resembling the city of Hatti has ever been located."

"So what did you discover, was there a clue or not?"

"Come over here and let me show you something, you won't believe what I've found."

Drew rose from his seat and followed the excited woman to the statue lying in its basket. He could not put his finger on it immediately but something was different. Bonnie reached and picked a small brush from the table next to the casket, it appeared to Drew to be a woman's make up instrument. Immediately she began dabbing at the surface with the instrument before speaking.

"Drew, do you see the line right where the language appears to change?"

Drew looked closely and noticed a fine line separating the two distinct cuneiform symbols.

"Yes, appears to be a point of difference where one is separated from the other." He said as he traced the line with his index finger.

"Now watch this," she said as she began to brush along that mark.

Drew stared, as the line of separation appeared to dissolve and begin to move slowly up the statue.

"What are you doing?" He asked as he leaned closer for a better look.

Smiling, she winked at him, "I'm erasing the Code of Hammurabi from history."

"You're what?"

Rising, she looked him straight in the eye and said.

"Drew, the Code of Hammurabi was placed over the Hittite writing. Apparently, and I'm only guessing mind you, the Hittite's used the stone first and placed this original text on it. Then, sometime later, the Babylonians must have acquired the stone, probably as loot from a war, and decided it would work for their use. They must have used this soft sand like mortar, filled the original text in, and then wrote over it. Don't you see, its not a few lines of writing at the bottom, an entire document has been covered over. Why it's like finding a Van Gogh under a fill in the dots painting."

Leaning closer, Drew replied, "I see what you mean it just dissolves and underneath is this other language."

Taking the brush from Bonnie, he began the process and watched with amazement as the sand mortar fell away.

"I'll be damned! There is a definite ridge here showing the depth of the undercut symbols."

Handing the brush back to the woman, he shook his head in disbelief.

"What have you been able to ascertain from the new section?"

"I'm convinced this stone was used in the temple of Tarhut that stood in the city of Hatti. Once I've completed the cleaning process, I may have a better understanding where the city was located. However, I'm convinced now I know where to start."

"Tell me," he pleaded.

"I'm certain it's in southern Spain, from what I've uncovered; I believe the Hittites are a lost Viking civilization that settled in Southern Spain. It has long been assumed the possibility existed; now I plan to prove it."

"Seems like a big task for a little lady who collects artifacts in Jacksonville, Florida." Drew chided good-naturedly.

A defiant attitude blazed in her eyes at the casual insult.

"I'll have you know Drew Wells, I have a Masters in Ancient Language and cultures of Mesopotamia, and I would have finished my PHD if it hadn't been for Aaron's generous offer to join him. I've often thought of going back, but never took the time. I'll have you know I'm well connected in the research aspects of my field and have a close friend who will help me. I'm sure together we can organize a dig and find the lost city of Hatti."

Placing her hands on her hips, she turned and strode across the room to gather her thoughts before her next attack on the self-righteous agent. Turning to face her tormentor, she added, "Would you like to come along and join in the fun, I think you would learn something.

"Gee digging holes in the ground in Spain sounds tempting, but I'm afraid I don't have the time just now. I'm involved in two murders, your former boss, Eckenstadt, and my FBI Director Clark."

The disappointment shown in her face, "I'm sorry to hear that, I think you would like my friend. He'll be at the service tomorrow, I'll introduce you, perhaps he can change your mind."

Chapter 17

His whole body seemed to sag as he made his way from the garage to the back door of his apartment. Bo was exhausted; he and Doe had spent the better part of the last two days running down leads on the suspect, Randy Edwards. Placing the key in the dead bolt, he slowly manipulated the device and the door slid easily open. Flipping the light switch next to the entrance, he gazed around the room out of habit as he entered. Resetting the latch, he suddenly stopped cold.

It was not anything he saw, it was that instinct that had saved his life in the past, something was wrong, but he could not put his finger on it. His eyes scanned the kitchen from corner to corner; still, it all seemed perfectly normal. Quietly and efficiently, he moved across the room with his Glock in hand, placing it against the doorframe, as he stared down the dark hallway. Nothing appeared to his eyes as they adjusted to the darkness. Moving down the confining corridor, he stared into the bedroom first before continuing on to his office.

The small converted bedroom, turned office, was dark. As he peeked in, he was framed in the doorway by the moonlight slipping in the hall window.

The flash from the muzzle registered in his brain before he heard the soft whump of the silencer. Instantly, Bo jerked sideways and without hesitating returned fire. The resounding boom of his Glock filled the room and the acrid smell of sulfur assailed his nostrils.

Immediately his assailant released another round, and again Bo responded with return fire. This time a groan emanated from the corner and a form pitched forward falling on the writing desk. As the body cascaded to the floor, Bo hesitated to be sure his attacker was disabled.

Wavering for only a moment, Bo approached the prostrate figure. Flipping on the desk lamp, he stared into the empty eyes of Randy Edwards.

The morning of the memorial service dawned bright and crisp with the first real touch of fall in the air. Drew checked himself in the mirror before heading out of the Marriott to his car in the back lot.

The drive over to Elms Funeral Home was short and the traffic was light for mid-morning. When he arrived, Drew parked at the farthest end of the lot and proceeded to the entrance. Room 3 had been designated for Aaron Eckenstadt and as Drew entered, he was surprised at the number of people in attendance. The room literally overflowed with men and women varying in ages from teens to the elderly. Looking around, he tried in vain to find Bonnie, but his initial effort was unsuccessful.

A short line stood lingering in front of the guest book. Drew dutifully waited his turn, and then migrated to a corner to wait. Again, he scanned the room for Bonnie, but to no avail.

"Did you know Mr. Eckenstadt well?" the short woman with blue hair and an impish smile asked.

Startled, Drew looked down and smiled in her direction before speaking. "No, not really, only a short time I'm afraid."

"You're that detective fellow, aren't you?"

"Now why would you say that?"

"I can always spot'em; you have that look about you," she added.

"Guess I'll have to confess. Yes, I am."

"Wrinkled suit gave you away."

"Mrs. Allen, so good of you to come, have you met Mr. Wells?"

Bonnie Lane stepped between the inquisitive older woman and shielded Drew from further scrutiny. He relaxed momentarily as she spoke to the woman, and then followed as she led him away to safety.

"Thanks, I'm not sure I could have stood up to the third degree from Mrs. Allen."

"Just a nosy neighbor of Aaron's."

"She had me pegged. Wonder how she knew I was with the Bureau? My suit isn't that wrinkled is it?" he asked, as he pulled at the crease in his coat sleeve.

Bonnie smiled and shook her head, what a silly question. Threading her way through the throng, she maneuvered her companion to a corner where a tall man was standing alone near the table with refreshments.

As they approached, he saw Bonnie and a smile lit up his face causing his eyes to sparkle in anticipation. The stranger was at least six foot four, Drew guessed. His long hair was streaked with flecks of gray and pulled back into a ponytail. His face was angular and his nose quite pronounced. The effect was further enhanced by a handlebar mustache that he felt compelled to twirl as he studied Drew.

As Bonnie reached him, the two embraced like father and daughter. Releasing the woman, he quickly re-scanned Drew to better assess this young adversary.

"Drew, I want you to meet a dear friend and colleague of mine, this is Dr. Lindsey Stringfellow. Lindsey, this is Drew Wells, the man I was telling you about."

Extending his hand, Stringfellow stiffened and said, "My dear sir, it is an honor to meet you." The brogue was as thick as molasses and Drew immediately pegged him as English. Later, he would be told Stringfellow was actually Scottish.

"Dr. Stringfellow, it's a pleasure," Drew said, as he received the firm handshake.

"Bonnie tells me you're in charge of Aaron's case. Have you caught the bastards who killed my friend?"

"I'm sorry to say we're no closer to solving the murder now than we were a week ago. However, I assure you we will eventually put the guilty parties behind bars. I'm sure Bonnie told you I have my suspicions, but we can't prosecute on hunches."

"Rightly so, yes. Well, good luck, Mr. Wells."

"Drew, Dr. Stringfellow is the person I was telling you about last night. I have nearly convinced him to join me in searching for the Lost City."

"Now, Bonnie, I told you that the community has been searching diligently for the city of Hatti for over a hundred years. Sadly, we have never even gotten close. Now you come up with this bizarre story about a Hammurabi's statue and hidden messages. I must admit I am intrigued, but this seems a little far fetched," Stringfellow said.

"It's not far fetched, Doctor. I can assure you, I've seen it, and Bonnie is telling the truth. I can't vouch for what it says since I can't read cuneiform. However, I can assure you she is genuinely excited about the find."

"Well, I plan to inspect it myself this afternoon, after the memorial. If it's what you believe, I'll move heaven and earth to finance the dig."

"That's wonderful, Doctor. Now if you will excuse me I must finalize my remarks for the service. Please feel free to work on Drew for me; I think he would make a wonderful addition to our team," Bonnie added, with a hug to the professor as she slipped away towards the podium in the front of the auditorium.

"Lovely gal, that Bonnie, one of my best students too."

"Oh, I didn't realize you were in the academic business, where do you teach?" Drew asked.

"I don't anymore. I'm professor emeritus at Harvard, the School of Middle Eastern Studies. Oh, I'm occasionally asked to lecture, but my activities are mostly in the research area now. Been there over forty years I suppose, seems like only yesterday. That's where I met Eckenstadt; we were students together all those years ago. Fine chap Aaron, I am going to miss him."

"Wish I could have gotten to know him better, everyone speaks so highly of him."

"Yes, upstanding, most upstanding, now what is this about you going on the dig? I thought you were with the Federal boys?"

"I am and I'm not going on any dig to Spain."

"Spain," he said, as his jaw dropped. "Did you say Spain? I was under the impression the dig would be in the Middle East, Syria, I assumed. Spain, hmm, that makes all the difference, certainly would be easier to get approval from the government. Now Syria is another case. Can you tell me more? Bonnie has been tight lipped about her find, except to say I will be amazed. I am anxious to get a look at the stone."

"I see I let the cat out of the bag, sorry I did that. I know she was going to surprise you. I can't tell you much more. She was adamant about the dig, as you call it, and taking me along."

Before Drew could continue, Bonnie's voice from the Podium interrupted his train of thought.

"Ladies and Gentlemen, thank you so much for coming to the memorial service. I know our friend and colleague, Aaron Eckenstadt, appreciates your kind consideration. Now if I may, I would like to begin the service with a short slide show that has been prepared especially for this occasion. I'm sure all of you will find it a touching tribute to our dear departed friend."

With that, the lights dimmed and a projector in the rear of the room blazed. Instantly, an image of a handsome young man striking a gallant pose jumped on the screen, with hat in hand, he appeared to be waving to all in attendance. A sigh escaped the audience as they all recognized the young and dashing Aaron Eckenstadt.

Chapter 18

"Well, what do you think?" she asked.

Looking up from the carved stone, he removed a handkerchief from his jacket pocket and wiped his temple. He had been studying the writing for more than an hour and she watched as his brows arched and he mumbled some incoherent comments from time to time. Afraid to interrupt his concentration, she could finally stand the suspense no longer.

"Well?" she pressed again.

"I think this is the greatest archeological find since King Tutankhamen's tomb was uncovered by Howard Carter. Bonnie, you may have the key to finding the city that has been missing for nearly three thousand years."

"I knew it, I just knew it!" she shouted, as she ran across the room. "This calls for a celebration."

As she poured the wine, Dr. Stringfellow rose from his kneeling position and stretched his lanky frame.

"Bonnie, this will have to be my last dig; I'm getting too old for this. I may be too old now, but I assure you wild horses couldn't keep me from coming."

Handing him the wine, she raised her glass in a toast.

"To the Lost City, may we bring it to light after all these years."

Stringfellow raised his glass and added, "To good friends and an exciting adventure."

Tasting his wine, the Professor placed his glass on the table and said, "I will make some phone calls in the morning to some friends with more money than they can spend. I am sure one or more will want to bankroll our effort. It will take a couple of weeks to get everything in order before we can begin. I will need you to be very involved. How will you handle Aaron's business?"

"I don't expect it to be much of a problem. I have a couple of interns who will be glad to run things for a few weeks in my absence."

"Good, I will call you tomorrow after I get a commitment and we will put together a plan of action."

Walking the professor to the door, she extended herself on tiptoes and kissed her mentor on the cheek.

"Good night, I will see you tomorrow."

Is Terrorist Organization targeting FBI?

Well it was inevitable; the media eventually had to find out the truth and feel it was their obligation to print it for the public. He laid the copy of the Post on his desk and leaned back with his hands behind his head. The article had been written by somebody named Darling, but Riley knew the editor and was sure he wouldn't have printed the story without at least two sources. The problem is they were right on the money. He couldn't find much wrong with their assumptions. They even had Bo and Drew assigned to solve the Director's murder.

Still, he knew he had to contact the editor and place a formal complaint. Maybe he could find out where the leak originated. Then again, he knew that was unlikely.

Removing the phone from the receiver, he was about to place the call when the door to his office opened and Janet stood with a somber look on her face.

"Yes, is there something the matter?" he asked.

"Mr. Boggs is outside; he needs a word with you."

"Send Bo in," he replied, as he rose and moved around his desk to meet the agent.

Bo entered as Janet exited and strode over to where Director Riley was standing. In his hand, he had a piece of paper that he immediately handed to Riley.

Taking the offering, he gazed at the picture and asked, "Am I supposed to know this person?"

"You are if you want to know the killer of Director Clark."

Staring down again, he said, "This is Edwards?"

"Yeah, that's our man."

"Looks dead to me."

"Should be, I put a 9mm slug in his chest early this morning."

"Gonna make it kinda hard to interrogate him now, isn't it?"

"Look, Doug, cut the cute remarks, I'm dead tired, and was almost plain dead. This guy broke into my apartment last night and was laying in wait for me. I'm just lucky that picture Crime Scene took ain't me instead of him."

"Sit down and tell me all about it."

Bo accepted the Director's invitation and slumped into an overstuffed chair near the window. Placing his feet on the small coffee table, he began his narrative.

"I got in after midnight, not exactly sure what time. Doe and I had been running down some dead ends looking for this character. We'd had no luck for the last two days; if I'd known he was looking for me, I would have gone straight home. Anyway, when I entered, I realized somebody else was in the place. I made a systematic search and found him in my office. He apparently had been there for a short period. He took a couple of shots at me, but missed. I guess he was surprised when I walked in on him and he just missed. Fortunately for me I was a better shot."

"Was he lying in wait or looking for something?"

"He had my files on the desk and I think he'd begun reading them. If I'd been later, he might have left and we would never have met. Hard to say, really."

At that moment, Doe Eys appeared in the Director's door. Seeing Bo in the chair, she ran across the office and approached him like a mother hen.

"Bo, I heard about the shooting. Are you all right?"

Without rising, Bo waved Doe to another seat across from him.

"Yeah, I was telling the Director what happened. I'll give you all the details later. Suffice to say I'm alive and healthy."

"I hope this doesn't mean we're up the proverbial creek. Was Edwards your only lead?" Riley asked.

"I'm afraid so, he was the only one on the job that placed the aerosol container in the vent system. He spent two days here coming and going. No one else signed in with him and his boss said he worked alone. Still, I've got some hunches. He left a vehicle out back of my place in the alley. We impounded it and are going over it with a fine toothcomb. I searched him myself, but he didn't have anything on him that would give us a clue as to where he'd been hiding. There was an I phone in the car we're going over now. All of his outgoing and incoming calls will be noted and we will pay a visit to the callers."

"Good, that sounds like the best thing I've heard since you walked through the door," Riley added. "Bo, I'm glad you're okay, sorry if I gave you the wrong impression. You look beat, why don't you go home and get some sleep. Doe can follow up on the I-phone and the two of you can start running down anyone you think is suspicious later."

Rising from the seat, he shook his head, "I think I'm going to take you up on that. Doe, why don't we go back to my office and I'll tell you what I have. Doug, I'll keep you apprised of my activities. By the way, have you heard from Drew yet? I haven't talked to him in a couple of days."

"Somebody asking about me?"

Turning to stare at the entrance, they all were surprised to see Drew Wells standing where Bo had entered only a few minutes earlier.

"Speak of the devil and he appears," Riley said, as he rose from his desk.

"Bo you look like shit, why don't you go home and get some rest." Drew suggested.

Staring around the room, Drew added, "What? Did I miss something?"

Bo walked across, shook hands, and then said, "I'm beat. Glad you're back, we've got a lot to talk over. Come on down to the office when you finish with Riley, and I'll fill you in with Doe."

With those final words, he and Doe exited, as Drew walked over and shook hands with the Director.

"Glad you're back, take a load off and bring me up to date."

"I don't need a seat, I've been sitting all the way from Jacksonville. I can fill you in while I stand."

"Suit yourself," Riley said, as he retired to his desk to listen to Drew's report.

"I'll be brief, unless you need more specifics. The Eckenstadt murder is not progressing well. I'm convinced that Girard and his girl friend Marie Louise, aka Mary Lewis, are behind the murder. However, I have no real proof. Someone dressed in a doctor's scrubs put poison in his IV. Of that, we're sure. We haven't fingered him yet and the other two have solid alibis. Still, they were after the same statue as Eckenstadt. That is motive enough for me. As I told you, the statue is a three thousand year old relic of the Babylon civilization. It now appears to be more than that and could be, well almost priceless.

"I've been working with Eckenstadt's associate, a Bonnie Lane. She believes the statue may be the key to a Lost City of Gold."

"City of Gold, are you serious? Sounds like a movie script to me," Riley chided.

"Yeah, well I thought the same, but the evidence apparently points to a lost civilization. I promised not to get specific, do you need more details?"

"No, no, as long as you are through with it, that's enough for me."

"I didn't say I was through, I just set it aside for a while. Ms Lane is putting together a dig in a few weeks and wants me to be part of it. I guess I could get out of it if I wanted, but to tell you the truth, I'm fascinated. Maybe after we put the Director's murder to bed I can get involved. I didn't think you would mind, really doesn't matter if you do, I might add."

"You're starting to sound just like Bo."

Chapter 19

▲▼▲▼▲▼

Stringfellow crossed the kitchen to where Bonnie was pouring the steaming hot coffee into china cups. Waiting patiently he said, "I see you brought out the fine china, are we celebrating this morning?"

Finishing her task, she handed the cup to her mentor and said, "Yes, I'm so excited I could hardly sleep last night. Please tell me you have good news?"

"Lets be seated and I'll tell you all about my efforts with the financing. First, however, tell me about your Mr. Wells, you mentioned he called, but you never got around to telling me what he said. Will he be joining us on the dig?"

Seating herself at the table in front of a pile of stacked papers, she blushed, "I did mention he called, well, he told me that he was now involved in an important assignment, and would be tied up for a few weeks. He wished us well and asked me to keep him informed of our progress. I must admit I'm disappointed he's not coming with us. We are going aren't we? I mean you did secure the funding from your rich friends?"

Leaning back in his chair he smiled as he crossed his legs.

"I'm pleased to tell you that we have been funded for ninety days. One of my sources will put up the financing for a portion of the digs treasure."

"Can we do that? I mean will the government let us sell off part of the find?"

"My dear, there are ways, if you get my drift? I have done this before so don't you fret about my methods. Suffice to say I will handle the intricate finances, I don't mean to patronize you, but the less you know the better."

"I understand, I want to focus all my efforts on the dig."

Spreading the papers across the table, she placed a large map of the Mediterranean area in front of them.

"I have my own theories, but I know you are more familiar with the Hittites and the area we discussed. Tell me your thoughts and I will tell you if I have a different opinion."

"Very well!" Pulling the map around, he placed a pair of reading glasses on his nose and scanned the area.

"Here is what I have gleaned from the stone, although it was not meant to be a map, it has many telltale signs that lead me to agree with your assumption of Spain as the location.

The stone tells a story of Tarhut the God of thunder who the Hittites believed was their main protector. He is the one who instructed them to leave their home and seek new lands to build their city. It tells of finding the land of milk and honey through the Pillars of stone, and building the city with its magnificent gold spires."

"Yes I saw that and I took it to mean the straits of Gibraltar."

"Quite so, I agree, from the narrative I am convinced the Hittite were Vikings who came from Norway four thousand years before the birth of Christ. From the narrative, they stayed close to the entrance to the Mediterranean so they would have quick access to the open waters of the Atlantic. At that time only the Egyptians were moving towards a modern civilization. The Romans and even the Greeks were still living in mud huts. The Hittites explored and built outposts everywhere within the region including Syria and Crete. At that time, the area was lush with vegetation and their city was magnificent by any standard of the day, but all that was about to change."

"How so Professor, what changed and what happened to the city?"

"Some of my theory is fact and some mere speculation, first the climate began changing as it is today. The area the Hittites had chosen was drying out and the rainfall was diminishing. Over a period of two thousand years, the land that is now known as the Tabernas Desert began to form. The Hittites realizing their mistake pulled up roots and prepared to move. It was about that time a war with the Babylonians who were emerging as a rival began. It is my belief that the Babylonians attacked the city and surprised the Hittites. They plundered what they could and left the city in ruins. Now comes the real speculation," he said with a twinkle in his eye.

Bonnie leaned forward, so close she could almost feel his breath as he began to speak in hushed tones.

"I firmly believe the Hittites pulled up stakes and left Hatti. They loaded their long boats and many sailed back to Norway. However, some chose to remain and moved to other locations like the area near the Golan Heights. In a few hundred years, the city was overcome by the desert. It now lies buried somewhere in a two hundred square mile stretch of desert that is expanding every day." He paused for effect as he continued to twirl the mustache.

"Yes, yes, go on is there more?" She pleaded.

Bonnie, I'm sure if we do our research wisely, we'll be able to plot the exact spot where the remains lie buried, and we will locate the 'Lost City of Hatti.'"

"When do we leave?" She fairly shouted leaping from her chair.

"As soon as all of the supplies are laid in and the ship is loaded, which I should be able to do in the next couple of weeks. Then we will sail with the supplies to the port of Almeria on the coast of southern Spain. From there we'll trek northeast one hundred and fifty miles to the Tabernas desert."

Continuing to twirl the mustache absent-mindedly he mused, "Have you ever ridden a camel my dear?"

She smiled to herself as she trod across the room to the window with the panoramic view of the city. Girard's headquarters location was on the penthouse level of one of the largest condominium complexes in southeast Florida. The view of the city and ocean were truly awe-inspiring. Today, Marie Louise was most satisfied with herself and the search she had instigated. The earlier call had convinced her the statue and its secret would soon be in her hands, holding her phone casually, she was startled to hear.

"Marchant here!' The sudden voice jarred her out of her daydream and she stumbled momentarily before she answered.

"Louis, oh I am so glad I caught you before you left," she said.

Marchant recognized the voice immediately as he seated himself in the leather chair behind his desk.

"I assume you have it or you wouldn't have called?"

"We have it in our possession, our mutual friend has acquired the piece and we now have a clear idea of its worth. I will be able to deliver it to you if you like, but there is more to the statue than we originally imagined. Do you have time to listen to my story?"

"Story, what story, you either have the stone or you don't, I warned you the last time my patience was wearing thin."

Raising her voice to a level that surprised even her, she spoke with a stern resolve. "Louis, I am tired of your empty threats. We both know they are meaningless, now please calm yourself and listen to my story."

Unaccustomed as he was to the rebuke, he nevertheless took a deep breath and replied, "Marie, this had better be good, I have little time for your games, now what is it you think I would be interested in hearing?"

Realizing she now had his full attention, she began her narrative. For the better part of the next fifteen minutes, she embellished the narrative she had received a few hours earlier from her partner. When she finished, she said, "Well what do you think now?"

The museum director sat stunned in his office.

"I don't know what to say really, I have never heard of anything so bizarre in my life. Are you sure, he knows what he is talking about? I mean could this be some charade to fool us?"

"I don't know why he would want to play games, there is too much at risk, there are two solid reasons he is telling the truth. First, the credit for finding the Lost City, which in itself would be the achievement of a lifetime. However, the treasure is what I am most interested in finding. A city of gold is worth millions, if not billions depending on how much is uncovered. Can you imagine the prestige the museum will achieve for funding the project?" She said.

"Funding, I don't remember agreeing to fund any project, have you made a commitment for me?"

"Marchant, if you want credit and a part of the treasure you will have to come up with part of the projects expense. I made the commitment for you. It is only a fraction of what we will receive for our investment. You will get all of your money back and a huge profit to boot."

He paused and rubbed his chin as he thought about her story. It all seemed preposterous but plausible, yet the Lost City had been discussed for over a thousand years. She was right of course; the prestige he would receive for participating in the project would be enormous. The Louvre would be given its just due and he would be the toast of society, in Paris and New York, not to mention all of Europe.

"How much will this cost me?" Marchant asked.

"I have pledged a hundred thousand American dollars for both of us."

"Very well, I will play this game with you. The reward is worth the risk. But, if you are trying to fool me, you will find I can reach across the water and make life miserable for you and Girard."

"Don't worry; I am confident in a few weeks you will be on the front page of the New York Times." She boasted.

Chapter 20

▲▼▲▼▲▼

The group of agents milled around the room making small talk as they waited for the meeting to begin. When Riley entered, they all turned to the entrance and the side conversations ended.

"Thank you, be seated!" he said.

At that moment, the door at the far end of the room opened and an embarrassed Bo Boggs tried to enter inconspicuously.

"Nice of you to make it, Bo, seeing as how you're the guest speaker."

Boggs hung his head sheepishly as he replied. "Sorry, Director Riley, I got hung up in the restroom."

The sudden laughter from the assembled caused him to redden even more.

"Never mind the excuses, sit down and I'll get to you in a moment."

Bo did as he was ordered and looked around the room in an attempt to locate his partner. Sitting near the head of the table was Drew with their new associate Doe Eys. Drew winked and nodded to acknowledge Bo's presence.

"Now as I was about to say, lady and gentlemen, the purpose of our meeting is to get everyone on board with the status of our investigation into Director Clark's death. I think all of you know by now the story was leaked to the press a few days ago. They have done everything in their power to make it difficult for us by sticking their noses into the investigation. I do have some good news, however. Some of you already know that Agent Boggs was instrumental in finding and eliminating the Director's murderer. I'll let him give you the details when I finish, but first I want to address the leak to the press.

It was discovered that a Bureau employee, a Mr. Thweatt, I believe," he said, as he glanced towards Doe for reassurance, "found it in his best interest to notify a writer who leaked the story to the Post. For his efforts, Mr. Thweatt is no longer an employee of the Bureau."

A slight murmur passed through the room. I must remind all of you this investigation is not to be discussed outside this room. If any of you have any questions I would suggest, no encourage you to bring it to my attention. If I'm not available, Agent Boggs and Wells have my complete confidence in the matter. Any questions?"

The room remained silent, so Riley continued.

"Bo, I think we'd all like to hear your report."

Boggs stood and strode to the front of the room. Placing some papers on the podium, he looked up at the assembled group.

"Thank you, Mr. Director. My report won't be long, unless there are a lot of questions which I encourage you to ask if I don't make myself clear."

Shuffling his notes, he began, "Agent Eys and I first discovered that the ventilation system to the Director's office had been tampered with and rigged to release a gas over a twenty four hour time frame. The air conditioning system had failed and a commercial service utilized by the Bureau was called. A Mr. Randy Edwards spent two days working on the problem and during that time placed an aerosol container with the poison Fentanyl in the system."

Bo continued his narration explaining how the poison acted and what led him and Agent Eys to discover the method.

After the discovery, he discussed the investigation and the subsequent shooting in his apartment. Ending his story, he looked around the room and asked, "Any questions?"

Two hands went up and Bo pointed to the closest Agent, Hank Barnes.

"Yeah, Hank."

Barnes asked a question about the poison and its possible connection to a terrorist organization he and his partner were investigating. Bo acknowledged the possibility and asked them to continue with their own efforts, but report any findings to him or Drew.

The second question was of a technical nature on the Fentanyl to which Bo deferred to Doe.

All eyes shifted to the Agent near the head of the table as she deftly answered the question with a flourish of acronyms. A follow up allowed her to again show her expertise in the chemical matter. When the subject under discussion was settled, Bo stacked his notes and turned the meeting back to Director Riley.

"Thanks, Bo, for the update. I wish I could tell you the investigation was closed with the disposal of Mr. Edwards, but that isn't the case. We still don't know why and by who the plot was perpetrated. I'm convinced it is a plot against the government and more attempts will be made on officials both appointed and elected. I have ordered around the clock surveillance of all known terrorist cells. The Secret Service is working in conjunction with us to guard all elected officials of the government twenty-four hours a day. This includes the members of Congress. I can't tell you the strain on all our manpower. I have volunteered our organization to help fill in as needed. Until we determine what organization and who the targets are, we won't get much sleep around here. That's all; dismissed."

Three weeks later
Port of Almeria, Spain

An old cargo trawler flying the Libyan flag inched its way against the protected pilings as its diesel engines ground to a halt. The tall, distinguished frame of Lindsey Stringfellow stood near the rail and peered at the non-stop activity all around him on the loading dock. The hustle and bustle of the goings-on always fascinated him. He could not help but wonder where everything and everyone was going in such a hurry.

"I'm so glad that's over," she exclaimed, as she joined him at his post against the rail.

Turning to acknowledge Bonnie, he said, "I told you it was permissible for you to fly over and meet me. It was your idea to join me on the five-day voyage. I again must apologize for the accommodations. On a ship of this nature you can't expect much better, it wasn't designed for women passengers."

"Oh, the cabin wasn't so bad, and the crew was all very nice. It was the bathing accommodations that were difficult."

"Bathing accommodations? Did we have bathing facilities?" He joked.

"You know very well what I mean," she added.

"I thought you did your graduate work in Belize, I would have thought the jungle and mosquitoes would have been a challenge."

"Yes, I spent nearly two months on a Mayan dig, but the accommodations were much nicer. I guess I was spoiled."

"My dear, you will find a dig in the desert will be a little more difficult. I'm afraid the bathing accommodations will be almost non-existent. You will get to know your partners by their smell even before you see them."

"All right, all right, I get the picture, when do we start?"

"Soon enough, I will provide you with one night of luxury before we begin. I have made arrangements at the *Hospedaria Del Desierto* on the edge of the desert for tonight. If all goes according to plan, we begin tomorrow."

Pointing to a man at the end of the pier watching the ship dock, Stringfellow said, "I think that's my associate, at least I hope so. It has been five years since we've seen each other."

Raising his hand, he waved in the other man's direction. Immediately the stranger removed his hat and waved in return.

"I think that answers my question. I believe you will find our guide a man of many talents. I have entrusted my life to him on several occasions."

The gangplank was shifted into place by two of the crew and assisted by several men on the dock. Within ten minutes, the tall man followed by the young woman, exited the old trawler and approached the man on the dock.

"Professor, it is so good to see you again."

The stranger was of medium height with a dark complexion. When he removed his hat, he had a full head of black hair that shined in the sunlight. His smile, however, was infectious and Bonnie found herself grinning back at the stranger in spite of herself. He was dressed in black with a woolen jacket even though the weather was nearly ninety degrees. She was sure he was most certainly Middle Eastern.

"Bonnie Lane, let me introduce you to my friend Achmed. We go back a long way, a long, long way," Stringfellow said.

"Ms. Lane, it is a pleasure," he replied, as he extended his hand.

Taking the offering, she was surprised at how rough it was to the touch. A little like shaking hands with a porcupine she thought.

"Your family is well I hope?" Stringfellow asked.

"Yes Professor, I have two more children now since we last worked in Croatia."

"My, you have been a busy fellow! How many does that make?"

"Eight, Allah has blessed me with six strong sons and two beautiful daughters."

"You are indeed a lucky man. Now tell me what arrangements to transport our goods have you made?"

Extending his arm towards the end of the pier he said, "I have trucks that will take us to the hotel at the edge of the desert. Based on the information you supplied, I have three. That should be enough. When we reach our destination, I have arranged for pack animals. Have you decided exactly where we are going?"

"Here, let me show you." Removing a small document from his jacket, he walked over to a cargo box sitting on the dock and unrolled the paper.

"Bonnie, please hold this end," he directed, as he placed it on the flat surface.

"Now here is where we are headed." He pointed to a spot a hundred and fifty kilometers north of Almeria and eighty kilometers east of Granada.

"I see," the other man replied, scratching his head.

"How long will it take us to reach our destination?"

"Depending on the weather, three or four days once we

reach the edge of the desert. At this time of year, we can get sand storms as the wind comes in from the *Sierra Filabres* to the north. If that happens, you just have to stop and wait. Nothing moves in a sand storm."

"I understand. The cargo is coming off now, that is the first crate. Achmed, you are in charge of the loading. I have a few details to handle with Customs and calls to make back to the States. We'll be inside the Customs office, let me know when you have it all loaded."

"Yes, Professor, I will come and find you," he said, as he hurried off down the dock.

Chapter 21

▲▼▲▼▲▼

"My word, Professor, you weren't kidding. I thought after the Cargo ship; well, you can only imagine what I thought," Bonnie said.

Stringfellow shook his head in agreement, "Yes, it is magnificent, and not something you would expect to find out here on the edge of a desert. The *Hospedaria* was built back in the sixties. At that time, there was nothing here at all. Then they began making those movies. What did they call them, the pasta cowboys? You know the ones with Clint Eastwood."

"You mean the Spaghetti westerns," she giggled.

"That's right, spaghetti. The desert here resembles the American west and it was a lot cheaper. The hotel was built to accommodate all of the movie people. A rich entrepreneur thought this would become a tourist area and built it to grand proportions. However, as you can tell, we almost have the place to ourselves."

"The marble columns and beautiful art motifs on the ceiling remind me of a church. I am truly impressed."

"Yes, well I hope you found the room to your satisfaction."

"Oh my, the suite would accommodate several people, and the balcony with the view of the mountains and desert was breathtaking," she said.

"Well, enjoy yourself tonight; tomorrow we begin to rough it on our way through the desert. Now let's have dinner, I understand the restaurant is also a cut above the best."

The couple made their way to the dining room and was seated near the veranda with a magnificent view of the mountains.

The menu was a plethora of local favorites and the wine selection was almost overwhelming. However, after the long and arduous boat trip, Bonnie was ready for a steak. She ordered the Sirloin medium with some mixed vegetables and a Caesar salad. The Pinot Noir was one the waiter recommended and the aroma that assailed her nostrils made her smile, as she brought it to her lips.

Stringfellow also preferred something substantial and he chose the rack of lamb. He knew the lamb was a specialty of the hotel and would be tender and flavorful. After a Dewar's and soda with a twist, he joined Bonnie with a glass of the Pinot.

When the food was served, they both dived into the task and ate heartily with little conversation, except to compliment their choices.

Finishing the main course, they both passed on dessert and accepted the waiter's recommendation for coffee.

The dark thick liquid was a heavy blend of beans grown in the mountains nearby, but it proved to be more than Bonnie could handle. After tasting the steaming coal black liquid, she placed the cup aside before speaking, "Professor, do you really think we will find it?"

Returning his coffee cup to the saucer, he twirled his mustache and leaned forward with a broad smile.

"Bonnie, I have every confidence in the world. I wouldn't have drug you this far and put you through that boat ride if I wasn't confident in our chances."

"Oh, I can tell you are confident and I'm excited, but why did you pick the area you showed us on the map this afternoon?"

"A very good question, and one I gave much thought. You see, the desert here is a little different from any in the world. Tomorrow you will see there is vegetation that grows through the vast wilderness. The rainfall here is not a lot, but when it comes, it arrives in buckets for a few hours. The land is not prepared for the deluge and most of it simply runs off. However, in the area we will be exploring there is a multitude of what are known as sinkholes. The runoff filters into these holes and goes off to some mysterious location underground. It's my belief, we will find signs of the Hittite city in and around this location. If I'm wrong, well we still have a lot of desert to explore."

"So you think the sinkholes are the key to the Hittite location?"

"Yes, I'm convinced that the city lies buried in an area no more than fifty kilometers square."

"How can you be so sure?" she asked.

"Bonnie, millions of years ago, this area was under the ocean. Then the mountains pushed up and formed a great lake. When the lake dried up over another million years, it formed a fertile valley. That valley is where I'm convinced the Hittites built their city of milk and honey. That's the location where we are heading in the morning, and will begin our dig. Now I have been saving the best for last."

Reaching into his jacket, he removed a small sack. Opening the top, he removed something and placed it on the table in front of Bonnie.

"What is it?" she asked, as she lifted the item and stared at it closely.

"As you can see, it's a shard of pottery. But not just any pottery shard, it's from the Hittite civilization of around two thousand BC."

Turning it over carefully, she asked, "Are you sure?"

"Positive, now ask me where it came from?"

"All right, I'll play your game, where did it come from?"

"This afternoon while you were scrubbing the grime from your trip off your body, I did a little browsing in the shops near the hotel. I found this pottery shard not a hundred meters from the hotel. The shop owner claimed he had secured it from a local who had found it in the desert. When I pressed him as to the exact location, he showed me on a map the region. It's from the very area I chose for us to explore."

Reaching across the table, she placed her hand on his, "Professor, I'm so thrilled I can't tell you how exciting this is. I couldn't have done any of this without your help, thank you for agreeing to lead the expedition."

"Bonnie, I'm pleased you felt confident and asked me to participate. I know Aaron would have loved to join us."

Bonnie yawned and stretched again before speaking, "I'm sorry, please forgive me, I'm exhausted and ready for bed. How about you? We have a big day tomorrow."

Stringfellow agreed and after paying the tab, and leaving a generous tip for their waiter, they rose and made their way out of the dining area. As they exited through the door, an unaccompanied man passed them following the host into the dining room. Bonnie only briefly glanced in his direction as she strode by and moved on towards the lobby. However, Stringfellow smiled and nodded slightly in acknowledgment.

The host seated the man at a table near the same veranda the couple had just vacated. When the waiter approached, he smiled his recognition before speaking.

"Oh, Mr. Marchant, so good to see you this evening."

Drew and Bo sat patiently as Director Riley paced his office from the window to the desk. Both men smiled as they remembered how his predecessor had traveled the same worn spot in the carpet.

"It's been a month and nothing new has transpired. I just can't believe this was a one-time killing. I'm sure Edwards had more on his plate than Director Clark. Bo, tell me again about the file he was looking at on your desk."

Bo shuffled his feet before speaking, "It was just my file on the murder and the people assigned to different areas of the investigation. I don't think it was anything out of the ordinary. It was for my eyes only. I didn't plan to use it in the investigation. I would have just added to it as we progressed."

"What about the AC Company? Have we checked them completely from top to bottom? Is that owner as clean and dumb as he pretends?"

"Apparently so, he's had a contract for over seven years and the most current one is in its third year. Never a complaint from anyone in the Bureau or other agencies he covered. I think he was set up, I'm pretty sure the whole incident was planned to perfection."

"How do you mean?" Riley asked.

"The AC didn't just go down on its on while Mr. Randy Edwards was employed at Eastern Shore Air Tec. Someone on the inside must have tampered with the unit and caused the malfunction. Air Tec didn't just stop by on a spot check; they don't get paid to do that."

"You think it was an inside job, someone in the Bureau set up Clark?"

"It's possible, but I don't lean in that direction," Bo said.

"What about the employee who called in the repair order?" Riley probed.

"She's been with the Bureau for over twenty five years and wouldn't know an aerosol valve from a spare tire. No, she couldn't have created the problem. Must have been someone else who was in here, possibly at night when the place was almost empty."

"You mean like the janitorial staff?"

"Yeah, I thought of them first, but have had no luck with that end. Nobody new on their staff and the same folks are working now that were working the service a month ago. Nobody has left suddenly or mysteriously."

"What about you, Drew, have you turned up anything of interest?"

Drew shook his head, "Sorry, I'm at a loss. Bo's been closer to it than me and I trust his judgment. I ran down a couple of employees who I thought might be suspicious, but came up with a dead end."

"So here we are, one month after the murder and no suspects except one dead hit man."

"It looks that way to us. What about Agent Barnes, has he had any success linking the terrorist organization to the murder? Drew asked.

"No, not really linking, but they're the most likely. We've received threats from them in the past, and we've always kept them in our sights. But they've only been talk to this point."

"There's always that first time." Riley suggested.

The three men looked at each other waiting to see who was going to offer a suggestion next. When no one spoke, the Director said, "As much as I hate to do this, Drew I'm going to release you from the assignment."

"What? You're kidding me right?"

"No, I have complete confidence that Bo and Doe can handle what we have for now. I may change my mind later and call you back. In the meantime, I'll allow you to return to the Art collector's murder."

"Why the change of heart, and why assign me back to Eckenstadt's murder? I thought you wanted to leave that to the local authorities?"

"If it were up to me I'd let it lie, but it isn't my decision. The President has been petitioned by the Iraqi government to return the statue. Based on what you told me about the alterations of the text, there might be some explaining to do. Do you think you could get it back in its proper order and see that it's returned?"

"I could, but I don't think that's wise. With the true message underneath, we could cause an international incident. I would suggest we make them a copy."

"Copy, won't they suspect?"

"No, if the one in the Louvre has fooled experts for all these years, I'm sure with modern technology we could do them one better."

"Look into it then. How long will it take you to come up with this duplicate?"

"Can't say until I talk to a few experts. I'll get back to you with some kind of answer within twenty-four hours. If that's all, I'm going to pack my bag. I have a trip ahead of me. I'll handle the statue and let you know when it's ready to be returned to our friends in Baghdad."

Chapter 22

▲▼▲▼▲▼

Looking at the Rolex on his left wrist, he realized although it was only ten PM in Washington, it had to be three AM in Spain. Still, he could not resist the temptation. Some information he had discovered during his recent investigation required him to alert Bonnie. He laid the airline confirmation on the desk and again checked the arrival time. He would be in Madrid by early evening if all went well and he made his connection at London's Heathrow.

Grabbing the satellite phone, he walked to the window of the Hyatt Regency and gazed out at the familiar outline of the nation's Capitol. Finally, the connection was complete and the phone gently buzzed as it tried to make the link. After the fifth ring, an exhausted sounding voice replied, "Yes, who is it?"

"Bonnie, this is Drew, sorry to wake you, it must be three AM, but this is important."

At the sound of his voice, she sat straight up and pulled the covers around her out of habit.

"Drew, is that really you? You're the last person I expected to call. Is something wrong?"

"No, not really, but since we talked a few days ago my status has changed and I wanted to give you a heads up."

"What are you talking about, your status has changed?"

"What I mean to say is I've been temporarily removed from the Director's murder and reassigned to Eckenstadt's case. I'll be free to assist you in your search. Just exactly, where are you right now? All I know is you left for Almeria on a boat last week."

She rubbed the sleep out of her eyes as she tried to comprehend everything that had been said.

"Yes, we arrived yesterday and had all of our material loaded on trucks and delivered to a hotel at the edge of the Tabernas Desert. It's called the *Hospedaria,* and it's wonderful. When do you think you'll arrive?"

"I'll be in Madrid tomorrow evening and it'll take me a couple of days to catch up to you, but there's more I need to tell you."

"Oh, what's that?"

First, I'm probably not going to join you right away; I need to do a little investigating on my own first."

"I don't understand, what do you need to investigate in Spain? Aaron was killed in Florida."

"Yes, but that leads me to the second part."

"Go on, I'm listening."

Drew began his short narrative and Bonnie listened intently. From time to time she tried to interrupt, but all she got in was "But, or what."

Finally, when Drew finished, he said, "Well, what do you think?"

Placing her house slippers on, she crossed to the window and stared out at the moon as it passed between two peaks of the *Sierra Filabres.*

"I guess I'm in shock, how can you be sure?"

Drew paused before speaking, "I'm not sure, nothing in this investigation is like anything I've been involved in before. I think there's a lot more to this than I've been able to turn up, but I'm sure of the part we discussed. Now I want you to be careful and not let any of this out of the bag. It's too dangerous to share with anyone, do I make myself clear?"

"Perfectly, however, I'm sure I'll be safe as long as my only interest is in the dig itself. Do you want me to do anything to help?"

"Absolutely not, I'll let you know when I'm in the area and will alert you to anything I feel important. In the meantime, keep your head down and that pretty little ass covered. Keep your phone with you at all times and I'll stay in touch. Now get some rest, but keep your eyes open."

The click in her ear told her he had disconnected and she placed her phone back on the nightstand. Looking at the clock, she realized it was nearly four AM. She'd have a hell of a time sleeping now, after the bombshell Drew had laid on her.

It was so preposterous she found it almost impossible to believe. Still, Drew was in a position to ferret out information and well, she had better take his advice and keep the entire story to herself. Removing her slippers, she slid back into the soft pillow top bed and stared at the ceiling for a few moments before closing her eyes. A smile creased her lips as she turned over imagining Drew lying next to her.

The soft tapping at the door alerted her and she made her way across the hotel room to the entrance. Staring at the clock on the nightstand, she realized it was barely seven AM. Still, since Drew's call she had been unable to return to sleep and finally got out of bed around five-thirty. Making a strong cup of coffee from the complimentary pot on the table, she called room service and had a plate of pastries sent up. What the hell, she thought; nobody out here in the desert to appreciate her figure anyway, might as well enjoy the last vestiges of civilization.

Another light tap greeted her ears before she reached the door and shouted, "I'm coming!"

Bonnie knew before she opened it that it was the Professor. He had said be prepared to leave early and she knew from experience what that meant.

"Did I wake you?" the voice from behind the door asked, almost apologetically.

Opening the portal, she smiled, "No, I've been up for quite awhile. I was too excited to sleep," she lied.

He was dressed in his bush jacket and jodhpurs. The boots were some kind of leather, possibly snakeskin she guessed, and his hat was straight out of the movies. Yes, he could have been 'Indiana Jones' in another lifetime. As he entered, he glanced across the room to the coffee pot and asked, "Enough for me a cup?"

"Certainly," she closed the entry and retraced her steps to the table where she poured him the last of the steaming black liquid.

"I was glad to see this was Maxwell House, not that syrup we had last night. It was too strong for my taste," she added.

Accepting the coffee, he sipped it before speaking, "I see you have been up for awhile, are you packed?"

"Yes," she said, pointing to her overnight bag on the bed.

"I'm ready when you are."

"Good, Achmed has the mules packed and loaded. We have a long trek ahead of us, the sooner we get started, the better."

"Well, as I said, I'm ready and excited about the trip. Will we see anything of importance today?"

"I'm afraid not, Achmed assured me the day's travel will be somewhat boring. We should reach the foothills of the Sierra's tomorrow, tonight we will camp in the open. 'The following day we will make our way through the mountain passes to the valley. The mountain stretch should take us at least two days. Are you sure you're up to it?"

At the mere mention of her frailty, she puffed out her chest and said, "I'll have you know I workout three times a week. I can bench press a hundred and fifty pounds and run five miles without a break. Does that answer your question?"

"Quite so, I meant no disrespect. I, well you know, men of my generation are used to dealing with frail ladies."

"Like I said, I'm not frail. I enjoy the physical regimen and am sure I can keep up, if that is what you meant."

"Yes, I'm sure. Well, if we're both ready, let's see what Achmed has for us."

Placing the cups on the table, Bonnie retrieved her bag and they made their way out of the room into the hall and down to the lobby.

"What about my camel?" she asked.

"Oh, I was joking about the camel," he laughed. "Even though there are a few around here, Achmed has pack animals for the boxes and we have some fine horses. Spanish blood and bred for stamina, I think you'll find them beautiful animals. You do ride, don't you?"

"Yes, I started as a small girl, my dad insisted I learn. Aaron and I used to go to the stables once or twice a year and ride some back trails. He was a fine horseman."

"Yes, I'm sure he was. Well here we are."

The pack animals were all tethered together, and Achmed was attending to some last minute details and didn't see their arrival.

"Achmed, are we ready to begin?" Stringfellow asked as they approached their guide.

Turning, he smiled and bowed slightly in Bonnie's direction.

"Almost, I have two men who will accompany us. They are locals and profess to know the area beyond the mountains like the back of their hand."

"Well, let's hope they earn their money. I'm sure we will be able to use their strong backs once we begin the dig," Stringfellow added.

Spying the horses tied to a post, Bonnie approached and asked, "Which one is mine?"

"The chestnut mare, I was assured she is most gentle with a good disposition."

"Everyone seems concerned about my frailty; I assure you I can ride with the best. What's her name?"

"Esmeralda," the Arab stated.

"You're putting me on?" Bonnie said.

"No, no, she is named for the peculiar color of her eyes."

Placing her hand under the horse's chin, she turned the head and looked closely at the animal.

"Well I'll be. She has one green eye."

"Yes, the owner thought that was unusual, he named her Esmeralda which means emerald."

"Well, old girl, looks like you and I will get to know each other quite well over the next few weeks." With that said, she placed her left foot in the stirrup and swung into the saddle. Cocking her hat to one side, she looked every bit the part of an American cowgirl in Spain.

"I'm ready," she repeated.

From the veranda a hundred yards away, a man appeared and stopped at the railing where he placed one foot on the bottom rung. He was dressed in a white linen suit and his appearance was distinctly European. Raising his coffee cup in a mock salute, he said to the assembled caravan, "I'll see you soon, my dear."

Chapter 23

▲▼▲▼▲▼

The British Airways flight from Kennedy was late, the weather had turned foul and Drew sat on the runway for over an hour.
He knew his connection to Iberia Flight 237 was tight at Heathrow, but the flight attendant convinced him Iberia was always late, as she handed him his Stoli Martini. Reassured he would have adequate time to make the connection, he settled in with a novel by his favorite author, C.T.Dowling.

The time passed pleasantly with good vodka and better reading. Arriving in London, he was disappointed to learn the Iberia flight had departed to Madrid right on time. The next flight was at eight in the morning and he had no options but to wait. He had a strong urge to call Bonnie, but not exactly sure if she'd be able to take the call; he decided to delay it until later when he hoped she'd be alone. Instead, he opted to call his partner Bo in Washington.

"This is Boggs, that you, Drew?"

"Yeah, had some dead time here in London, thought I'd check to see how you and Doe are doing? Anything new on that end?"

"Boy, do you have good timing!"

"What do you mean?"

"I mean you couldn't have planned it any better. You hadn't been in the air an hour when we had another attempt on a government official's life."

Drew stopped in his tracks before asking, "Who was it, where did it happen, were they hurt?"

"No, and it happened near his town house in Georgetown. It was Riley's boss."

"You mean the Attorney General?"

"I do, and he was damn lucky. One of the agents assigned to him saved his life and took a bullet in the thigh."

"Did the shooter get away?" Drew asked.

"No, another agent winged him before he could beat a retreat. He's in custody right now."

"Has he told us anything about who's responsible?"

"No, he's clean, no papers of any kind. We got nothing on his prints and he's as tight as a clam." All we know for sure is he's Middle Eastern, probably Saudi. He speaks passable English, but about all he'll say is 'I want my lawyer.'"

"Does Riley want me back?"

"No, in fact, I was supposed to call you if you didn't check in by this evening. To say he was pleased the AG wasn't hurt and we got the assassin alive, is putting it mildly. We're sure we can control this and it won't hit the newspapers. With the assassin in custody, we should be able to break this wide open."

"What are you going to do, torture him with some of your jokes?" Drew chided.

"No, not exactly, we've hinted to him he might be on his way out of the country."

"You mean?"

"Right, I mean Gitmo."

"Guantanamo? We can't do that; he was captured here and will have to stand trial here. Besides, they're closing that place after all the bad publicity."

"He don't exactly know that. He hasn't seen any legal beagles yet and we have him isolated for the time being."

"Good work, Bo, wish I could have been there. Tell Riley I'm delayed in London, but expect to be on my way again in the morning."

"Glad I'm not with you. I can't believe you wanted to go traipsing around in that damn Spanish desert looking for treasure, when you couldda been here in the cold and snow."

"Duty calls, I need to try and hook up with Bonnie. Let me know as soon as anything new breaks, I'll keep you posted on a daily basis if I can."

"Roger, tell Bonnie babe hi for me, see ya."

With that, Bo hung up and Drew folded his phone and returned it to his jacket pocket. He still had eight hours to kill in this airport until the next flight to Madrid. Might as well find the nearest bar and see if he could stir up any excitement.

The shadows were creeping towards them from the purple mountains in the distance as Achmed urged them on. Bonnie realized her best riding days were in the past and her butt was just plain sore from the eight hours she had spent in the saddle. A soft breeze was in their face and it was a relief from the steady heat they had experienced for most of the day. The first day had been, as the Professor predicted, nothing to write home about. They had stopped three times to eat and relieve themselves, seeing nothing except a few vipers that lived under rocks near the trail. From time to time, vegetation poked its head up here and there to test the heat before fading away into the sand. The dust and sand was ferocious. Every speck of wind carried sand and grit into her face attaching itself to her riding clothes. She spent a good portion of the morning, using her broad brimmed hat to beat the collection from her clothing. Finally, with little to show for her efforts, she gave in and let it have its way. "Would this day never end?" she asked herself.

The Professor had been unusually quiet and when she tried to make conversation, he was quick and short with his replies, perhaps tonight around the camp he would open up. Something appeared to be bothering him and it annoyed her he wouldn't share it.

Finally, Achmed raised his hand as a sign to halt. He dismounted and turned to face them.

"We will camp here, please to help me with the pack animals. We will not make a full-fledged camp, only a fire to keep any wild creatures away that might be curious."

Esmeralda gratefully halted as Bonnie swung down from the saddle. Rubbing her backside with little concern for the men around her, she stretched and took in the scenery. Achmed had selected a sight near a large outcrop of rocks. The wind had partially subsided and only a cool breeze approached timidly from the north. The two laborers were busy helping Achmed with the pack animals, and had already unloaded some of the camping equipment.

"May I help?" she asked.

Their guide smiled timidly and replied, "No, I think we have it, you may make the coffee if you wish. We will need a fire, can you make one?"

"I can, if you have matches," she teased.

Removing the box of fire making instruments from his pack, he handed it to her.

Bonnie accepted the offering and began her search for kindling to begin the task.

Within an hour, the fire was blazing and the bedrolls were laid out in a circle around the small controlled inferno. The coffee had already been poured and Achmed was now busy with some mysterious concoction he was preparing for the evening meal.

When she thought the moment appropriate, she approached Stringfellow, "Are you all right? I mean, you appear as though something is bothering you."

"What? Oh no, I'm fine, just a lot of details on my mind. I'm beginning to have doubts about my assessment of the situation. I was so positive the other day of our goal, but now?" He paused before continuing, his brow was furrowed and he looked every bit his age.

"I know this will be my last dig, I was so hoping that it would be a major discovery. But what if it isn't, what if we find nothing? I just can't stand the thought of failure."

Bonnie continued to stare, and realized no matter how confident he had appeared earlier, he was no different from anyone else. Self-doubt always haunted those who undertook lofty goals and difficult tasks.

"Professor, don't doubt yourself, you have put in a great deal of time and research. Don't forget I also studied the stone before you, and came to the same conclusions. I agree with your assessments, this is the only place the Lost City could be. We'll find it, I know we will."

"Yes, yes, you are right. Only, it is quite stressful and the people who financed the dig are expecting a major return on their investment."

"Who might they be, may I ask?"

"Oh, no one you would know. Don't bother yourself, I'm the only one accountable."

A slight tinge of red appeared in her cheeks as she fought back the urge to reply with a cryptic remark. Bonnie hated it when people treated her like a little girl. She knew all of the major players and although she did not carry the weight of Stringfellow, she could have as easily put this dig together without his assistance. The anger of the demeaning comment slowly subsided and she re-grouped her thoughts before speaking.

"Let's not focus on what might be, let's be positive. We'll find the lost city and both of us will be remembered for the foresight and effort of our discovery."

"The food is ready, if you are," Achmed proudly proclaimed.

Stringfellow stood, and as he did, he placed his arm around Bonnie's shoulders, "You're right, we'll find it, and even if by some chance we don't, the thrill is in the search."

Cxapter 24

▲▼▲▼▲▼

When she awoke, the sun was just peeking over the top of the Filabres and the cool morning air refreshed her aching body. Bonnie wished she could take a shower, but that was impossible. Still, Achmed assured her the base camp would have a make shift facility he knew how to improvise. She was looking forward to that, but it was still at least two days away. She removed a soft cloth and wiped her neck and face. No need for makeup out here, no one would notice anyway, just clean and sanitary were her goals.

At first, the sound was barely perceptible and she had to strain to hear it. The steady hum was unlike anything she had ever heard before. It almost pulsated as it made its way in on the morning breeze. Yes, it was gradually getting louder as she listened. Now she no longer had to strain to hear it. The rhythmic buzz was coming from the direction they were heading, the purple mountains in the distance.

"Professor, wake up!" she urged him, as she shook his arm.

"What, who, what's the matter?" he asked, as he sat up in his bedroll.

"Listen, do you hear it? It's been getting louder for the last few minutes. What is it, do you know?"

Cocking his head to one side, he listened in earnest. Tossing the covers aside, he leaped fully dressed to his feet.

"Achmed, Achmed, wake up! Listen, what do you make of it?"

The guide scrambled to his feet and turned his head to one side. The two laborers sat up and they all listened to the mysterious noise.

"What is it?" Stringfellow repeated.

The two Spanish laborers began jabbering amongst themselves and Achmed immediately joined them. Suddenly, he stared at Stringfellow and proclaimed. "It's hoppers, they're coming."

The Professor returned the man's stare and asked again, "Hoppers, what the hell are hoppers?"

"Why, they're small locust, ones that cannot fly yet. They are coming and they eat everything in their way. All of the vegetation around us will be stripped from the vines. We must calm the pack animals and find shelter. They will show us no mercy and their swarms can be deadly."

"Locust, here, now?"

"Yes, they only do this every five years. They will eventually begin to fly. They may be as many as, I don't know how many. They stretch for miles and it will take them hours to pass. Hurry, we must hurry!" he said, as the three men began to collect the horses that had already become nervous and were snorting and stomping with fright.

"Locust, he must be joking, they are the dumbest locust I've ever heard of, out here in a desert," Bonnie retorted.

Packing her bedroll, she placed it back on the pack animal that was by now in a near state of terror. "There, there, girl, everything will be all right. We want let them get to you."

Turning, she left the frightened pack animal and strode over to where Esmeralda was standing and stomping her foot in protest to the ever increasing hum.

Again, she patted her steed and whispered soft reassuring words in the chestnut mare's ear. The soothing sound and gentle hand seemed to help as she stopped her nervous twitching.

"Where are we going?" Bonnie shouted across the camp that was now nothing more than a memory. The professor had already mounted his black stallion and pointed in the direction of a small foothill no more than a mile in the distance.

"There, where the professor is pointing, we will try and make shelter against the rocks, hurry!" Achmed shouted.

Grasping the reins, she flung herself into the saddle and kicked Esmeralda in the ribs with her heels. Immediately the mare leaped forward and bolted in the direction of the foothills. The Professor was right on her heels with Achmed and the laborers following close behind. Looking over her left shoulder, she saw the first sign of the migration. Half a mile, maybe less, she saw a mass of black moving unevenly along the ground towards them. The dark shadow appeared to be a river of oil as it flowed and ebbed along the floor of the desert. Strain as she might, she could see no end to the tide of terror. Esmeralda was now at full gallop, and although Bonnie was an expert equestrian, she held on for dear life as the terrified animal fled the noisy intruder.

It seemed longer than it must have been, but finally she reached her goal. Pulling the reins in with all her strength, she halted the frightened mare grudgingly.

Her trained eye searched the immediate area as the Professor pulled up beside her. "There, over there, beneath the overhang!" he shouted.

Bonnie immediately saw the plan and dismounted leading her steed to the shelter. The rock had a slim ledge that extended at least ten feet from the base and was a natural refuge against the wind and rain. Esmeralda seemed immediately reassured as she entered the darkness created by the over hang.

When Achmed and his helpers arrived, they all led the animals under the ledge as Bonnie had done.

"Please to help, we need to unpack the tents, hurry!"

All hands joined in the task and untied several nylon packs that would normally be used for shelter in the open. Achmed and one of the laborers climbed on top of the ledge as Stringfellow and the other man tossed the edge of the nylon to them. Placing rocks and small boulders on the tarp, they soon erected a wall against the oncoming intruders. At the base, Bonnie assisted by shoving other rocks on the bottom to hold the material taught. It seemed like it took an hour, but in truth only a few minutes. When the wall had been erected to Achmed's satisfaction, all hands entered the sanctuary and waited. The breathing of the five sounded like a small windstorm as each person tried to catch their breath.

They only had a few minutes to wait, as the surge of the locust reached their location. The sound was terrifying as they all tried to reassure the frightened animals. Esmeralda was surprisingly calm now. It may have been the darkness, Bonnie could not be sure. Nevertheless, she continued to whisper in the mare's ear. As the locust reached the outcrop, hundreds, if not thousands of them hopped into the nylon and bounced off. The tarp continually waved in the breeze of insects. At first, Bonnie was as frightened as the horses, but as the minutes turned into hours, she was able to calm herself. As she watched, only a few of the insects made it beneath the nylon material into their shelter. They were small and ugly creatures. What possible use they served was beyond her capacity to reason. Still, they were here for a purpose she thought, as she squashed one of the repulsive insects beneath her boot.

Looking down at the glow of her Seiko, she realized it was after three PM. They had been in their shelter for nearly seven hours, and the locust continued their onslaught against the nylon material. Little had been said among the group, but now her stomach was beginning to growl as she realized she had missed two meals.

"Yes, I'm hungry too," Stringfellow said, as if he could read her mind.

Achmed had the same thought and reached into one of the saddlebags, removing several packages from their place of concealment. Handing them out he said, "Eat, they are good for you, and the taste is tolerable."

Accepting the package, Bonnie quickly opened it and consumed the ingredients in a couple of bites. Well, it wasn't chocolate, but it had a rather sweet taste and she looked longingly towards Achmed. He immediately understood the meaning. Reaching in the bag, he produced several more packages and offered them to the group.

"How much longer do you think we'll have to stay in here?"

Achmed shook his head, "I think not much longer, I'm sure they must be mostly past us by now."

Almost before he finished speaking, the sound died off and then stopped completely. The nylon tent hung limp and each of the members looked at one another. Achmed almost timidly raised the edge of the flap and peeked out.

"It is good they are gone."

Bonnie was quick to follow his lead, she led Esmeralda out from the protection of the shelter, and then stopped to gaze around.

The entire area was now barren and where scrub bushes had been before, nothing remained. The landscape was stripped of all vegetation and the sand looked as if it had been smoothed with a fine rake. Only a few of the insects remained on the ground around the outcropping. The weakest always die, she thought.

Joining her, Stringfellow shook his head and said, "Might as well make camp here. It's too late to make any time now, we only have a couple of hours before dark."

The four-wheel drive vehicle was making good time as he again checked his map. The town of *Albacete* was disappearing in his rear view mirror and the darkness of the countryside was returning to envelop the jeep. The flight to Madrid had been uneventful and he planned his strategy loosely as he stared at the map in the seat beside him. If he could believe the chart Hertz had given him, the town of *Murcia* was a hundred and fifty miles further to the east. When he reached it, he would have to replace his vehicle with some kind of four-legged transportation. He didn't consider himself a first class horseman, but he knew his way around a saddle from lessons he had taken as a child.

The problem he would have would be reading the terrain around the desert. His route would bring him in from the north, while Bonnie and her entourage would be approaching from the south. They had discussed the valley and its approximate location, however, a mile or so in either direction and he could find himself lost and going in circles. Well, it wouldn't be the first time, he reasoned.

The vehicle sped on through the inky darkness and Drew found himself pleasantly surprised at the consistency of the road. He had half expected a gravel expressway, but the asphalt was smooth, straight, and well marked. The full moon began its journey from beneath the horizon, and his thoughts turned to the beautiful woman out there somewhere. "What is she doing right now?" he asked himself.

Chapter 25

▲▼▲▼▲▼

Having wasted the entire day cowering under the outcrop from the attack of the locust, she was tired and disgusted. Another day thrown away, would they never get to the site? How she longed to get her hands dirty digging for the mysteries of the Hittite civilization. She had walked away from the camp and was now a half mile in the desert somewhere north of the base camp. The night chill was coming in on a cool breeze and she shuddered as she planned her retreat to the warmth of their fire.

    When asked later how she saw it, she would reply, she had more felt it than seen it. Stopping, she could not decide if she should investigate, or return to camp. "What the hell?" she thought, "Might as well enjoy what's left of the daylight." Striding in the direction of the object, she again, was amazed at how the locust had stripped everything in the area. The desert that had resembled Arizona that morning now appeared more like the Sahara.

    When she reached it, she was even more puzzled. It protruded from the ground a few inches and she realized immediately it was man-made. A small cap of bronze or copper covered the end. She went to her knees and reached across to pull it from its place of concealment.

It did not budge, stuck as tight as if it were glued. It felt metallic and had ridges along the edge. Yes, carved ridges, she was sure. Slowly, she smoothed the sand away from around the article and began to dig her way down. The object continued its stubbornness as she again tried to pry it loose. After fifteen minutes of effort, she had excavated a couple of gallons of sand, but the object continued its obstinacy to her efforts.

The digging now allowed her to see it was at least two feet in length, three inches in diameter, and had a slight arc in the portion she had uncovered. Brushing away more sand, she saw additional markings along the length of the object. The article was definitely metal, but in places there remained remnants of a leather material. The light was now failing and she knew if she wanted to get it free, she would have to call for assistance.

Leaving the digging, but placing her hat atop the object as a marker, she hurried back to the campsite.

Stepping off the curb at Pennsylvania Avenue, he crossed the intersection and decided to walk back to his hotel. Bo was not amused after his conversation with the President of the United States. She was not in the best of moods and he was sure the old gal had rather seen Drew than him, but he was what she got.

As he passed the art shop he heard, "Hey, good looking, how would you like to buy a working girl a drink?"

Startled, he stopped and glanced in the direction of the voice. Approaching at a brisk pace with a large smile was his partner, Doe Eys.

"Oh it's you, thought I was gonna get lucky," he said, with a smirk.

"Luck, you don't need luck, a big good looking guy like you," she replied.

How bout buying me a drink and filling me in on your meeting with the boss lady?"

"Sure, there's a tavern on the corner. Never could understand how one could be this close to the White House, but after all, it's America."

Another half block and the two agents entered the establishment and made their way to an empty table near the back. As they slid into the old booth, Bo flagged down a waiter and ordered two drafts of a local vintage.

Doe waited patiently as she noticed Bo apparently clearing his mind and trying to sort out what he would tell her.

"Not a lot to tell, really. Maybe next time I'll take you along. Course she'd rather have Drew, as you might imagine."

"Who wouldn't?" she joked, "Sorry, Bo, just kidding. Now tell me about the meeting."

"Okay, well first she was pleased we apprehended the assassin. He still hasn't said much. Wish I could have five minutes with him, I think I could persuade him to level with us. All the same, they're so hung up with prisoner's rights nowadays that he's getting better treatment than the King of Saudi Arabia. I think he'll fess up for a plea bargain; they're trying to convince him he'll fry if he doesn't. You know, I don't think the bastard cares. Probably would've like to been killed at the sight. They all want to be martyrs, you know."

"Yes, you're right. Well, what are we supposed to do in the meantime? I mean, does this expand or reduce our effort?"

Bo shook his head and accepted the beer the waiter placed on the table before disappearing into the darkness of the pub.

"No specific directions from the boss. She's leaving it all up to Riley. He told me on the way out to maintain our surveillance on the officials and determine the exact people responsible for the murder and the attempt on the AG."

"I thought that was obvious with the member of the 'Sword of Islam," or whatever he's calling himself now."

"No, I agree, kinda wish Drew was here. He always has some harebrained scheme that seems to work and ferret out the bad guys. Nevertheless, he ain't and all you and the President got is me, so I suggest we start at the beginning and review all the information we have. I'll call a session with the team leaders for first thing in the morning and we'll compare notes. There has got to be something we're missing. I just feel it."

"It's over here; I marked it with my hat. There, I told you I hadn't imagined it," Bonnie said, as she half-dragged the reluctant Stringfellow along.

Arriving at the site of her dig, it was now nearly dark. Only a little light played off the peaks of the mountains as Stringfellow knelt and examined the find.

"Some kind of scabbard, I'd say," he announced.

"Scabbard, you mean like as in sword and scabbard?"

"Yes, could have been out here for several thousand years. Must be from some battle, probably lost by a soldier, although?"

His voice trailed off and Bonnie could see he was in deep thought.

"Yes, is there more?"

"Just doesn't seem to fit. I mean, this is more of a cavalry officers, something like you might find with the Greek or Roman officers. Oh well, we'll find out soon enough. Here, hand me the shovel."

Bonnie had almost forgotten the trowel she had retrieved and was carrying. Handing it to her mentor, she watched as he began to dig. With years of skilled excavation behind him, he handled the tool like an extension of his arm. He quickly made short work of the job and placed the instrument aside. Placing both hands on the protruding scabbard, he exerted a great deal of effort with almost no result. However, a small movement indicated they were close to the point of extraction.

Again, he retrieved the trowel and continued to dig around the base of the find.

"Here, bring me that light," he demanded.

Bonnie did as she was asked and handed it to him. Turning on the high beam, he flashed it around the base of the hole. After a moment, a slight gasp escaped his lips.

"What's wrong? Is there something the matter?"

Without uttering a word, he pointed in the direction he had been working. There on the very end of the sheath was a bony hand grasping the hilt of a sword firmly entrenched in the scabbard. However, it was not just any hand, but one of royalty with rings of colorful stones on each silent finger holding the instrument of death, and reluctant to give it up for any reason.

Bonnie pulled away at the sudden realization that someone had died holding the prize. Now they had to excavate the entire area to determine what happened and who had died here. If they were lucky, it may have something to do with their search for the Lost City. If not, it would still be a find worth the extra effort.

Almost a mile away at the edge of darkness, a lone figure stood silently observing the scene. Removing the binoculars from his eyes, he handed them to an aide and stood pondering what he had seen. Removing a silver case from his jacket, he extracted a filter tip cigarette, and immediately lit it with a Zippo. The flash could have been seen in the failing light if anyone was looking in his direction, but no one was.

"They've found something already. I wonder what it is and if it has anything to do with the search? They are still two days away from the planned sight."

Shaking his head, he continued to stare as the last vestiges of sunlight gradually slipped into the abyss of darkness.

Chapter 26

▲▼▲▼▲▼

The sun had risen to its apex and the heat was intensifying as the five labored at their assigned task. Bonnie wiped her brow with a soft cloth and turned her face away from the burning ember that seemed to follow her everywhere. From a touch to her cheek, she realized she was getting a good case of sunburn. Absent-mindedly she had forgotten to apply the lotion that morning while the breeze was still cool to her face.

"There, let's stop, we have quite a bit to ponder," Stringfellow announced.

Achmed and the two men hurried away from the large hole in the ground and headed for the shelter of the shade where they greedily consumed the water from their provisions.

Looking down into the pit, Bonnie was amazed at what she could see. A skeleton astride a horse's frame was buried beneath all that sand. He was in battle gear and his outstretched hand held the sword and scabbard that had been torn from his waist and held aloft as though it might shelter him from the elements.

"Well, what do you make of it?" Stringfellow asked his former pupil.

"Do I get extra credit if I'm right?" she quipped.

"You always were a smart aleck, even when you were in my class. Oh, you thought I didn't understand all those wisecracks, but I did. Yes, I'll give you extra credit because this is so far from the norm I would be surprised if anyone would ever put it here in the Tabernas Desert. Go ahead, tell me your deductions."

Bonnie knelt to be closer to the horseman and felt his tunic that had been covered for so many centuries. She smoothed the ruffles, then touched the helmet and stared at the unusual headband, before gazing back at the professor.

"I'd say Roman cavalry, sometime about 4th century BC."

"You'd be wrong! Look closer at the horse's bit and the stirrups, they should have been your first clue," he exclaimed.

Bonnie's feelings were bruised, but it did not keep her from challenging her mentor. "What's your guess then?"

"No guess, I know for a fact it's Macedonian."

"Macedonian? You mean Alexander's army?"

"I mean one of Alexander's armies. Although I can't be sure until we excavate the entire area, my guess is it belongs to General Ptolemy."

"Wasn't he supposed to be Alexander's closest ally? I thought he died fighting the Egyptians."

"Yes, most historians have placed him there, but the truth may never be known. Some of us of my generation believe he was Alexander's lover."

Bonnie snapped a disrespectful look at Stringfellow before speaking, "Lover, you mean he was homosexual, 'Alexander the Great' the mightiest of warriors, gay?"

"Not exactly gay, Bonnie, after all he had a son and two different wives. No, I think the term more accurately would be bi-sexual. Not so uncommon in that time if you remember some of my lectures. The Romans and Greeks were considered enlightened in their sexual preferences by their bi-sexual activities. In my lectures I always proposed that after Alexander conquered the known world, he returned to Alexandria and died of boredom."

Yes, that is the accepted theory."

"Well, he died all right, but I think he was saddened over the loss of his lover."

"Why, professor, you're a romantic!"

At that, Stringfellow burst into laughter, "Bonnie, you always have to have the last word."

"So what if Alexander was bi-sexual as you claim. How does that have anything to do with this find? For that matter, what does this find have to do with our plan to locate the Lost City of the Hittites?"

"One question at a time, young lady, one question at a time. First, if this is Ptolemy, and I think it is, but only further effort on our part will determine that fact. It may change the face of ancient history as we know it."

"I don't understand," she repeated.

"Let me restate my hypothesis. First of all, no Macedonian army was every remotely supposed to have traversed into this part of the known world. However, our friend here is living proof, pardon the pun, dead proof that is a lie. Next, the Hittite city of the lost is supposed to be in Syria. We are now proposing that to be a lie and it is here. We may never know why these two cultures came together on this plain in the middle of a desert that has so little to offer, but I have a theory on that too!"

"You mean give up our search for the city?"

"No, on the contrary, I propose the city is somewhere near here, if not right under our very noses. While you were sleeping last night, I sat up for several hours pondering this proposition. I think we would miss a great opportunity if we didn't fully excavate this sight."

Bonnie gave no visual sign of disappointment as Stringfellow paused before continuing.

"Well, do you agree with my deductions or not?"

"You're still the professor and I guess I'll always be the student. I must defer to your judgment on this issue. You've had much more experience in these matters than I."

"Tut tut, don't shortchange yourself, you were one of the brightest pupils I ever had the good fortune to come across," he admonished her.

Bonnie smiled with pleasure at the compliment before replying, "Thank you for your kind words, but as I said, I'll defer to you in this matter. Still, what will our benefactors say, you know the ones who financed this dig. They were expecting us to find the city of the Hittites, and oh yes that small matter about the gold."

"Bonnie, if your old professor is right, we may have it both ways. I took the liberty last night of placing a call on my satellite phone and talked at some length to my contact. She was most excited about my story and gave me permission to use my own judgment on when and where to dig. I sent her a photo of what we had uncovered and she said she would get back to me if further instructions were needed. So there, you see, we can do as we think prudent."

At that moment, the professor did something totally out of character. A change in his demeanor was followed by the reaching across to Bonnie and smoothing a lock of her hair back from her face. She sat mesmerized at this action and started to speak, but was interrupted.

"Bonnie, there is one more thing I need to tell you before we go on, it is difficult for me and no one but you will know. You must not mention it to anyone."

Puzzled, she said, "Another secret? My, you are full of surprises today. What could it be, let me guess."

"Don't make light of this, Bonnie, I am very serious."

At the change of tone in his voice, she cocked her head to one side and said, "What is it?"

Stringfellow said nothing for several seconds and the pause was uncomfortable to the woman. Finally, he cleared his throat before speaking and said, "This is my last dig. Oh, I know I have said that before, but you don't understand my meaning."

"What are you getting at?"

"I'm dying. The doctors have only given me a short time to live. Of course, when I got the news I was devastated as anyone would be. I sat around for several days contemplating my life and my legacy. I came to realize I have no legacy of significance. Then out of nowhere, you called with this wonderful opportunity. To me it will fulfill a life's dream."

"Oh, Professor, I don't know what to say," she mumbled, as she leaned forward and hugged him affectionately.

Accepting her embrace for a few moments, he finally pushed her gently away.

"Bonnie, I don't want your condolences, I want your help. If we can prove this is Ptolemy and he is here, it will jar the world of my peers."

Regaining her composure, she wiped a tear from her eye and said, "Why is this find so important?"

The gleam had now returned to his eye and he charged forward,   "Because this will prove the Macedonians left Egypt to fight the Celts here in this god-forsaken place and ran unexpectedly headlong into the Hittites. If this battle beneath our feet had not taken place, Ptolemy would have been able to defeat the Celts and unite the kingdom of Alexander. The fall of the Roman Empire would have happened much sooner and the past you have studied would not have taken place. I believe this one battle changed the face of history for all time."

hardly a consolation as he was moving way to fast towards the unknown. Twisting the steering wheel, he again tried to right his direction, and for a moment succeeded, as he was now moving forward. All too quickly, the sandy landscape grabbed his automobile like quicksand and turned him sideways once more as a sense of helplessness took hold. He felt the car begin to lose its integrity and start to slip over onto its side. No time to check his seat belt, he took a deep breath and gave one more mighty jerk of the wheel. For an instant, but only an instant, he had it, but just as quickly, he lost it. The auto tipped and rolled over onto the passenger's side door. If the speed had been greater, it would have rolled and he never would have remembered anything else. However, the sudden change in mass caused the car to decelerate immediately and spinning once more for good measure, it came to a complete halt in a cloud of dust.

His heart was racing and the adrenalin rush was one he would never forget. Slowly, his breathing moderated and he was able to compose himself. Checking his seat belt, he undid the clasp and removed the harness from around his body. There was no smoke, and thank God, no fire. He slipped free from the restraint and exited the vehicle through the driver's window. Half stumbling, half-falling, he stood erect and looked around. As his eyes adjusted to the darkness, he at first saw nothing unusual, but then he noticed something that seemed quite odd. Leaving the vehicle where it lay on its side, he half walked, half stumbled forward another fifty yards before stopping. Leaning over the edge, he stared down a hundred yards to where the river raced away to the west. His knees suddenly became wobbly like jello and he felt the need to sit down. The vehicle had come to a halt less than half a football field from the edge of the abyss. The road had ended because there was simply no bridge. "So much for warning foreigners," he thought.

Dangling his feet over the edge of the precipice, he realized how lucky he had been. Shaking his head, he contemplated his next move.

After a few minutes to gather his senses, he slowly rose from the edge of the ravine and turned to return to his vehicle. Walking to where the pavement ended, he paused and looked down to ponder the large square hole near his right foot.ABteen feet away another similar hole resided. Scratching his head, he wondered what was missing.

"A barrier, must have been the damn barrier," he mused to himself.

Glancing around in all directions, he noticed in the bushes several yards away the edge of a man made object. He stumbled in that direction and realized it was the fence. Someone had removed the obstruction and placed it along the side of the road, but why go to all this trouble?

Then a feeling like someone pouring ice water on his neck shocked him into the realization they might still be here watching. His right hand expertly reached for the weapon holstered around his shoulder and removed it in one smooth motion. As he did so, he dropped to one knee and glanced in all directions looking for anyone who might be observing him. The reassuring feel of the Glock 22 gave him immediate relief as he remembered how he resisted the transition from his old model 17. The new weapon was superior in every way, but Drew hated change and fought it unconsciously whenever pressed to do so. Pushing the trivial thought from his mind he felt more confident with the weapon in his hand. The superior firepower the new handgun possessed was worth the small inconvenience of his old weapons smaller size.

Scanning the perimeter, he was startled as he saw something moving in the distance. However, it was too far away to make out clearly. The object was large and moving awkwardly towards his position. Shifting his angle in the direction of the new threat, he squared the handgun in a classic firing position with both hands steadying his aim.

"Hold and identify yourself!"

"*Senor,* are you all right?" the voice from the blackness inquired.

Drew again squinted from his squatting position and glared back into the gloom of the night. As the odd outline continued its approach, it began slowly taking shape. Finally, Drew could begin to make out a small man in a dirty linen jump suit leading an animal. Later Drew would find out it was more precisely a burro.

"*Senor,* I said are you all right? Do you speak English or *hablo espanol?*"

"I speak English," he said, with cautious relief as he rose from his shooting position.

The little man stared with both eyes locked on Drew's weapon. It was obvious to the Agent the stranger was frightened at the imposing figure aiming a handgun in his direction.

"Oh, sorry, thought you might be one of the bad guys that tried to kill me." Holstering the Glock, he smiled at the stranger and held his other hand palm down as a sign of friendship.

"Why you no stop? The warning sign is very clear, Road ends, detour ahead."

"I must have missed it, that is if there was a sign."

"That's funny, the barrier is missing. It was right here yesterday," the little man with the returning smile said, as he wandered back to the road's edge. "Look, you can see where the post was secured. It was a big sign in red and said *Alto,* Stop. I have seen it many times."

"I wish I'd seen it once, it's over there in the bushes if you want to help me replace it. No sense in someone else running over the edge of this cliff."

The two men approached the discarded barrier and proceeded to drag it back to its appropriate station. Lifting both sides, they inserted the long poles into their proper location.

Removing his big hat and displaying a rumpled head of black hair, the smiling stranger with the chipped front tooth replied, "My name is Carlos, I was on my way home. The old bridge is a half kilometer over there. It will take us to the village of San Marcos where I live and you can call for help."

Slapping his pocket at the mention of calling, Drew realized his satellite phone was in the car seat when the crash occurred.

"I have a satellite phone, that is, if it didn't fly out of the vehicle when I capsized. Why would they build a wonderful highway like this and not build a bridge?" Drew inquired, as he retraced his steps to the motor vehicle lying on its side.

"Something about funding, a political thing. The bridge cost much more than was expected and one of the bureaucrats ran off with the money. It is like a futbol, as you would say. They are supposed to build one in five or ten years. In the meantime, they are using the old one lane bridge a half kilometer over that way. There was a sign about two kilometers back."

"I'm sure there was, I just missed it like I missed the barrier. Can you report this? I'm sure the authorities would like to investigate the barriers removal and the missing sign."

"Yes, I will call from the village. Are you ready?"

After searching the car, Drew found the phone between the console and the passenger's seat. Retrieving the instrument, he paused as he assessed his situation. Without transportation, he would have to wait for the rental agency to bring him a replacement. Might as well follow Carlos to the village, perhaps he could get something to eat while he waited. Hoisting his suitcase, Drew shook his head in the affirmative and began to follow the burro and the little man along a well-worn path to the one lane bridge somewhere in the distance.

Chapter 28

Drew smiled, as he looked up from the plate of food he was consuming on the rough-hewn table with the linen tablecloth. Carlos had been a perfect host inviting him into his home and introducing him to his wife and two small children. The little boy and girl giggled as they peeked out from behind their mother's skirt at the funny looking visitor. The woman was now busy cleaning the utensils from the evening meal as their guest finished the remains of the mysterious stew she had prepared. He was not sure what was on his plate, but it was good, and he was starved. The concoction consisted of flat bread, beans, onions, peppers, and what he thought might be mushrooms. However, he could not be sure. It was held loosely together with some kind of gravy-like paste that was brown and thick, with an intriguing flavor. Nothing that would be on the menu at his favorite restaurant in Kansas City, but right now it was a gourmet delight.

"So why you here in Spain, Mr. Wells? Who you think is trying to kill you?" Carlos asked casually from across the small table, running the questions together so quickly he made Drew almost laugh.

Placing his fork on the side of his plate, he wiped his mouth as his mother had taught him before replying.

"Don't know if I can answer the second question, but I have to confess they've made several attempts. I hope to find out before they can complete their assignment. What did the authorities tell you about the sign and the barrier when you called them?"

"Nothing, only they would be around in the morning to be sure it was properly back in place. They said it was probably kids playing a silly prank."

"Kids? Prank? Silly? I hardly think so, but they're entitled to their opinion."

"You did not answer my other question, why you here in Spain? Looking for international spies or something? I have never seen anyone carry a gun like that except the police."

Pushing the plate away, Drew looked Carlos straight in the eye. The penetrating stare made the small man almost sorry he had pressed the stranger for an answer.

"No, actually I'm here to meet some friends south of here in the desert. We are looking for a missing civilization. She is with an archaeologist and they are certain they're onto something spectacular. I thought I would tag along to see they didn't get into any trouble. They left a week ago and I'm trying to catch up."

"Oh, I see, they really believe they will find something out here in the Tabernas?"

"They seem to be convinced there is a lost civilization of some sort out there. Why, do you know where this city might be?"

Carlos broke out into a small chuckle and the children followed suit as the little girl leaped into her father's lap playfully.

"Oh, no, not really, only there are strangers that come around occasionally. They spend some time south of here near the foot of the Filabres. I have been told they are looking for gold."

"Have they ever found any?"

Stroking the little girl's dark hair, he again showed his chipped tooth, "No there is no gold, only fools' gold. Some of the people in the hills place things for them to find so they will stay longer. Here, like this," he said as he reached across the table and handed Drew a small vase.

"So they are salting the dig with pottery to keep them around, I don't understand."

"Yes, salting, that is the word they use. It keeps them interested for a little while, and they continue to spend money while they are here. It is good for business, as you Americans would say."

"I see capitalism in action," Drew chuckled, as he joined in the levity.

"Say, then you must know where this valley is located in the northwestern portion of the desert? I'm supposed to meet them there in a few days. If you could lead me to the spot, it would certainly simplify my situation and save me a little time."

Carlos accepted the map from Drew and glanced at the small spot marked with the x.

"Yes, I have been there many times, there are caves along the edge of the desert. That is where the sand ends and the Bad Lands begin."

"Bad Lands?"

"Yes, many of the *banditos* live there and you don't want to go poking around by yourself. I will show you. Of course, I must charge you for my service."

"Well, I would expect to pay you whatever is fair."

"Good, now that we are going to work together you need some supplies."

"I bet you know where I can get those too," Drew added.

"Yes, I can get them for you. By the way, what did your rental car company say about your vehicle?"

"They plan to deliver a replacement in the morning; I got a four wheel drive one this time. Can we use it for the trek through the badlands, or will we need pack animals?"

"No, the vehicle should work out fine; I would hate to have Maxmillian carry the entire load again. He is getting so old and he sometimes forgets what he is doing. Why I woke up one morning and he was gone! I searched for three hours and found him wandering around in circles. Lucky I did or he would have starved."

"Well, we can't have Max wandering in circles, is there somewhere I can sleep for tonight? I know there aren't any hotels around here, sorry to keep being a bother."

"No, no bother, you can sleep with Max in the stable. There is a nice soft pile of new hay I put there yesterday. Max won't mind, he likes company."

"Wonderful, well show me the way and I'll get out of the kitchen, thank you for the fine meal." Drew rose from his chair, bowed to Carlos' wife and followed him out the door. Shaking his head and laughing at his luck, Drew passed from the house into the star filled night towards the barn where his bedfellow Max awaited.

Looking up from his paperwork, Bo acknowledged his guest with a headshake before speaking, "Come in, Doe, what's on your mind?"

"Oh, I wanted to bring you up to speed on some things I've dug up recently in my investigation. Haven't seen you in two days, you got your head in paperwork every time I peek in," the agent replied, as she pushed a chair away from the desk and placed her briefcase on the floor next to her feet.

"Sorry, this job is a little more administrative since Drew took off for Spain."

"Well, if you have some time now I'd like to cover a couple of items with you and get your approval before I proceed on one."

"Certainly, glad you came by, would you like some coffee?" he asked, pointing to the pot on a burner in the corner of the office.

"No thanks, I've had your idea of coffee before. It would take the hide off a construction worker."

Suit yourself," he said, as he walked over and poured himself a cup of the syrupy black liquid. Doe watched as he spilled a few drops on the credenza and neglected to wipe it up as he returned to his desk.

"Been reviewing some of this report the CIA sent over yesterday. Our friend down in the lockup has an interesting background. With this record, we can put him away for a long time if we can tie the shooting of the Attorney General to Director Clark's death."

"That's our job, I mean to be sure he's guilty and—"

The ringing of the desk phone interrupted Doe's thoughts and Bo instinctively picked it up without thinking.

"Yeah, what is it?"

The voice of his secretary on the other end informed him he had a guest in the lobby that was insistent on seeing him.

"I'm tied up right now with Doe. We got a lot to do, so tell him to come back when I'm not so busy."

Listening to the response, he wrinkled his brow and pulled unconsciously at his left ear. After a few moments, he exhaled softly and said, "Okay, send him back."

Placing the receiver back in the cradle, he turned to Doe. "Sorry, I have an unexpected visitor, you'll have to come back. This may be important. I'll call you when I finish."

Picking up her briefcase, Doe smoothed her skirt as she prepared to leave the office. Moving effortlessly down the hallway, she passed a distinguished looking man with gray wavy hair in a blue blazer who smiled as he moved silently by.

The light tapping on the door alerted Bo to his guest's arrival and he stood to greet the stranger who was insistent on seeing him.

"Mr. Boggs, my name is T.C. Darling and I have some information about the Director's murder I think you will find interesting," he stated matter of factly.

"Have a seat Mr. Darling, and just whadda ya think you know about Director Clark's death?"

The writer grinned self-consciously and settled in the chair Doe had just vacated. Crossing his legs, he began.

"Before I answer that, I must ask you a question Mr. Boggs."

Bo was uncomfortable with this man and being put on the defensive wasn't what he enjoyed. Nevertheless, he reluctantly agreed.

"Depends of course, but I have a lot of questions for you so answering one isn't unreasonable I suppose."

The smile increased and Bo suddenly felt like the canary in a cage with a rather large cat staring at him as if he was on the menu. Shaking off the feeling, he pressed. "Well, what is it? Go on Mr. Darling!"

"Is it true you are a Presidential Agent? I mean, I've never even heard of a Presidential Agent."

Bo was dumbstruck by this man's forthright attitude and apparent amount of inside knowledge.

Leaning forward on both elbows, he tried to increase his stature behind the desk as he replied.

"You got me at a disadvantage, Mr. Darling, but yes I'm called that by some in the department. Now could we press on? I'm rather busy and you interrupted a meeting I had with my partner. I've got a few important questions concerning the murder, if you don't mind?"

Realizing he had made his point, Darling slumped back in the chair before responding.

"All right, but I reserve the right to ask you some more questions about you and Mr. Wells, if my information proves useful. Do you agree?"

"Fair enough, now you said you have information on the Director's death. If that's true, why haven't you come forward with it before now and how do you come by this information?"

"Mr. Boggs, a journalist has his sources and you know I'm not going to reveal them to you. The information however, has only recently come into my possession. I've spent the last two days trying to verify its validity."

"You say you're a journalist. What paper do you work for?" "Well, I'm not exactly employed at the present time, I freelance for several of the local rags. I've wrestled with this information for a couple of days and finally decided it was my duty to come forward and tell you what I know."

"I'm listening!"

"Very well, here it is. As I said, a source I use from time to time came to me with this story. Since I've been interested in you and your partner, Mr. Wells, I realized it was just what I needed as leverage for the novel I'm writing about the Bureau's two Presidential Agents."

Bo felt uncomfortable with this scenario, and tried not to show his emotions, as he grimaced.

"My source said the prisoner you are holding for the murder of Clark and attempted murder of the Attorney General is a diversion. It seems he is merely a pawn, and although he did make the attempt on the AG, it was not a professional job.

"I would agree with that, but he did make the attempt on the AG," Bo stated firmly.

"Yes, all that's true, but if you've talked to him you know he can barely speak two words of English. He's fighting Jihad and is a dupe. They want you to think it's a Muslim conspiracy. It's easy to jump on the Muslim bandwagon, and all of you fell for it.

Now Bo's interest was peeked and a vein in his neck pulsed as he tried to contain his excitement.

"I just know you're going to tell me who the real culprits are, aren't you?"

Darling relished the hold he had over the agent and drew it out as long as he could, finally he almost whispered.

"I think you will find the murderer someone who dumped a body in the Gulf a couple of months ago. You remember the Eckenstadt murder?"

Bo repeated the man's last comment, "Eckenstadt, you don't mean?"

"Yes, the very same one," Darling stated matter of factly.

"It would at first seem to me you are mad, but let me think on this for a moment. What's the motive?" Bo demanded.

"You're the investigator, Mr. Boggs, I'm only the messenger. I've given it some thought, but I don't presume to understand the criminal mind. I think you need to look closer at Girard Enterprises. If you haven't figured it out by now, they are the ones that were responsible for Eckenstadt's murder. A rather interesting couple that runs the business, I should think you would find them involved in all kinds of illegal things. I've met Jean Paul before and he is a charming devil, if I may say so myself. I'm not as impressed with his girl friend and partner, but I think she is the brains behind all of this murder and intrigue."

Bo twirled a pencil he had been holding and said, "All I have is your word against theirs. What I need is cold hard facts, not accusations. Yes, Girard Enterprise has been on our radar. They are, after all, an international company with their fingers in numerous businesses. We suspected them in the Eckenstadt murder, but not the Director's."

"My source is a disgruntled employee who shall we say does unsavory things for Girard. He has close ties to an illegal element and I have never known him to be wrong. I realize he is trying to make things difficult for Girard, but his motive was money. Cash is always an agent of the devil. I can only assume he was short changed somewhere along the line and saw a way to get even and profit from it. I have him on a retainer so to speak, and I will try to get more information if you find his accusations to be accurate."

Rising from his chair, Darling placed his hands on his hips before speaking again, "Good luck in your investigation, and don't forget your promise. I'll be in touch soon for the interview I'll need for my book. Let me know if you want me to try and get more information from my source."

Bo watched as the journalist passed through the exit. Raising his voice appropriately and with all of the authority he could muster.

"Mr. Darling!"

Turning to face Bo, he replied, "Yes?"

Smiling now at the change of roles Bo said, "I'll be getting back to you and don't leave town. Don't even think about leaving town. Do I make myself clear?"

The journalist smiled right back as he replied, "I knew you were going to say that."

Rising from his desk, Bo reached for the coffee pot, but before pouring the cup, he slammed the pot back down.

"No Pain, No Gain!" he shouted.

Leaving the J. Edgar Hoover building, Darling fairly floated down the steps on an invisible cloud. The two young agents entering the facility stared at the stranger with amusement as he skipped down the pavement and up the street.

Chapter 29

▲▼▲▼▲▼

The fire smoldered as Stringfellow stirred the flickering vestiges of the flame. Bonnie watched as the hypnotic effects of the dying embers worked their magic on her imagination.

"I've given it some thought and I think we should move on," Stringfellow said, matter of factly.

Bonnie knew this was coming as he had alluded to it all day and now he was planning to finalize his proposal. She remembered how he had postulated in the classroom and anyone who took a different position was often buried under a barrage of data. Now he felt compelled to present a case to her.

"That's not necessary," she replied.

Stringfellow was somewhat taken aback as Bonnie spoke from her mind without him having the benefit of her thoughts.

"I beg your pardon?"

"Oh, I'm sorry I was thinking the same thought myself and I didn't want you to feel you have to justify it to me. I agree totally, only I wish we knew what we'd found out here all alone in the desert."

After three days of digging and finding nothing but the solitary rider, two pack animals, and what must have been two servants, they were exhausted and confused.

"I tell you, Bonnie, I don't know what to think, a man of apparent importance alone except for two servants in the middle of the Tabernas Desert. Oh, I'm sure the cause of his death is quite simply a terrific sand storm. Poor chap must have been buried under tons of sand for more than a thousand years. Now another storm has allowed him to resurface, but for what purpose was he here? I most assuredly thought my deduction of Alexander's general was correct. His tunic, his dress, and his saddle all fit the time. That is correct, I would swear to it on my mother's grave! Still, what was he doing out here by himself? Was he coming or going? We may never find out. Therefore, I suggest we pack up the remains that are of value and send them back to our base by one of the laborers. How say you to this idea?"

"Sounds like the most logical approach, I must admit the area we dug up is the size of a football field. If there were anything else close by, I'm sure we would have found it by now. Shall we leave in the morning?"

"Yes, I will get Achmed to complete the packing and supervise the transfer back to the city. When he finishes he can meet us at the sight we have deemed the most logical place to begin our dig."

"Well, now that we agree on that, can we talk for a few minutes about the lost city?" I have been thinking about it since we left the States and except for the other night, we have talked very little. I know you had a lot of work to do pulling this all together and ordering supplies. The funding was a major priority and I was amazed at how fast you pulled that off. I don't mean to be nosy,

but you seem to get quiet every time I try to discuss the details. Is there something else wrong, I
mean other than your health, or do you not fully trust me yet? I assure you I am quite capable and I'm confident in my ability."

"Oh, it's not that, not that at all."

"What is it then?"

Tossing the stick away he had been using as a tool to stir the fire, he leaned back and stared into the heavens. The stars flickered back and shone brighter than anywhere Bonnie could remember.

"There is more than I told you the other night, I mean about my health. I wanted to tell you the rest, but you got so emotional I just couldn't bring myself to tell you everything. I have been keeping something from you until I could be sure. Do not take what I say lightly, I wouldn't mention it if I wasn't sure. Bonnie, I think you are in danger. I'm sorry now I brought you, but I don't know how I could have left you behind. You are so hard headed and I wasn't sure at first, but now," his voice trailed off into a whisper.

"Danger, what on earth are you talking about Professor?"

Tapping his pipe out on a rock, he began.

"It all started a long time ago, many years before you were a student of mine. You see, I've been here in the desert before, back in the late sixties when I was a young adventurer seeking excitement and was indestructible. Oh, I know what you are thinking, the old fool is merely reminiscing, but no, there is more to it than that. You see, Aaron and I were here together all those years ago."

Bonnie felt a chill run up her spine as she listened to the man she respected more than anyone weave a tale that left her speechless.

"We were both right out of school and contracted by a large museum. They had suspicions and information about the existence of the lost city. It was Aaron's and my first experience and we were terribly excited, as you can imagine. There was a large team of mostly young and inexperienced former students. However, that did not slow us down. We had enough enthusiasm for a thousand experienced archaeologists. For three months, we searched the area in and around the Filabres Mountains. Even though we searched every likely location, we found nothing. It was frustrating, but our enthusiasm never abated. One morning our site leader called us together to tell us the work was being terminated. The results of our effort were disappointing and the cost was escalating to a point that could not be sustained. I was devastated and so was Aaron. We were told we would be back in a couple of years when we could justify another search, but that never happened.

You remember the sinkholes I mentioned earlier. Well, Aaron and I were convinced we could find the city if we searched them, but our leader overruled us and tried to make us feel foolish. It seemed so obvious to us, I never understood his reasoning. The next morning we began packing and left three days later.
I stayed with them another six months and was continually frustrated by their inability to make good decisions. Finally, I got fed up and accepted a position with the university that I had been seeking. My life was then transformed into an academic one and my priorities changed. Aaron left shortly after me and you know his story. He finally settled in Jacksonville and we kept in touch over the years. I lost interest in the dig for a time, but Aaron would always bring it up in our discussions. The fire still burned within him and he always hoped to return.

Every year I expected to open the papers and see where some young fools had found our city, but it never happened. When Aaron told me about the Hammurabi stone, I must admit I almost laughed at what I considered a preposterous suggestion. Aaron however had some insight and tried his best to convince me. I tried to listen with an open mind, but it seemed preposterous. He finally gave up and we never spoke of it again. I knew he believed the stone in the museum was a fake and the real one had much more to offer. I'm sure if I had insisted we would have pursued the stone together and who knows, if we had, he may not have been killed and the three of us might be sitting here around this campfire together. So you see, I am here as much for Aaron as I am for myself."

Bonnie sat there silently taking in all of the information the professor was dispensing. Finally, she felt emboldened to say, "Aaron never mentioned the dig to me. The story you have told me is quite fascinating and gives me a warm feeling about our work. I know Aaron is with us now in spirit. Nevertheless, I still don't understand why does that make it dangerous for me. Why dangerous?"

Rising from his sitting position, he pulled unconsciously on his mustache as he walked away from the fire. At first Bonnie thought she had pushed him too far, but then he began to speak.

"I have every reason to suspect the museum has gotten wind of this and is watching our every move."

"You're saying the museum will try to stop us? Are they so pompous they feel that they should have first right to every find?"

"My, you are naïve, the museum I am talking about thinks they invented history and they have the right to all finds first."

"You mean?"

"Yes, I mean the Louvre in Paris and their Director of Antiquities, Louis Marchant will stop at nothing to claim the find as his own. He is here, I saw him back at the hotel where we stayed. Oh, he doesn't know I recognized him, but I did. When I saw him, I put two and two together. He is a shrewd and calculating man with a lust for glory. This find would make him a chapter in the history books, so you see he will stop at nothing to put his name on the find."

"But we have the map, with all of the identifying locations. He will never be able to find the site. You said yourself he would never suspect the area you mentioned."

"That will not stop him, he will follow us with a group of thugs and steal the glory if he can. Now do you understand? We are merely an inconvenience to him and his kind.

To murder is simply a noun in the dictionary, it means nothing to his kind."

Chapter 30

▲▼▲▼▲▼

When the rental agent pulled up in front of Carlos' humble dwelling, Drew was stunned at what he delivered. Quickly his mind reminded him he had asked for a four wheel SUV, and yes, that is what had been delivered. The two small children burst from the house like rockets on the Fourth and began to climb in and out of the vehicle as if it was a new swing set. Carlos, like Drew, was taken aback. To say it was red is an understatement, more like a fire truck in color and size.

      Drew was accustomed to something smaller, much smaller. His Corvette had been a purchase he made after a long period of deliberation. After all, a man who had driven a Toyota for most of his adult life obviously takes a car purchase seriously.

Walking around the vehicle, he accepted the keys from the agent. After signing the appropriate documents, Drew handed over his keys to the wrecked vehicle back near the unfinished bridge. The agent remarked he had seen the wrecked car on the side of the road and would have it towed. After the insurance settlement, any additional charges would be forwarded to Drew for payment. As the young man departed, Drew stepped back and looked once more at the massive new Escalade SUV.

Carlos began packing the vehicle almost immediately and had already stored the camping gear and most of the food supplies before Drew could lend a hand. He had also procured some pick axes and shovels for the mysterious dig Drew kept referring to in his conversation.

It was nearly ten a.m. when the duo pulled away from the little homestead, with Carlos waving good-bye, and headed south. For the first twenty kilometers, the landscape changed little as small trees raced by and Carlo chattered on about the trip. Drew kept his thoughts to himself and sat silently listening to Carlos ramble on.

Soon the terrain began to change, the trees fell away, and only small scrub bushes hugged the roadside. A dull gray seemed to be the color of the day as Drew pushed the Escalade along at eighty kilometers an hour. Ever alert for any more misplaced signs, he felt somewhat at ease with Carlos by his side.

The temperature outside the vehicle climbed to over a hundred and the air-conditioned SUV was earning its rental fee Stopping only twice for restroom breaks, the hours passed as the sun drifted lower and the shadows crept across the road. Drew was intent on making as much time up as he could after his mishap of the previous evening. Soon the Filabres Mountains loomed up in the distance and promised them their goal would soon be reached.

"Mr. Drew, I think it best we stop somewhere along here. The paved road ends soon. I don't want to drive on the dirt in the dark. We are getting close to the place I told you we needed to be careful crossing."

"You mean the bad lands?"

"Yes, that is what I mean. That looks like a good place over there, why don't we stop here?"

Drew agreed and slowed the vehicle as he left the asphalt and moved gradually over to an outcropping of small boulders. Stopping the Escalade, he opened the door and stepped out into the soft sand. Stretching, he stared around at the scenery. Nothing had changed in the last two hours -- sand and scrub cactus, a few boulders and the setting sun as it slid slowly behind the mountain range.

The two men removed a few instruments for cooking and Drew prepared a makeshift bed in the back of the vehicle while Carlos arranged the cooking utensils and set up the fire.

The little Spaniard was all efficiency in his preparations. It was as though he had done this a thousand times and for all Drew knew, he may very well have. Soon an efficient fire was glowing as a tripod of sorts held a kettle above the flame and Carlos was busy mixing mysterious ingredients from cans and a bag of produce he had stored in the vehicle. The smell was intriguing and Drew found himself staring at the fire and wondering when the concoction would be finished.

"I am almost done, Mr. Drew, please to get the metal plates from the pack over by the boxes."

Drew turned, determined the location Carlos meant, and secured two plates that reminded him of his military days. All he needed was a canteen and an M-16 to feel right at home.

As the thought of the rifle passed, he decided it might be a judicious time to check his weapon. Pulling the Glock from the shoulder holster, he methodically popped the clip and insured himself the gun was fully loaded. Closing it, he removed the safety and hefted the weapon for balance.

Carlos looked up from his culinary work and noticed Drew going through the motions of a police officer. He smiled to himself as it somehow made him feel a little more secure to know his new friend was ready and competent to meet anything they might encounter.

The meal was finished and consumed within an hour and after the meal, Carlos cleaned up his utensils and poked the fire. Drew pulled his map from the vehicle and sat down to chart their progress. The two had traveled at least three hundred kilometers and were as Carlos said, close to the Filabres. Tomorrow they would reach the mountains and traverse the mountain road for another hundred kilometers searching for the valley. Drew considered calling Bonnie, but decided it was too late and he was too tired. Besides, he was hoping to surprise her and Stringfellow.

Carlos had already tossed a sleeping bag alongside the fire and was dozing when Drew returned. The temperature had dropped at least forty degrees and according to Carlos, he would need a heavy blanket. Drew had spent time in Tucson in his former career and was accustomed to the desert and the dramatic temperature shifts.

Leaving the fireside, he ambled back to the Escalade and slipped into the back of the SUV where he had made his bed.

The stillness of the night and the cloud covering the moon made it easy for him to fall asleep.

It must have been a few hours; he could not be sure as he stared at the luminous hands of his Rolex. He thought it was two-thirty, maybe three-thirty. Why he awoke was another mystery. He listened for a while but could hear nothing. Slithering from beneath the cover, he slipped his shoes on and strolled over to the still smoldering campfire. Carlos was turned on his side and for all practical purposes was totally out. Drew took a small stick and stirred the fire until it leaped back to life. Gathering a few branches from around the area, he stoked the flame and watched as it greedily consumed the small wooden pieces.

The sound was almost non-existent, but it was there. Again, he heard it and again it confused his senses. It was getting louder and closer. Without any hesitation or alarm, he slowly returned to the SUV. Reaching inside as if to get an insignificant article, he removed the Glock from its holster, and palmed it into his pocket so it could not be seen.

Turning, he strained to see if anything or anyone had appeared. Still it was only darkness that greeted his searching eyes. There it was again; however, this time he recognized it. How could he have not figured it out sooner – hooves, horses' hooves shuffling slowly across the sand and dirt! Now a quiet whiney and snort of a disgruntled animal assailed his ears. Then the sound grew quicker and louder as the animals broke into a gallop. Still Drew feigned ignorance of the impending danger.

His mind raced as he assessed his options. Not knowing the enemy was the major problem. Were there two or three, or just how many? Did they want his money or his life? He'd find out soon.

Bursting into the campfire circle, a dozen riders on sturdy steeds reigned in with drawn pistols leveled at Drew. So much for shooting it out, he was outgunned and out numbered.

Carlos awoke with the arrival of the uninvited guests and pulled his blanket up around his neck as if it offered protection. For a few agonizing seconds, they all stared at each other.

"*Senor*, place your weapon on the ground, the one you removed from the car. Do it very slowly, if you value your life."

Drew thought he knew hardened mercenaries when he saw them, and these twelve men fit the bill. Slowly he retrieved the Glock from his pants pocket. Placing it carefully on the ground, he stepped away and glared back at the man who had spoken.

The leader was dressed in riding attire similar to that befitting western movies Drew had seen. As the man dismounted, his spurs jingled and his hand carved boots of exotic leather shone in the flickering moon light. On his head, he wore a wide sombrero pulled tightly by a drawstring against his unshaven chin. A short jacket similar to a military one covered a white shirt with frills of lace around the collar and sleeves. The pants were a tight fitting knit material that hugged his muscular frame. The coat and pants were black with a slight trace of ornamental stitching that added to the effect. It was hard to tell his age, but Drew would guess mid-forties. Besides the stubble on his face, his black hair was streaked lightly with gray, and his almost black eyes bored into Drew as he tried to look nonchalant in this awkward position. The bandit was a stern looking man, and Drew assumed he would not hesitate to shoot him as casually as a rattler if he made any missteps.

Approaching Drew, he handed the reins of his horse to one of his compatriots and eyed the American up and down.

"If I am right, you are Americano, no?"

Drew found the confrontation stimulating if not a little frightening but mustered up all his bravado as he spoke, "Yes, American, my name is Drew Wells and yours?"

The group of riders broke out into laughter as though Drew had made a joke on their behalf.

"Is that funny?"

"You don't know who I am. Your friend over there on the ground does, don't you?" He pointed at Carlos who was visibly shaking beneath the blanket.

"*Si*, you are Edmundo Rafael Castillo *senor!*"

"*Si*, that is correct!" the stranger acknowledged.

"What is it you want from us? We have very little money, but you are welcome to it." Drew began to reach for his wallet when Castillo stopped him.

"Mr. Wells, I may take your money or I may not, it all depends on you. But first I have some questions for you."

"Questions all right, what would you like to know, Mr. Castillo?"

"Call me *Rafe*, all my friends do," he said, as he waved a gesture towards his men.

Again, a convulsion of laughter cascaded down from the other horsemen.

"Come walk with me so we may have some privacy."

Castillo began to stride off into the darkness followed by Drew who was thinking this was the strangest thing he had ever encountered. A bandit, in the middle of a Spanish desert, dressed like a cowboy out of a western, wanting to make small talk. Well, he'd play along and perhaps eventually get the upper hand.

Castillo holstered his Smith and Wesson 38 as if he dared Drew to try something. Drew noted the action, but made no move to create a conflict.

"A federal agent from Florida in the middle of the only desert in Europe, kind of a strange place for you to be nosing around isn't it, Mr. Wells?"

Drew was stung by the remark but remained nonchalant as he replied, "You have me there *Rafe*, and how may I ask, do you know so much about me?"

Stopping now that the two were several hundred meters away from the campfire, *Rafe* smiled and Drew noticed his perfect set of white teeth.

"I know everything about you, Mr. Wells. I try to research my adversary before I ever meet him, and you are no exception."

"What is this charade you're playing, *Rafe*? Who are you really? Your little game is tiring me."

"So you think this is a charade?"

Drew stepped back and gave Castillo another once over, before speaking.

"I'll tell you what, *Rafe*, you're a perfect imitation of a badlands cowboy, everything anyone would suspect but, that's the problem."

"Go on."

"I must admit you had me for a moment, I really believed you were a *bandito* that hid out here in the Filabres and preyed on unsuspecting travelers."

"Now you don't?" Castillo questioned with the hint of a smile approaching his lips.

"No, the casting is too perfect, but you played the part well. Tell me *Rafe,* what is all this dress up cowboy all about, who are you really?"

Castillo tossed his head back and roared with laughter.

"Mr. Wells, they told me I could not fool you, but I thought no, I have fooled everyone else, why not this American agent. I had to meet you anyway, so I planned to make it fun for both of us. But you spoiled it for me; I wanted to see if you were as smart as your reputation. I must admit I was not disappointed. What was it that gave me away?"

"Your teeth."

"My teeth, oh I see, my teeth weren't old and yellow and missing. Yes, you are right, I never thought of that. My mother was such a stickler about my dental care when I was a boy. I guess you never stop following mother's instructions."

"Now are you going to tell me what this elaborate charade is all about?"

"Of course, I am with the *Centro Nacional de Inteligencia,* the CNI, our version of the FBI and CIA combined. I am one of many undercover agents who are trying to infiltrate the Basque separatist organization. I am out here because some of the bandits in the Filabres. No, I may say all of them are with the Basque organization. My mission is to infiltrate and monitor what their plans are. As you can see, I have accomplished my mission and am learning much about their organization and its leaders. All of the other men with me except two are Basque, so our conversation must be kept between us. The Basque are a hardened bunch and are unshakable in their attempt to cause us embarrassment on the national scene."

"What the hell has that got to do with me?"

"Nothing really, except you are going to be digging around looking for historical artifacts that are important to the Spanish government. In Basque controlled territory, I might add. Your Director Riley called our Director *Roldan* and asked for assistance. He said you were here to help two American archeologists who were searching for a lost city. You see how it eventually filtered down to the agent in charge of the area. That is me, so here we are. My instructions were to meet you and explain my position and put myself at your disposal." Reaching across, he extended his hand, and Drew took it with relief.

Chapter 31

Yawning, Bo stared at his wristwatch and realized it was well past midnight. The Randy Edwards file was lying loosely all over the work area where he had searched in vain for a missing clue. He had pulled the Edwards and Girard files again to review the facts of the assassination and to see if anything in the records might ring a bell. Bo was convinced Edwards and Mary Lewis aka Marie Louise had some connection. As he asserted to Doe, he would stake his life on it.

Shoving the Edwards file away in disgust, he again retrieved the Lewis file and began to study it with renewed interest. Ten minutes into the process, he rubbed his eyes and yawned again. Then a light bulb exploded in his brain and he stabbed at the document with his forefinger.

"That's it - Carlisle!" he shouted.

There on the page in front of him was the connection he had been searching for all this time. He was such an idiot to have overlooked it twice before. Now he had the connection.

Of course, the first time he missed the name of the school where Edwards received his degree in air conditioning maintenance was at Carlisle Community College in Omaha, Nebraska. Sliding his hand over to the Lewis file, he found a notation scrawled in pencil by someone after the document had been typed near the bottom of the page. Bo read aloud, "Attended Carlisle College, Olathe, Kansas. This wasn't on the data base file! How can stuff like this slip through the cracks? If I hadn't picked up the hard copy I would have missed this completely. I'm going to fry somebody's ass for this."

Tracing the note with his forefinger, he stopped on the town, Olathe. Going back to the file for Edwards, he did a similar search and stopped on Omaha.

"Hmmm, I'll bet you a dollar to a *Krispy Kreme*, somebody transposed Olathe for Omaha. Probably working late like me and simply assumed it was her hometown in Kansas. Olathe, Omaha, damn close if you ask me."

Bo retrieved his laptop from across the room and Googled Carlisle Community College. The little *Sony Vio* leaped to life and a full page of options came to the screen. Squinting as he scanned the page, he picked the best sounding one and selected Open.

Again, the computer blinked and a full page complete with a picture of the administration building and a current schedule for the Indians football team with ticket information appeared in the upper right corner.

Bo carefully scanned the page and reviewed several options available to him.

"Aha!" exclaiming to himself, he selected students by year, and opened another tab. Going back to the files on his desk he quickly pieced together the years and then selected 2003.

The laptop hesitated for a moment, but then spit out a page with a list of names in alphabetical order. Scanning his options, he finally seized on Randy Edwards, Scottsbluff, Nebraska.

The computer opened another panel and a picture of Bo's assassin stared back at him from the page on the machine.

"One down and one to go."

Selecting Print, he sent the file to the inkjet, then returned to the previous page and scanned for Mary Lewis.

No luck, Mary Ellen was as close as he could come.

"Something's wrong, this must be the right place, maybe the year." Again, checking her FBI file he deduced she might have been a year behind her friend Edwards.

Returning to the laptop, he tried 2004 and hit enter. A new list with some repeats like Randy Edwards and Mary Ellen reappeared. This time, however, behind Laurie Kirkpatrick was Lewis, Mary. The picture did not do her justice. She was a little more homely than the runway model photo in her dossier on his desk, but it was the same person. It showed her hometown as Olathe, Kansas and her interest of study was listed as Liberal Arts.

So there it was, Randy Edwards, the assassin, and Marie Louise, the business tycoon, were college classmates, albeit if for only a year. They had ample opportunity to get to know each other.

"This is more than a coincidence; it could show a relationship that led to motive, and motive leads to murder," Bo muttered.

Satisfied with himself, he poured a cup of cold leftover coffee and settled back in at his desk. A smirk appeared in the corner of his face, as he reached for his I-phone.

Punching in the number, he waited.

A sleepy voice on the other end answered after four rings, "Hello."

"Doe, you asleep? You ain't going to believe what I found in the file tonight."

"Bo, is that you? Don't you know it's nearly one AM?"

"Yes, yes, I know, sweetie, but I just found the connection between Randy Edwards and Girard Enterprises. I want your sweet ass in here bright and early, I have a lot of work for you to do on our friend, Marie Louise."

The connection clicked off and Doe was left holding a dead line.

"Sweet ass my foot, how dare he call me that!" Then with a self-satisfied smile, she laid her head back on the pillow. "I'm glad he noticed, he's such a cutie."

Carlos was still shaking as the twelve riders thundered away into the darkness.

"Mr. Wells, how you do that? How did you keep them from killing us?"

Drew ignored the question as he strode over to the Escalade and reached for his duffel in the back seat. Finding it, he rummaged around for a few moments, discovering the bottle he was looking for he returned to the fire. Before replying to the Spaniard, he produced two small glasses and poured the golden liquid into the tumblers, handing one to the little man.

"Here, I think this calls for a celebration."

"Celebration, what are you talking about, celebration? What are we drinking?" Carlos stared at the amber colored liquid and sniffed it to see if it was recognizable. "Phew, this is strong stuff. I don't drink alcohol, my wife would kill me if she finds out I have been drinking. What is this stuff? I think I could start a fire with this."

"It better be strong, I paid a hundred dollars American for it. It's Don Peron Tequila. I was saving it for a celebration when we find this lost city. But, after our close call I think we can sample a small bit tonight."

With those words, Drew threw his head back and downed the firewater in one thirsty gulp. Carlos watched the proceeding and when Drew continued to stare at him, he copied the American and downed the drink in a like fashion.

"Ay, yi, yi, that is powerful stuff," He found himself saying in a high-pitched voice.

"I knew you would like it. Now what was it you asked me? Oh yeah, how did I talk my way out of being murdered by the meanest man in the Filabres?"

"Yes, how did you? They say Castillo has killed over twenty men for no reason. I thought for sure he was going to shoot you when you walked away into the dark."

"Wish I could tell you it was a brilliant bit of double talk on my part, or I scared him into thinking the Bureau would hunt him down like a dog to the ends of the earth if he harmed us. However, it was simple, I bribed him."

Carlos watched as Drew poured another drink for himself and proceeded to down it as quickly as the first.

"You bribed him, with what? He didn't take your wallet, did he?"

"No, nothing that mundane, I offered him a bigger piece of the pie."

"What is this pie you are referring to?"

"Carlos, when you have nothing of value, you offer something that seems unattainable to most men. In this case, I offered him a share of the gold in the lost city. Now if I had the gold, or could even guarantee to find the gold that would be one thing. In my case however, I made him believe we know where it is and it is only a matter of time until it is in our possession. For this promise, he guaranteed me no one would interfere with our effort. Seems fair to me, how about you?"

"You promised Edmundo Rafael Castillo, the meanest man in the Filabres, a share of something you don't have, and he promised to protect you until you deliver it to him?"

"That about sums it up nicely. Are you sure you wouldn't like another shot of Tequila?"

"No, *Senor,* you are crazy! Castillo will cut off your privates if you don't deliver this gold."

As the little man shuffled away back to his bedroll, he shook his head and began mumbling to himself in Spanish.

Drew laughed softly, it was a good story even if he did say so himself. Now Bo would tell him how ridiculous it all sounded but perhaps Carlos actually bought it. What really happened was a lot less dramatic and not nearly as entertaining.

After shaking hands, the Agent for the CNI advised Drew he and his men would be in the neighborhood and would make it a point to keep an eye on Drew's companions. If they had any problems, they were to contact him immediately. Until then he would continue to play the meanest SOB east of Madrid. Drew reasoned telling Carlos the truth was not that important or in his best interest. The fewer people who knew the truth the better, Drew knew there were some real outlaws laying in wait somewhere.

"What the hell," he thought, "one more shot should do it for me." The warm feeling in his stomach told him the tequila was working and he would have no trouble falling back asleep.

Chapter 32

▲▼▲▼▲▼

"Marchant is where?" she shouted across the room at the young man who had just delivered the news.

"Miss Louise, our representative in Paris informed me half an hour ago that Marchant had left his office. He checked with one of his sources and discovered the Director had booked passage to Almeria, Spain. He has been away for three days, so it is certain he is there by now. Our contact was also able to determine Marchant procured a legal permit from Madrid to undertake an archaeological site excavation. However, he was unable to determine where in the country that information was deemed confidential, so he wouldn't pursue it without further instructions from us. I thought you would want to know this immediately."

She felt her blood pressure begin to rise to one ninety and she knew she was losing control of her emotions. Afraid to completely explode in front of her employee, she waved him away with "All right, you did the proper thing. Now go and find out where he is planning this dig, and bribe the usual petty officials if you have to. Now hurry, man!"

As the young man turned and scurried away, Louise rose from her desk and began pacing the room, she needed to think. She had assumed that Marchant had bought everything she had been telling him about the statue and now the search for the lost city. Her calculations on the profit from this discovery had run upwards to well over a hundred million dollars on the black market. Of course, she had planned to see that Marchant got all of the credit for himself and the museum. The credit she knew was more important than the money to the crazy Director of Antiquities, while she had no need for credit. Now he had taken it upon himself to go chasing off into the desert on his own to interfere in her well laid plans. By now, he had probably employed a group of thugs to impede or disrupt Stringfellow and Bonnie Lane.

How much more did he know? Obviously enough to lose faith in her. Well, in that case she would have to change her plans. She had been so involved with the death of Randy Edwards and his connection to her and Girard Enterprises, that she had lost control of the dig. She knew that Wells and Boggs would eventually piece together her connection in the Clark murder.
That would have to wait for now, Randy had taken the fall and they would have to be extremely lucky to tie her to him.
 For now, she would turn her attention to the two naïve archaeologists searching for the city. Stringfellow was such an academic fool she had never concerned herself with his part in the plot. When he called her with the suggestion she fund the dig, she couldn't believe her luck. Bonnie Lane had tried to convince her

the statue she had was fake and worthless. Even though she made a good case, Marie Louise knew better.

After all, it was Stringfellow who first brought Eckenstadt and the statue to her attention. Back then she thought this would simply be another artifact to add to her collection. She would buy it from the old fool and resell to the anxious Marchant. She had known of his interest in the Code of Hammurabi for some time. The fake in the Louvre was an embarrassment he had long lived with and wanted to correct. He told her privately his predecessor had been a fool to try to pawn it off on the public. Marchant felt it his obligation to fix the mistake that had lingered in the museum for all these years.

Now with the Antiquities Director meddling in the find, she had to hit upon a way to divert him and reclaim the prize for herself. She then would either pass credit to Marchant as she had originally planned, or have him eliminated and keep the discovery quiet. With Marchant, Stringfellow, and Lane out of the way, she would then sell off the entire lot of artifacts one at a time.

However, if she were going to take control, she had to go to Spain. Reaching for her phone, she punched the red button. When her male secretary answered, she demanded, "Get me passage to Almeria, Spain. Arrange for some of our special employees to join me. I think three should be enough. Do I make myself clear? Good!"

Hanging up the instrument, she paused for a moment as she contemplated what to tell Jean Paul. He was constantly on her mind these days. Their personal life had deteriorated to such a point she knew he was having an affair. She suspected he was fooling around with that little bitch he met at their opening in Orlando. Yes, she would now have to decide how to dispose of the big fool. First, she had to be sure everything was in her name.

There could be no slip-ups like some the well-publicized entertainers had made recently.

"She has just purchased a ticket to Spain! Louise is leaving the country! Shall we intercept her?" Doe shouted, as she burst through the door of Bo's office.

"Spain, she can only be going there for one purpose, she must be planning to get involved with the archaeological search Bonnie Lane and her academic friend have initiated. No, let her go, we'll monitor her movements. I'd better call Drew and get him in the loop. Good Work, Doe! Did you find out anything more about Marie Louise and the Randy Edwards connection?"

"Yes, I was in the process of running down another witness when the information about the tickets came up. Thought you needed to know that first."

"Are we going to Spain?"

"Sorry, Doe, you can't leave the country, only I can join Drew."

"Damn, Bo, you get to have all the fun."

"I know, I know, now tell me about Edwards and Louise."

"You don't know how hard it was to pull all this together; I better get a raise for this."

"It's your job, never forget that," he said with a touch of sarcasm.

Placing the briefcase on the corner of his desk, she rummaged around, pulled out a manila folder, and opened it. Laying the contents down, she preceded to hand Bo several sheets.

"First, the connection, here's a picture of her and Edwards at the opening of a restaurant in Omaha taken in 2004. They are listed by name and are said to be nearby students who are dating. I have followed up on contacts who were classmates of hers and gotten a pretty good picture of our little lady. She was some hot item, I can assure you."

"Her class picture made her look like a bookworm. What made her change?"

"She was only at the school two years. She and Edwards dated briefly before he was asked to leave. She stayed on for another semester, then dropped out. According to one of her girl friends, she was always scheming. Wanted a short cut to success and big money. School was too slow for her so she decided to chase her dream in Hollywood. Her friend said they talked once when Lewis thought she was getting a role in a musical, I think it was 'Rent'. Remember, it was a big hit a few years ago?"

"No, I don't remember, don't go to many movies."

"It was a stage play, but no matter. Apparently, it didn't work out and she never heard from her again.

So you can imagine the girl's reaction when standing in a supermarket line one day, she picked up the Enquirer. There on the cover was Mary Lewis with the wrestler, Jean Paul Girard. She was now called Marie Louise, but the girl said there was no doubt about who it was. Since then, she hasn't given her much thought until I called and inquired."

"Interesting, what about Edwards? After they broke up, you said he was asked to leave school. What was that all about?"

"Thought you'd never ask. Seems Mr. Edwards was accused of breaking into one of his professor's office, and while copying some tests, he was caught in the act. He agreed to leave quietly and not be expelled. From what I was able to gather, he did just that."

"Wait a minute," Bo said, as he pulled a document from his desk. "It says right here he got a diploma from Carlisle in AC maintenance, a two year course, and according to his boss over at Air Tech, he has the proper credentials to work on the equipment."

"Not from Carlisle, he doesn't. Of course it sounds like our Mr. Edwards simply had the diploma printed somewhere at one of those rag shops. Apparently he has been using it for several years."

"Guess you're right, not too surprising, same thing happens in most technical fields. If the guy appears competent, he never gets questioned."

"Have you pieced together why Randy Edwards would want to kill Director Clark? That's the big stretch, if you ask me?"

"I agree, but the answer is no, I haven't. I'm still working on a promising connection concerning Marie Louise. I've been able to determine that Edwards has a bank account in the Cayman's with three hundred thousand dollars stashed away. Don't think he'll need it now. But here's the interesting thing I discovered - - seems Eastern Shore Air Tech serviced another art collector who died mysteriously several months ago. I'm checking to see who the tech was that handled the account. If my suspicions are right, I'll find that Mr. Edwards dropped in and planted a little surprise in his air ducts. I think we'll find that Marie Louise was in the process of trying to secure some valuable piece of art from him just before he died. Doe that would be undeniable evidence."

"May I help in that search, since I'm not going to Spain?" Doe pleaded.

"I was just going to ask if you'd like to participate. Now as for Girard Enterprises, they have a long and interesting history with the law. They were investigated for dealing in stolen artifacts five years ago. We got involved when it appeared they were dealing with drugs with the Colombian Cartel. It was never proved and finally dropped. They were found guilty of procuring stolen artifacts from Honduras and Belize. They pleaded guilty to a minor infraction, said they didn't know the items were stolen. Somewhere along the way, drugs may have been smuggled in with the artifacts. I'm still looking, it's a stretch, but I'll find it, if it's there."

Chapter 33

▲▼▲▼▲▼

They reached the end of the paved highway three hours ago, but continued down the dusty, sandy road now marked with only a few modest signs. No matter, Carlos was familiar with the terrain and occasionally when Drew would drift off the path, he was quick to correct him. The two men continued into the foothills and through several ravines that contained minute traces of water. The liquid flowed from the higher elevation and reaching the end of its journey, pooled in the sand until the sun made quick work of it.

Carlos grew quiet and Drew realized the small man had finally run out of family history to share with his companion on the trip. Drew was thankful; as he was sure, his right ear had a cauliflower appearance from the constant jabbering. Carlos was now snoring blissfully with his hat pulled down to shield his eyes from the noonday sunlight. Drew realized he was on his own with directions. However, the road had straightened into a steady climb and it appeared as though it would remain this way for a while.

When his satellite phone on the seat began to vibrate, he looked around for the source of the annoying sound, and realizing it was the phone, grabbed it up, and flipped it open.

"Wells here."

The voice from the other end was a familiar one that made Drew smile when he recognized it was his partner.

"Ya found any senoritas to travel with until you meet Bonnie?" the voice boomed with a garbled tone that made Drew realize he was probably eating the proverbial ham sandwich.

"Your warped sense of humor fails to make an impression on me, what's going on in the big city?"

"Not much, just doing the usual FBI stuff, tracking down murderers, catching terrorist, getting shot at by assassins, the normal crap. How's your vacation?"

"Bo, if I told you all the things that have happened, you wouldn't believe me. I missed you so much I decided I could use some help so I got a Bo substitute. He's efficient, polite and can cook. Not to mention he knows the territory. I'm thinking about trading you in when I get back."

"I know you're just jerking me, but that's okay I got some news for you."

"I hope its good news and a raise, this desert is hot and sticky and no fun, nothing like Hawaii or Mexico."

"Sorry, but no, funny everybody wants a raise, you remember 'No Pain No Gain?'"

"Yeah, the logo on the boat? What about it?" Did you track down the source?"

"Yes I did, it was right under our nose, can't believe you missed it when you started suspecting Girard Enterprise."

"Girard, why are you asking about that? Aren't you devoting all your time to the Director's murder, or has Riley pulled you off that?"

"No, he hasn't pulled me off and wait till you hear what I've come up with since you left. I've been able to tie Marie Louise and Randy Edwards together."

"Bo, you're confusing me. What do Girard Enterprise, the Eckenstadt murder, and Director Clark have in common?" Drew asked, with a touch of confusion in his voice.

"We have definitely fingered Edwards as Clark's assassin. The trace of Fentanyl in the AC duct and the nozzle are circumstantial, but should be convincing with other evidence I've acquired placing Edwards at the scene. I have some more legwork to do first, but I'm sure Louise has her hand in this and I'm searching for the connection. May take a few days, but I'll persevere."

"Louise and Edwards, I'll be damned, you have a vivid imagination. How did you put them together? This has got to be a hell of a coincidence or there is a lot of intangibles I'm unaware of going on."

"Yeah, imagine my surprise when a journalist walks into my office a couple of days ago and tells me Girard Enterprise is responsible for the Director's murder. I almost dropped my shorts when I heard that. At first I thought he was just taking pot shots at them, but he had some convincing evidence that we should have had and didn't. Since then I've been burning the midnight oil literally. Once I got to digging, it was amazing how it started to come together. Found a notation in our file on Louise that placed her at the same school where Edwards went in Omaha. I can't tell you all the coincidences and mistakes our investigation has missed. Thanks to Doe, we were able to determine they knew each other at school and even dated briefly. A good lawyer would say that's a bit circumstantial and maybe it is, but I'm still working the facts."

"Damn, Bo, good work! I seem to remember she went straight from high school to California to make it in the movies. Where did I miss Edwards in her life?"

"I thought that myself, but like I said, her file had been amended and a note about the school was added in pencil at the bottom of the page. Lucky I pulled the hard copy cause it wasn't on the data base."

"Still, that doesn't tie her to Clark's murder. Edwards could have been working for anybody. On second thought, here's an idea you might want to pursue, you may find the murder connection in California. Director Clark came from there, in fact, he was the Attorney General under Governor Rutherford. When Rutherford was elected President, he brought Clark along to be Director of the FBI," Drew suggested.

"Really, I didn't know that, I'll check it for any connections out there when I get off the line. Oh, well as you can see the Director's murder has come a long way since you left. After I check the California connection, I'll be in contact with you. I hope I have enough evidence to make a case and get arrest warrants.

Oh almost forgot, the other reason I called was to inform you that Marie Louise is on her way to Spain."

"Here, what the hell is that all about?"

"You forget, we got a tail on her and are keeping up with her whereabouts. When she booked a ticket to Almeria, I realized she was sticking her nose in the archaeological affair."

"I'll be damned! When is she leaving?" Drew quizzed.

"She's in route right now, should be there in four to six hours, I'd guess. Soon as I tie up a few loose ends over here, I'm coming to join you if you like. My number one suspect has left the country and I should have enough evidence to detain her."

"Good, well bring some more tequila when you come, I'm almost out."

"Tequila, sounds like you're working real hard over there. I'll get back to you before I leave and we can decide on where to hook up."

"Good, I'll see you soon, and again, good job Bo." Drew shut the phone off and replaced it next to him in the seat. Nodding his head, he began to mull over all the new news Bo had imparted on him. Edwards and Louise were sweethearts. Now isn't that cozy, but what in the hell could her and Girard's motive be to kill Director Clark?"

After hanging up on Drew, Bo thought for a minute and glanced at his Tag Heur. It was getting late, but Janet would still be in Riley's office. Maybe if he was careful he could avoid the Director, he wasn't ready to tell him what he and Doe had found. Deciding to take the stairs, he padded up the three flights. Could stand to lose a few pounds he reasoned as he reached the stairwell door. Passing through, he continued down the hall until he reached the Director's spacious office. Somehow, he never thought he would see Riley in the big chair, but goes to show ya, he reasoned.

Janet was sitting prim and proper and just putting some of the final touches on some correspondence for the Director when Bo stuck his head in the door.

"Not interrupting anything, am I?"

The grandmotherly senior administrative assistant grinned when she recognized Bo's voice.

"No, no, come in Bo, did you want to see the Director? I'm sorry he's out."

"No, actually I wanted to see you. I need something and only you can find it for me."

"Well, it's nice to be appreciated around here, what is it you need?"

Bo eased his way into the reception area and sheepishly asked, "Do you still have access to Director Clark's files?"

"Why yes, I had them put in the basement archives several weeks ago after I cleaned out his office. However, everything that was pending and current was give to Director Riley. I know he has taken action on several outstanding issues. Why do you ask?"

"I'd like to know if he had a file on Girard Enterprise that might not be a part of the data base. You know, something he might have maintained in private."

Tilting her head, she gave Bo an inquisitive look," Funny you should ask, he had that file right before he died. He gave it back to me that Thursday and told me to put it away. He said he was finished with it for the time being. I gave all the active files to Director Riley and didn't think anything about the Girard file. I hope it's not important, did I do the wrong thing?"

"No, Janet, if you could find it for me I'd like to evaluate the Director's notes. I'm sure there is nothing to it, just a coincidence. Girard is a person of interest in my investigation and I can't leave any stones unturned. You understand?"

"When do you need it?" she asked.

"How about right now?"

"Oh dear, well I was just about to lock up any way. Would you like to accompany me down to the archives? I don't like to go down there alone this late."

"Scared the boogey man will get you?" Bo joked.

"Bo, I know I'm being silly, but I can feel his presence still here in this office. I was with Director Clark for many years in several jobs. You know he asked me to come with him when we left California six years ago. My daughter lives in upstate Maryland and well I thought it would be a good chance to see my grandchildren. Of course, I fell in love with the place. Umm, now what was I saying?"

As the two exited the elevator Bo prompted, "You were saying how long you had been with the Director."

"Oh yes, we have been working as a team for nearly twenty years."

"My, that is a long time. I'm sure you miss him more than anyone."

Stopping in the hall, she stared at Bo and said, "Bo, I think I can still hear him calling me sometimes. You know I'll look up from my desk and start to say yes, Director Clark, I'll be right in, and then I catch myself. I remember he's gone and there is no one in that dark office. It's kind of spooky, you know?"

"Yes, I can imagine. Well, here we are."

The couple strolled down a long aisle and Janet found the cabinet she was seeking. After producing a key, she opened the top drawer and fumbled around until she removed the right document.

"Here you are Mr. Boggs, I hope it helps you in your search."

Chapter 34

▲▼▲▼▲▼

It took them another day and a half, but they finally reached the site Stringfellow was searching for on his map. Achmed was still away with the remains of the mysterious rider in the desert, as Bonnie had begun to call him, and while the two remaining laborers were efficient enough, without Achmed's leadership, they needed constant prodding. The travel to the *Filabres* was uneventful except for one small storm that slipped in from the north without warning. It only lasted a couple of hours and was little more than a nuisance.

As the group plodded to its final destination, Bonnie's excitement grew. The mysterious rider had peaked her interest. She now could feel the thrill of the hunt she had as a student. When this was over, she would have to rethink her career, had she made the right choices? She was afraid she had not. There were always two or more to choose from in life and she was beginning to think she had chosen the easier one too often. After all, going to work for Eckenstadt had been straight forward. She was broke and out of work at the time. His generous offer led to part ownership in the antiquities business that was now worth several million dollars and was all in her name. Still, she wondered how she would have felt if she had pursued her passion and spent more time in the field getting her hands dirty, than at cocktail parties schmoozing rich entrepreneurs.

Then there was her personal life, which seemed a mess to her. She had sacrificed personal happiness for success, not that she had not had her share of flings and an occasional one-night stand. She was no naive virgin. Still, she had crossed paths with few men that came up to her high standards. Until that is, she met Drew Wells.

Drew was not what she would have expected, nor pursued if given a choice. Still, he had a special something that fascinated her. When this dig was finished and they had secured the Lost City, she and Drew were going to get to know each other better, a lot better.

Stringfellow halted and held up his hand to the others. He was staring intently at the rock formation and comparing it to a map he was holding. Stepping down from his mount, he removed his large brimmed hat, and wiped his face with a handkerchief. Nodding now, he turned to Bonnie, "This is it, and I remember it as if it were yesterday. Aaron and I sat right on that set of boulders and discussed our opinions every night. The camp was there near the base of the foothills and our last dig was over there," he said, pointing off to a spot a half mile away to the north.

"We will make camp here," he announced, as he pointed to the laborers and they obediently stepped down from their horses and moved the pack animals over to the spot where he was pointing.

Bonnie removed her right foot from the stirrup and lifted her leg over the saddle horn and loosening her left foot, dropped easily to the ground like the true equestrian she was.

"Professor, it's so big, I mean all this area to cover. How will we accomplish it?"

"Not so, Bonnie, I remember most of the places where we looked and can discount them. I want to search where Aaron and I decided was the last best possible place."

"Lifting his hand, he pointed over her shoulder towards the rock face of the base mountains.

Bonnie turned and stared at the odd rock formation. A chill ran up her spine as she wondered if it could possibly be the hiding place of a civilization thousands of years old missing from the face of the earth.

The desk clerk at the *Hospedaria* looked up from his guest list and watched as the beautiful woman escorted by three burly men approached his station. Straightening to his full height, he offered his best smile before speaking.

"May I help you, madam?"

"Yes, you have a reservation here for Marie Louise, I presume."

He knew he did. He had just seen it a few moments before, but in his most efficient manner, he scanned the list before him.

"Ah yes, madam, I believe you have three rooms, the penthouse and two connecting suites for the gentlemen."

"That should be sufficient, would you have the bellboy secure my luggage and take it to my room."

"Certainly, if you would not mind signing our register, please."

Pushing a document in her direction, he waited while she signed her name with a flourish-reserved for most countries presidents.

As she handed him back the document, she asked, "Do you have a distinguished French gentlemen in his mid-fifties, small mustache, registered?"

The clerk never hesitated, why you mean Monsieur Marchant, I presume."

"Yes, I take it he is staying with you?"

"Sadly no, he left three days ago, but he will be back. I do not know precisely, but he has an open reservation. Would you like me to notify him of your presence when he returns?"

"No, I would like to surprise him, would you please send word to me if he returns?"

"Certainly, madam, mums the word."

The bellhop arrived at the desk with a gurney, placed the three bags on it, and hung a garment bag on the hook.

"This way, please."

After the bellhop departed and her hired help settled into their accommodations, Marie Louise strolled out onto the terrace. With a cool glass of Chardonnay, she admired the same mountain scene Bonnie was mesmerized by a week earlier.

Her mind wandered as she planned her course of action against Bonnie and Stringfellow. Memories flooded in and the mountains reminded her of California and her early days with Girard. Their plans were simple and her ideas fresh. In those days, Jean Paul was involved in the day-to-day activities of their new and thriving business. The opening in LA was a major one and they did everything to roll out the red carpet for the celebrity clientele they were catering. Marie was thrilled as one movie and TV celebrity after another passed through their portals. Time flew by and success appeared to be within their grasp.

Marie found herself watching as Jean Paul catered to his rich friends. More and more, she stood by disapprovingly as he provided them with recreational drugs for their amusement. It was no wonder, he came from a similar culture, and it was the cost for doing business she was told. In those days, she was afraid to ask him where he was getting the illegal substance. Marie worried and wondered if this would not cause problems down the road.

Eventually she overcame her fear and felt free to imbibe with the clientele. It was almost two years to the day from the opening they were raided. The local District Attorney, a man named Mark Whitaker, encouraged by the State's Attorney General, John Clark, issued warrants for their arrests on drug trafficking and stolen art.

Only quick thinking on Marie's part kept the entire episode from getting out of control and making all of the newspapers. Utilizing Randy Edwards's unique talents, she was able to alter the state's case. Then with her attorney, they pleaded to a lesser offense of stolen artifacts. The DA a new and aspiring politician, found the quick and easy conviction what he was looking for and agreed to the lesser charge. Of course, after Randy Edwards introduced himself to the star witness, they had a much weaker case. One or two of the papers ran the story, but it was over so quickly that it had no legs to prolong the headlines.

However, Marie never forgot the embarrassment and expense the episode caused her new business. Those who meddled in her affairs would find it did not pay; she would exact her revenge no matter how long it might take. After that misstep, she pushed Jean Paul aside and asserted total control of managing their enterprise. Jean Paul took it all in stride and quickly relegated himself to more self-ingratiating activities, while Marie made plans to exact her revenge.

Thinking back on those days, she shook her head and finished the Chardonnay as the sun ended its restless run across the heavens. As darkness slowly ebbed into the desert, Marie Louise returned to her penthouse and refilled her glass. Tonight she would dine in the four star restaurant she had heard so much about and tomorrow she would plan her activities against Stringfellow and Marchant. Nevertheless, for tonight, perhaps after dinner, she would see what kind of companionship she might be able to arrange. Yes, Jean Paul was not the only one that could test the waters. It was a shame about Randy, he had many redeeming qualities.

Chapter 35

The two agents sat across the table, oblivious of each other, intent on piecing together the puzzle of Director John Clark's mysterious death. Bo was busy analyzing the Director's personal file, as Doe reviewed the material she recently received from the California Attorney General's office in Sacramento. The couple had not spoken for over an hour and you could feel the intensity in the room as they absorbed every detail of their search.

Looking up and rubbing her eyes, Doe scanned the wall clock and was surprised to see it was nearly eleven PM. They had been at this work for nearly eight hours with no break for supper.

Finally, pushing her chair away, she said, "Bo, I think I have probable cause but it's still a little bit weak. Are you willing to listen, I'm gonna need your help?"

Out of habit he began tugging his ear, raised his head from his hunched over position, and replied, "Whadda ya think you got?"

Standing, Doe placed her hands behind her back like a classroom teacher about to pounce and started to pace. She began with, "First of all, as you know, Girard Enterprise had a run in with the law early on at their inception. In 2012 in LA, they were cited for drug trafficking and dealing in stolen art. The DA had a weak case, but I believe due to personal consideration, by that I mean political aspirations, he proceeded to build his case and issue arrest warrants. However, he was a shrewd politician and proceeded to run his scenario by the Attorney General's office. From what I can gather, he made his case out to be a slam-dunk. At that time, Director Clark, who was the AG, was deeply involved with Governor Rutherford's Presidential run and accepted the DA's assessment of the case."

Stopping to gather her thoughts, she gazed at the little Greek who was taking in her story and piecing together his own scenario.

"That's it?" Bo asked.

"No, there's more, but here's where I need your shrewd mind."

"Go ahead, I'll try and help if I can."

"Well, for some reason, there is no reason stated in the file, the charges were reduced and only dealing in stolen artifacts was brought against them. Girard Enterprise pleaded *nolo contender*, and they were slapped on the wrist with a token fine with no admission of guilt on their part. I'm surprised with the DA's willingness to reduce the charges. As I mentioned, the DA was an up and coming politician and it was speculated he would run for Governor when Rutherford left. He could have been looking for the easy conviction and was just adding notches to his gun to keep his numbers high.

Anyway, Girard Enterprise was fined fifty thousand dollars and given no jail time. Shortly after this incident, Marie Louise took control of the day-to-day activities of the company. Jean Paul's title changed from President to CEO, and our friend Marie became the President with all the power. If that was all there was, then we wouldn't have anything to go on at this point, but there's more. I think you will find this as interesting as I did."

"And what's that?" Bo asked.

"About eight months later, the DA, Mark Whitaker, was killed in an automobile accident."

"That's not unusual; lots of people are killed in automobiles."

"Hold on, I'm getting to the interesting part. Seems Whitaker was coming back from a fund raising dinner in Malibu, and his car ran off the road. He was pronounced dead at the scene. His blood alcohol level was over the limit, but just barely. At first, it was thought to be a case of DUI with the DA the only casualty. A few days later, the car, which was impounded by the county, was inspected per their usual procedure. The brake line was found sawed partially in half. The fluid had leaked out and our friend Mr. Whitaker had no brakes. That combined with his slower than usual response from alcohol, is what killed him."

"They never found who or what caused the break, I take it?"

"Correct, it was officially classified an accident. What do you think? Was our little friend the bitch from the east, and her hired hand Edwards responsible?"

"You're right, that's a stretch, the DA probably made a lot of enemies in his job, Marie Louise being just one. However, wait until you hear what I have from the Director's file, it ties in neatly with your scenario."

"I'm breathless with anticipation."

"According to Director Clark, he and the DA were convinced that Girard was involved in a myriad of art theft and drug trafficking activities. The only problem was they couldn't prove it. As to your question, why the case was reduced to the lesser charge is because their star witness, a Mr. Ralph Long, met with a premature death. At least that was the assumption. Seems he disappeared the week before he was supposed to testify. Now you know, surprised that wasn't in you file. Anyway, without him, they were relegated to accepting lesser charges or dropping the case. So, they participated in a plea bargain Girard initiated and accepted the fine with no admission of guilt."

"Case closed?" Doe asked.

"Not hardly, Clark was convinced that Girard was responsible for the witness disappearance, but they couldn't prove it, or for that matter even find a body. As you know, John Clark hated to be bested by anyone, especially common crooks like Girard and Louise. He instructed the DA to continue the investigation and bring new charges later when the evidence supported it. Clark's file didn't mention the death of the DA, only the case was set aside when Rutherford was elected President. Clark became his chief of staff for a year before he was appointed to the Director's chair. The files were left to his replacement, but no further action ever took place."

"So Louise and Girard got away with murder on more than one occasion it would seem."

"Yes, the day before he died, Clark pulled this file he kept on Girard and reviewed it. I can't say for what reason, only he knows and well," Bo's voice trailed off and he closed the document in front of him.

"Sorry, Bo, I know how close you were to the Director. What do we do now?"

"We keep on keeping on, I'm positive the bitch from the east, as you called her, and her former killer, Edwards, were responsible. It seems our Marie Louise has a long memory and won't hesitate to eliminate anyone that crosses her path. I suspect she knew Clark had a long memory and she was anxious to eliminate him. Drew had better be aware of that. I'm gonna join up with him and see if we can find out what Louise is up to in Spain. I'm leaving you in charge here. You'll have your hands full while I'm gone. We know for sure that Edwards was on Louise's staff and we both know he was a killer without conscience. I want you to connect the dots. Check on that account in the Cayman's and see if you can't determine precisely where the funds came from. If they won't cooperate, use one of our tech guys and hack the system. I know it's not accepted practice, but the death of Clark warrants unusual methods. The new guy Taylor we hired away from Social Security can make it happen, we used him once before. When you find that information, or for that matter anything you think of significance, call me immediately."

"Anything else?" She asked.

"Yeah, I started checking on Randy Edwards's whereabouts at the time of Eckenstadt's murder. I'll bet you he was the mysterious doctor seen in the hallway that day at the hospital in Destin. In addition, from what you told me he knew how to cut brake lines. Randy was quite useful to Marie, I'm sure she misses him. Now one more thing, when you get a minute, run those two ideas on Edwards down and see if you can't tie him into both of those cases."

"When I get a minute! Damn, Bo, there's enough legwork here for three people. This may take awhile."

"Doe, I'm a good judge of character and talent, and you got both. Put those pieces together and you'll get that raise you were asking about and one other thing."

"What's that?"

"Permanent assignment to work with Drew and me. Now get your butt out of here and get some rest. Tomorrow is going to be a long day for both of us."

Chapter 36

Bo tipped the cab driver ten bucks and quickly made his way across the parking lane towards the entrance to Reagan National Airport. Hurrying to make the early morning flight to Madrid, he was not sure he had remembered everything to pack. No matter, he could procure whatever he forgot at the airport or a local store when he arrived. Dodging a Mercedes and a Tahoe, he glided to the curb like a quarterback running a naked bootleg. Glancing again at his timepiece, he shuffled onto the curb and in thru the revolving doors. It had been several years since Bo had flown a commercial airline and he knew it was going to be a hassle, even with his ID. People with guns get special attention and Bo dreaded the bother. Even though he was prepared, his schedule would be close.

The bag was a carry on he had had for many years and the edges showed the wear and tear of constant circling of carousels. Approaching the first security checkpoint, he pulled his ID and headed towards the front of the slow moving line. People holding baskets containing their personal belongings as well as their shoes, were patiently accepting the dehumanizing procedure they were required to endure. When the little Greek passed ten people and pulled a security guard aside, several of the patrons looked on with obvious displeasure.

Displaying his badge with all the courtesy he could muster, he gave his story to the security person and watched the man's face when he opened his vest and displayed the Glock 22 handgun neatly holstered inside. The security guard was new and flushed a deep red at the sight of the gun. Asking Bo to wait politely, he waved in the direction of another guard and asked him to join them. The other man strolled with an arrogant attitude in Bo's direction. Arriving, he glared at the little man causing the disruption and said, "What's up, Fred?"

"This gentleman claims to be an FBI agent and wants to pass through security. He has proper identification and is carrying a gun and well, I thought," he stopped in mid-sentence and waited expectantly.

"May I see your identification, sir?"

Bo again politely removed the badge and ID passing them over to the senior officer. The man examined the documentation carefully and thoroughly before handing it back to Bo.

"Looks in order, Agent Boggs, new?" he remarked.

"Yes new, now may I go gentlemen? I have a flight to Madrid leaving in twenty minutes and it's still a hike down the concourse."

The security agent nodded and saluted courteously as Bo lifted his overnight bag and briefcase. Returning the smile, he saluted back before turning and hurrying off down the crowded corridor.

Reaching his destination, Bo approached the gate agent even though he had his boarding pass. Anxiously he waited while a woman accepted her seat assignment, and then strolled back to her seat to wait. Again, he flipped his badge open and presented it to the agent as he had been instructed. The representative, an African American who towered over Bo, accepted it and passed it back commenting, "Are you armed?"

"Yes," was all Bo felt compelled to reply. The agent nodded and reached under the counter. Handing Bo a red card, he said,

"Please give this to the attendant in first class, Mr. Boggs. We have been expecting you, have a nice flight."
Pointing to the gateway, he motioned Bo to pass to the front of the line. Again, Bo headed straight for the agent taking boarding passes and passed through the checkpoint. Inspecting his boarding pass for seat assignment, he stepped into the cabin of the American Airlines 767 and maneuvered towards seat number 6B. Tossing the battered travel bag in the overhead, he placed his brief case in the empty seat beside him before slumping into 6B. As he began to remove his jacket, he remembered the holstered weapon. Hesitating, and not wanting to cause alarm, he reached inside his jacket, unsnapped a clasp, and carefully removed the entire unit. With practice, Bo learned to do this without bringing attention to himself. Folding the holster and gun together, he placed them into his brief case. Across the aisle two seats over, a man in 6D, reading a magazine, observed the procedure with apparent indifference. Turning the page he appeared absorbed in his article.

Looking up from a file he had removed from his briefcase, Bo was pleased to see the flight attendant approaching.

"May I get you something to drink, Mr. Boggs?"

Acknowledging the woman, he replied, "Yes, do you have a Samuel Adams?"

The beverage arrived with a courtesy smile from the attendant before she resumed her travels down the aisle in search of new orders. Bo placed the beer on the drop down table in front of him and resumed reading his notes.

His itinerary would take him to Madrid with a short hop down to Almeria and then a rental to the mountains. It looked like a small jog on the map, but he knew better. The information in the file folder was some Drew had sent him and he wanted to be sure he was knowledgeable of the lost city before he arrived and joined in the investigation. Unknown to Bo, he was taking the same flights and traveling the same paths as the prey he was tracking. With only minimal luck, he would arrive in Almeria and find Marie Louise at the hotel. However, luck was not in Bo's favor this day. That very morning, the Louise entourage, including her bodyguards, had left for the northern *Filabre*s and a rendezvous with Bonnie Lane and Stringfellow.

After careful review, he felt confident he was familiar with the terrain and the players; casually he laid the file aside to concentrate on his beer and his own personal thoughts.

Commercial flying wasn't so bad he rationalized if you flew first class and the government picked up the tab. Of course, he was used to flying the Director's personal Gulfstream V more often than not. A smile creased his lips as he remembered 'The Beautiful Babe', his own personal P51D Mustang he had lovingly restored and flew for several years. The incident in the State of Quintana Roo in southern Mexico was most unfortunate. The drug cartel that shot him and Drew down almost killed them both. They were lucky; still, he missed the old girl.

Recently, he had acquired a new P51 from a retired colonel in Texas who owned three, two of which he had restored and the third he used for spare parts. Bo was happy to pay him the ridiculous price he was asking just for the World War II relic's frame. He had shipped it to his facility in Gaithersburg and planned to restore it in his spare time. Of course he had little spare time these days. He was short on parts himself, but found a company in Miami that had begun making new ones for the old warhorse. They were better and more expensive, but what the hell, it was only money. If you can't spend it, what's the use in having it? The project was bigger than he remembered and it was not half finished. At this rate, he was another year away from completion. The smile slowly faded, as he closed his eyes and leaned his head back with happy thoughts.

Sliding to a stop at the unexpected intersection, Drew scratched his chin as he attempted to read the Spanish. All references to English had disappeared when the road turned to gravel and dirt. After all no sane tourist would be driving around in the *Filabres* Mountains. Unable to determine the exact meaning, and realizing he could not afford to make a mistake, he reached over and swatted Carlos on the Sombrero.

"Hey, get up and earn your keep!"

The little Spaniard jerked at the rebuke and removed his hat from his head. Rubbing his eyes, he stared around and looked at the sign that had confused Drew.

"You want to go left here, we are not far now. Let me see the map again."

Drew dutifully handed him the map that was lodged between the seat and the console. Yawning now, he folded the document into another quadrant and pointed for Drew to see.

"It is here, only another fifty kilometers. Do you need me to drive?" he asked pleadingly.

"Oh, all right, if you insist. I need to relieve myself anyway."

Both men opened the doors and exited the vehicle. Stepping only a few feet away from the Escalade, they proceeded with the natural body function. Zipping his pants up, Drew went around to the passenger side and exchanged places with Carlos. The small man fiddled with the seat adjustment and finally arranged it to his satisfaction. Dropping the lever into Drive, he accelerated tossing gravel in his wake.

Unaware of the three riders on a hillside above the auto, Drew and Carlos continued down the path towards their rendezvous. The three men kicked their horses in the ribs and moved off in the same direction.

"Are you going to call the senorita and tell her we are coming?" Carlos asked.

"I tried while you were dozing, but can't get a connection. Darn mountains are causing some problem with the satellite, I guess. I'll try again in a few minutes."

At that exact moment Bonnie was hefting a pack laden with tools she would need for her dig. Stringfellow was already at the sight and had been patiently plotting out the procedure for the last hour. Bonnie had slept in and when she awoke, the sun was already high in the sky. Embarrassed, she scrambled to ready herself for the days work and hurried to join her mentor.

"Sorry, Professor, I just couldn't wake up."

"That's okay, I needed to plan this extraction anyway. You know how it is, ninety percent preparation and ten percent perspiration."

"Somehow, that isn't how I remember it," she joked.

"You never went on a dig with me, then."

"What have you accomplished so far?"

"Here, look at this. I have decided we can start here at the edge of this sinkhole. I have dropped a line in and the depth to the base is more than a hundred feet. We will have to rappel down the side until we reach the landing. From there we will proceed into the base of the mountain. I think we will find some signs of human activity near the edge of the hole."

"My, you are optimistic, sounds so easy the way you explain it. All I remember from my efforts in Belize was dig, dig, and dig. Sometimes we found shards and a few bones that we spent hours brushing until we could remove them. Your way sounds a lot more fun."

Chuckling softly, he shook his head, "Yes, you have to be optimistic under these circumstances. Why, I remember once in the Valley of the Kings we - oh well, that was another time and another lifetime ago. There will be plenty of time for reminiscing around the campfire at night. I'll try and not get distracted again."

As Stringfellow spoke, Bonnie looked up at the steep face of the rock not ten feet away. It stretched into the sky for what seemed to be forever. About half way up it jutted out and a ledge formed a small platform before soaring into the sky again. The ledge reminded Bonnie of a nose and she said, "You know, professor, this range of rock resembles a face. I know I must be crazy, but I would call it an old person with a large nose and look at the recesses, they look like eyes."

"Amazing you noticed," Aaron said the exact same thing over fifty years ago. It was almost as if he were speaking through you. I know now we will be successful, that is a good luck omen.

At the mention of her former partner's name Bonnie felt saddened immediately, but threw back her head and dabbed at her eye where the tear was forming and said, "Yes, I can feel him sometimes, I think you are right, he's with us and we will not be denied.

"Come on, then help me widen the crevice so that we may enter the gates to the lost city," Stringfellow exclaimed.

Chapter 37

He was not accustomed to roughing it in the open spaces of a desert where the temperature routinely climbed to one hundred and ten degrees Fahrenheit. No, Marchant was polished and refined, someone accustomed to the finer things in life. Gourmet food, the best of wine, all of the creature comforts he could obtain. From his office at the museum, to his private collection, an apartment in Paris, both were overflowing with rare and valuable artifacts, some acquired legally, and some through other methods too sordid to mention.

Alas, now here he was in this god-forsaken place, doing what he asked himself. Recently that question more than not popped into his mind. In the past, in situations like this, he would routinely hire the appropriate people to acquire the objects he sought for the museum, or for his personal collection. Now, for some reason he felt compelled to chase after Stringfellow and his female friend, Bonnie Lane, himself. Well, no matter, they were on the verge of a great find that he would proclaim to the world as his own. If anyone tried to interfere, he would dispose of them post haste.

Camped several miles away and sheltered in the foothills of the mountains, he was out of view of Stringfellow's site. No one knew of his presence as he observed them from afar. This very morning he watched as the two explorers began their descent into the hole in the ground. Even though he detested the arrogant Stringfellow, he admired and envied his sense of adventure. When the sun became unbearable, Marchant quickly tired of the proceedings. With nothing to entertain his imagination, he found it appropriate to retire for rest and refreshment.

As he sipped the cool chardonnay, he stared into the distance and his mind wandered to thoughts of his former partner Marie Louise. What was she doing now he questioned. Yes, he had given up on her excuses, taking the entire matter into his own capable hands.

With nothing else to do until Stringfellow and his associate emerged from the hole in the ground, he decided to rest and plan for the task that lay ahead.

Returning to his tent, he yelled at one of his hired help advising him that he was not to be disturbed. Raising the flap, he entered his well-appointed tent and removed his broad brimmed hat. Tossing it onto a makeshift table, he sat on the edge of the cot and removed his boots. A nap was in order; he had plenty of time to check on his quarry in a few hours.

She had expected it to be pitch dark in the sinkhole as she descended into the bowels of the earth. Therefore, you could imagine her surprise as the sun light from above filtered in lighting her way down the narrow passage. Rappelling down the sheer incline like a mountain goat, she began to wonder if Stringfellow might be mistaken. How and why would an ancient civilization lie at the bottom of this hole in the ground? Was there an earthquake that caused the subterranean location?

When he first proposed the idea, she jumped at the thought because it was unique and she so wanted to believe it. After all, if Eckenstadt and Stringfellow both had come up with the plan, it had merit. Her current mentor and former partner were brilliant minds, and their ideas were always sound.

However, this shaft was bare and showed no signs of human intrusion at any time in the past. Somewhere down below Stringfellow was still plodding ahead, but no matter how hard she scanned the blackness, she could see no sign of him. Finally, out of frustration and concern, she called out hoping to get his attention.

"Professor, can you hear me?" she spoke in a normal tone of voice. Nothing but silence greeted her waiting ears, so boldly, with more volume, she tried again.

"Professor, if you can hear me, please shout out."

"Professor, if you can hear me, please shout out," from far below an echo came back. Then as she strained, she thought she heard a faint voice filtering up to meet her.

"I'm here; keep coming, you're getting closer. I'm on a ledge."

Relieved at his reassuring tone of voice, she accelerated her descent and within a few moments, saw his outline on an outcrop that seemed to hang far over the abyss. Kicking her feet, she pushed herself in his direction as he reached to grab her. His grip was still strong and sure, and she quickly slid onto the ledge beside him.

Gasping for breath, she stared down into the darkness.

"Are you sure this is safe?"

The twinkle in his eye told her he was about to lie, "Yes, of course. This rock formation is part of the granite substructure and has been in this position for a hundred million years or more. It was probably formed when the mountains pushed their way up from the sea floor."

"When did you get to be a geologist?" she asked.

"Oh, in my business you are an archaeologist one day, a geologist another, and sometimes even a paleontologist. You'd be surprised what I could tell you about dinosaur bones," he added.

"Professor, nothing you tell me surprises me anymore. Still, what do you think? This seems very deep in the ground for a city like the Hittite's Hatti. Are you sure, we are not headed in the wrong direction? I would have thought an earthquake may have caused the disappearance, but surely we would have seen some signs by now."

"No, I can't be sure; I must admit my theory isn't as sound as when Aaron and I hit upon it forty plus years ago. Now I, well, I'm not as confident. I would've thought we might descend a few hundred feet before we saw signs of the ancient civilization. Still, I would like to explore a few more of these sinkholes to satisfy my curiosity before ruling it out."

"Fair enough, I'm willing to assist you. For now though, I think I'll return to the surface. This hole is creepy and desolate. Shall we have the men pull us both up?"

"No, you go ahead first, I'll be right behind. There is a small opening over here I want to inspect before leaving. I was about to do it when I heard your call. It shouldn't take me more than a few minutes," he said, pointing towards a dark recess in the wall."

Bonnie shook her head in the affirmative and said "Suit yourself then, I'll see you on top."

After gaining his concurrence, she looked up and gave two sharp tugs on her line. Immediately, a return signal came back and she was instantly lifted off the ledge and up into the dark, like an angel ascending into heaven.

As she looked down, Stringfellow followed her progress for a few moments before turning and entering the recess. Immediately she realized the ascent was not what she expected. The laborers were instructed to pull at a steady and reasonable rate of speed. She found herself hurtling upward at an alarming tempo. From time to time, she would strike the side of the shaft scraping her clothes and banging her knee painfully on one occasion. No matter what she tried to do to slow the ascent, she had no control. Looking up, she observed the small opening in the floor of the desert growing closer. The sun was almost directly overhead now and shone straight down making it impossible to see the laborers. Cursing under her breath, she again scraped her elbow as she popped into the sunlight.

Before she could utter a word of condemnation, someone grabbed her around the waist and placed a hand over her mouth. Instinctively she kicked and fought the personal intrusion. Trying to focus, she found it impossible coming from pitch black to bright sunlight. Then another pair of hands grabbed her and placed a cloth over her nose and mouth. At first, she thought they were trying to smother her, but then she smelled the strong odor entering her lungs. Where had she smelled that fragrance before? The hospital she realized, it was chloroform, her mind screamed. At the comprehension she was being drugged, she kicked out with all her might and began to swing her arms wildly about. A small amount of satisfaction was achieved when she struck one of the assailants in the face, but it was short lived. It took only a few moments as the chemical began to work. Ever so slowly, she began the deep descent into another black hole of fear.

Stringfellow was satisfied that the small cave was insignificant after he followed it into the edge of the wall facing. It quickly shrunk in size and when he stopped, it had dwindled to about two feet in height. Even though he was sure, it continued for a bit, he was not nimble enough to crawl on his hands and knees far enough to determine its importance. Removing his hat, he beat the dust from it as he returned to the ledge. Looking up, he could not determine if Bonnie had reached the top or was still ascending. Nevertheless, he gave two gentle tugs on his line as a signal to raise him.

Funny, the rope felt suddenly limp, and then he realized it was gathering in slack around his feet. Somehow, it must have come loose from its mooring above. Stepping back, he looked up and watched as the remainder of the line fell crazily towards him.

In only a moment, the end of the line struck the ledge and then bounded over the precipice into the darkness below. Stringfellow quickly grabbed at the rope and stopped its free fall. Standing, he again looked up and shouted.

"What's wrong, the line came loose. Can you hear me?"

"Can you hear me?" echoed back from somewhere along the shaft. A cold chill ran up his spine as Stringfellow realized he was all alone in this dark hole.

Awakening from the drug-induced sleep, she struggled as she realized her hands and feet were bound tightly. Slowly the haze lifted and she stared across the storage tent. As her eyes adjusted, she saw the two laborers staring back at her with fear in their eyes.

They were both bound in a similar fashion to her, and both had gags in their mouths. It was now dark outside and Bonnie assumed she had slept for several hours. Her mind raced trying to determine who would find it necessary to tie her up. Gradually, as she reasoned through her situation, she realized the professor was nowhere in sight.

Determined, Bonnie began the slow process of trying to free herself. Although her hands were bound tightly, she knew with enough time, she would be able to wiggle them free. As a child, she and her older brothers often played cowboy and Indian. Being the youngest, she was always the one tied to the stake. If she could escape them, this would be a piece of cake. The two bound laborers watched as she wiggled and squirmed in her sitting position. After several minutes of effort, she felt the knot slip a minuscule amount, and then her right hand moved with more freedom.

At that precise moment, the tent flap was thrown open and a large Caucasian male with a bandage over his nose, followed by a petite woman, entered the tent. As the woman passed around the large frame of the man, Bonnie gasped as she recognized Marie Louise.

Rising in her sitting position, she tried to put on a confident air, even though she knew now she was in the hands of the devil.

"So, Miss Lane, we meet again, I think you remember Carl, he was the one that picked you up that morning at your place. Carl has many useful purposes. However, he was careless and you left your mark on him. You may leave us now," she said to the man. He bowed slightly and gazed at Bonnie with contempt as he exited.

Bonnie's mind raced as she searched for a clever dialogue to confuse the sinister Marie Louise.

"I demand you untie me, and just exactly what is the meaning of this? What have you done with the professor? I told you when I met you I didn't have the statue you were looking for and I still don't. If you don't release me immediately, I will report you to the authorities."

Marie looked at Bonnie as if she were the biggest fool she had ever met. Then she said, "Miss Lane, we both know you secured the original Stone of Hammurabi and aided by the government, you still have it stored in a secure place. A fake was shipped back to the government in Baghdad. But even if I didn't know all that, I would question what you are doing here in the *Tabernas* Desert of Spain. This isn't exactly what I would call an all-inclusive resort vacation. As for reporting me, I think you should assess your situation better. You are the one that is tied up. Now you can make it easy, or you can make it hard. For your information, Carl knows many persuasive methods to get you to tell us what you know. After you broke his nose, he would relish the idea of making you talk. Now why don't you explain to me your reason for digging in these mountains in this remote part of the world?"

Bonnie was now in full anger mode and she knew that Marie Louise was right. Still, she did not want to give her the satisfaction. "I don't have to explain my activities to you. However, I have nothing to hide. If you must know, Professor Stringfellow and I are searching for the site of a battle that we believe took place near here. I often assist him in archaeological digs. Now, what have you done with the professor?"

"Miss Lane, you are a liar, you haven't been on an archaeological search since you were a graduate student. If you insist on lying to me, it will make your meeting with Carl come that much sooner. Suit yourself, you will remain tied up here in this tent until you change your mind and tell me the truth. As for now, you may sleep. In the morning, I will have Carl pay you a visit. That will give you something to look forward to. As for your accommodations, I think you will find after the sun rises, the temperature in here will do likewise. The temperature at mid-day can reach well over a hundred and ten degrees Fahrenheit. That may loosen your tongue even sooner. If you change your mind in the meantime, just call out. I will be close by, and oh yes, don't even think about escaping, there is nowhere to go for a hundred kilometers. Your bones will bleach in the sand if you make the attempt."

"What about the professor?"

"The professor, oh, he is close by; I have left him in that hole in the ground. I'm sure he is getting hungry by now. He stopped calling for you a couple of hours ago. I hope he is all right."

Laughing at her own joke, she lifted the flap and exited the tent, leaving Bonnie staring wide-eyed with fear she could no longer hide.

After a few moments, her anger turned to action, and she began with renewed effort on her bindings.

Chapter 38

Drew closed the satellite phone and placed it in the console beside him. Carlos was still driving and the pace was slow, but steady.

"Still no get the lady to answer?"

Deep in thought, Drew did not reply as he wondered if something could be wrong. Of course, the satellite they used for the link could just be in the wrong position. It happened occasionally and usually caused only a minor delay in connections. Still, he had been trying now for the better part of two hours. According to his map, they were close to her camp, but did not have the exact bearings to find them. When he was given the coordinates she did not know the specifics, but by now, they would have been on site for several days.

"Huh, what, you said something?" he finally replied.

"I asked if the lady no answer. You have been calling for several hours. I think I can come close to the valley by your description, but, well, it would be easier with more information."

"Yeah, sure, well they don't answer and until they do we are stuck with wandering around these mountains. Go ahead and take us to the spot you think is the most likely."

"*Si.*"

Drew returned to his map and tried to make out the position from his own reckoning. He had little luck reading maps and to him they were always a mess of jumbled lines. Where was Bo when he needed him? That mathematical mind would pinpoint the most likely location in short order. If Drew had known of Bo's location he would have been surprised to know his partner was only fifty miles south heading in his direction.

As the Escalade bounced down the gravel and boulder strewn pathway, Drew placed the map aside and stared out the windshield. The night sky was dark, but the headlights illuminated the narrow roadway as they plodded along. It was now nearly ten pm and Drew was considering telling Carlos to pull over and make camp for the night.

From a half mile away, the horseback riders who had been following them, continued to trail the slow moving vehicle as it progressed along methodically picking its way around small obstacles. If the two travelers had been in a small plane flying above the landscape, they would have been surprised to know they were less than five miles from the campsite they were seeking. However, they would not know this until they almost drove into the front door of the encampment.

Finally, weary of the bouncing and apparently fruitless effort, Drew told the small Spaniard to pull off the roadway and make camp.

Close by, the campsite of Bonnie and Stringfellow was dark, except for a small fire in the middle of the encampment. Surrounding the fire were two men with AK 47's drinking coffee and making small talk to pass the time.

Deep in the sinkhole in the ground, Stringfellow was not passing his time idly as he waited to be rescued. Using his flashlight sparingly, he had moved away from the ledge and made a small place for himself in the recess of the granite wall. It was surprisingly warm and he would swear a slight breeze seemed to emanate from the darkness of the recess. He had given up calling hours ago; whatever was the matter up above was out of his control. It seemed to him that Bonnie was either being held captive or had been. Well, he didn't want to think of the other possibility. For what must have been the fifteenth time, he illuminated his light and shined it around the small site he had chosen to rest. Playing the light off the black recess, he decided he would try to widen the hole and see if it went anywhere. He knew he couldn't climb the sheer walls out and this may be his only hope.

    Opening his pack, he removed the small trowel he used in excavation and checked for spare batteries for the light. Yes, he had an entire pack of the double A's he would need for his effort. Good, he was now comfortable he would have several hours of light if he managed it carefully. After that, he didn't know what he would do.

    Licking his index finger, he held it aloft to confirm his suspicion. Yes, there definitely was a small breeze blowing from inside the black hole in the wall. With this encouragement, he began in earnest to widen the fissure. As he worked, the perspiration trickled down his forehead and dropped to the floor of the cavern.

    An hour passed and he had made noticeable progress. Getting down on all fours, he stared into the blackness. Was he imagining things or was there a small flickering light coming from deep within the mysterious hole? A smile creased the corner of his mouth and he shook his head as if to say yes, there definitely was.

    Lying flat on his stomach, he kept the trowel in his left hand and began to crawl cautiously into the small passage.

At the same exact moment Stringfellow made his entrance into the opening, Bonnie pulled her right hand out of the bindings. She was sweating from the exertion, even though it was comfortably cool in the tent. She had been trying to free her hands for the better part of four hours, although time had no meaning to her as she worked. The two laborers who were tied across from her had given up and were dozing blissfully.

    She must be careful, a guard had been poking his head in the tent flap every hour as near as she could tell. It was almost time for his check now so she needed to be careful. Her wrists had been bound behind her back around a stake in the ground used to support the tent. Now she deftly removed the last of the bindings and frantically scanned the tent looking for something she could use to defend herself. Even though she was securely tied, they were careful to remove anything that could be used as a weapon. Rubbing her wrists, she thought she heard someone coming. Immediately she placed her hands behind her and hung her head loosely in front. The tent flap opened and one of the two guards peered into the dark recesses of the supply tent. Noticing Bonnie and the laborers sleeping, he dropped the flap and walked back to the circle where the fire was slowly dying.
Instantly she reached around and began working on her feet. It took her only a few moments and both were released from their bonds. Now what to do, should she wake the laborers and free them, or escape on her own? What about the professor, she couldn't leave him at the bottom of the sinkhole. Her mind raced, and she realized she needed help. "Drew, where are you? I need you now!"

    If she only knew how close he was, she would have had some comfort in that realization.

He had seen them arrive that afternoon and was shocked at the realization it was Marie Louise and her band of hired killers. Although Marchant was prepared to attack Stringfellow himself, he had no stomach for an all out war with someone he knew was more cunning and treacherous than himself. He had waited around all afternoon to see if they would leave and when it became apparent they were going nowhere, he decided it would be in his best interest to depart. His men had packed their belongings and the jeeps were loaded waiting for his command.

As he leaned on the boulder observing their campsite with his digital binoculars, he noticed something peculiar. Refocusing his glasses, he swore he saw the woman crawling from beneath the tent and slip away into the desert. He had watched earlier that day when she was pulled from the sinkhole and drugged into submission. It had been six hours since that episode and the realization that his former partner Marie Louise had taken control of the dig site.

He tried his best to follow the woman as she made her way away from the tent, but she slipped into the darkness and was gone. Turning, he motioned to his men and joined them as they prepared to leave. In a few minutes they had started their vehicles and were on their way back to civilization.

Bonnie still had no plan; she was trying to put as much distance between her and the camp as possible before they discovered her absence. She stumbled and fell on several occasions and scratched her arms on small prickly scrubs that were growing in abundance around the campsite. After a few minutes, she was several hundred meters away and stopped to catch her breath, while the two guards continued talking and smoking around the campfire. The remainder of their entourage including Louise were sleeping in the tents Stringfellow had set up for her and himself. Bonnie's mind continued to race as she beat herself up emotionally for abandoning her mentor. How would she get him out, she repeatedly asked herself. Try as she may, no answer was forthcoming. Therefore, with great reluctance, she turned and began fleeing in a northerly direction toward the mountains.

Chapter 39
▲▼▲▼▲▼

By now, they must know she was missing and were searching for her. As she fled, she continually looked back over her shoulder for any sign she was being followed. Perhaps she would elude them she hoped, as she scrambled along the base of the mountain range. Eventually, she knew she would have to hide somewhere, perhaps now would be a good time to find a spot before she was forced to make a hasty and bad decision.

     The small boulders at the base of the range turned larger as they approached the solid granite that jutted out of the floor like monoliths to a forgotten god. Squeezing through a gap between two large pillars, she stopped abruptly, catching herself before she fell into another of Stringfellow's sinkholes. Studying it briefly, she noticed this one was wider but no doubt just as deep and foreboding as the one she had rappelled into earlier that day. Without a flashlight, she could not tell where it went, or how abruptly it descended into the bowels of the earth.

Her indecision was short lived, and she forged ahead to see if it was a place that could provide her with cover from her pursuers.

Carefully, she placed one foot on the edge of the large crevice and then another on a second protrusion that jutted out lower and wider. She continued this process until she stopped abruptly.

"Steps, these appear to be steps," she uttered under her breath.

Where could they lead, she wondered as she continued her flight into the unknown. Disappearing from the surface, she entered a vertical shaft that spiraled steadily downward as a warm breeze wafted up to greet her like the devil's own breath. The stone steps kept their regular interval and she found herself dropping eight to ten inches for each stride she took. Although the moon was dipping in and out of the clouds, she was surprised to notice she could see the descent perfectly. In fact, the deeper she went the lighter it appeared to become. After ten minutes of steady decline, she stopped and stared around at this passage she was blindly following.

Looking in all directions, she noticed something carved or scratched into the wall like ancient graffiti. Approaching, she wiped her hand across the scratches and removed layers of dirt that had collected over a millennium. The marks were a pictograph and she followed it along the wall lower into the cavern. After several minutes of cleaning, she stepped back and studied the work. At the top of the picture was a ship, a single mast vessel shown sailing on a turbulent sea with a stiff breeze in her sail. Several men were in the positions of oarsmen while another stood on the bridge operating the tiller. Drawing closer, Bonnie was able to discern the men in the picture wore their hair long and braided hanging from beneath helmets. Studying the ship more closely she noticed on the bow of the craft a fearsome looking creature, a dragon of some kind meant to frighten away sea serpents she presumed.

    As she moved down the stairway, the ship gave way to two large pillars of granite with the ocean crashing upon their base. At this point, she placed her hand on the wall and continued as though she were reading a term paper. Next, the landscape changed to tranquil scenes of a harbor with many ships like the first. The farther she went the sea gave way to fields of grain growing in the distance, while women could be seen harvesting the crop. Gradually the panorama changed again and showed people fleeing in large numbers back to the sea and boarding the ships anchored in the harbor. The next panorama showed a great sea battle in progress between the people on the wall and another power. Bonnie studied the new invaders carefully and concluded they must be Egyptian. It was apparent the invaders with superior numbers were winning and the sea people fleeing. Bonnie's mind raced as she tried to piece together the meaning of the pictures. Then the pictographs stopped and the story ended along with her theory.

    What could it all mean, if only the professor were with her, he would be able to translate it more precisely.

Absorbed with deciphering the cuneiform, she had completely forgotten the people who must surely be searching for her. Looking around she could not decide whether to go on or turn back. The area below her still seemed to have enough light for her to push on, but the way out beckoned to her and she struggled to decide. Turning away, she slowly continued her descent down the stairway.

He had dozed for what must have been no more than thirty minutes. Dropping the AK 47 suddenly jarred him awake and he quickly retrieved the weapon from where it lay at his feet. Stretching, he rubbed his eyes and gazed at his wrist watch. It was past time for him to look in on the woman in the tent, but what if he were a few minutes late, she was not going anywhere. Looking around, he observed his partner snoring lightly as he lay by the fire. Deciding not to wake him, he strolled over to the tent, and raised the flap. Peering in to check on the hostages he began his inventory, the two laborers were still in place, one with his head on the others shoulder. As he scanned across the tent, his mind screamed something was amiss. The woman, where the hell was the woman?

Shining his light around the small space, he noticed a trail in the sand floor that led to the back of the tent. He immediately raced to the back and saw where she had ripped the material as she slipped underneath.

Jumping up, he exited the tent and scampered around to the back. Shining his light, he saw her tracks where she slipped beneath the fabric and stole away into the desert.

Ms. Louise was not going to like this and he dreaded telling her, but he had no choice. Retracing his tracks, he returned to the campsite kicking at the sleeping body of his partner. Hurriedly he relayed the story to the other man as best he could. The two men looked at each other and decided to make a preliminary search before waking Ms. Louise. With any kind of luck, they would find the woman before she got too far from the campsite.

Bonnie eased her way down the gradual incline and continued her descent along the passageway. The path had begun to widen as if to accommodate more people. The light was still tolerable but Bonnie realized she would eventually run out of the precious commodity. After a half hour of carefully picking her way around boulders, stalagmites, and an occasional vermin that made this place its home. She stopped and stared incredulously at the amazing sight that befell her eyes.

    On the wall next to the opening was a torch she realized was used for additional light. She removed the object and wondered if it could still work. Then almost as though a ghost from the past could read her mind, she noticed the two pieces of flint lying on a ledge at the base of the torch. Removing the small stones the size of walnuts, she struck them together to test her theory. Immediately sparks flew from the instruments and fell harmlessly to the floor.

    Saying a little prayer, she placed the torch on the ground and carefully positioned herself over it where the sparks would fall on the blackened and charred end. Steadying herself, she again struck the two blunt objects together and watched as a shower of sparks jumped from flint to the ancient object on the ground. Again, and again, she repeated the action. On the third attempt, a small fire burst from the corner of the torches black and oily covering. Seizing the instrument from where it lay, she began to blow gently trying to nurture the flame. Encouraged by her efforts, the fire rose up to meet her. In less than a minute, the torch was blazing as she held it aloft.

    Waving it around in front of her, she gasped at what befell her eyes. No, it was not the lost city, but what appeared to be a temple of worship.

    Before her, a great amphitheater spread out over a space of two football fields in size. Carved into the rock itself, were stadium seats that encircled a platform or a stage used for some kind of performance or ritual. The theatre extended outward towards a large pit with an altar behind it. On the altar were carvings of creatures devouring men as they engaged in a great struggle. Climbing the steps to the altar, she held the torch aloft as she came closer. She did not see it at first, and when she did, she let out another gasp. Standing over twenty meters high was a statue of a giant, or God, she could not be sure.

His features were those of a young warrior dressed for battle. Looking up at his countenance, she approved of his handsome features and the helmet upon his head. Long braided hair fell to his shoulders and framed the perfect face. The nose was straight and small and looked almost feminine. His mouth was closed and a grimace seemed to be the best way to describe his pose. Dressed in a robe with fur around his shoulders, he held aloft a large blunt instrument in his right hand and a shield in his left. The instrument was not a sword or a bow as one might expect, yet she knew it had an important meaning. The instrument appeared to be a large hammer held in his palm. She followed his gaze as it filtered down to the ground where a serpent was coiled and ready to strike. The God like creature was apparently preparing to strike the snake with his weapon. It was all happening too fast and Bonnie wanted to sit down and draw a representation of the scene. Of course, she did not have the materials or the time. Blinking, she tried to take in everything and hold it in memory so she could describe it again to the Professor.

   When she looked back at the statues face, she swore he had turned his head slightly in her direction and was staring into her eyes. "That's funny," she thought, she had not noticed at first, but now with his gaze on her, she saw his eyes as they blazed like burning coals. Mesmerized, Bonnie could not look away and continued to stare at the glowing objects the size of small oranges.

The hypnotic effect was calming and she felt as if all the tenseness in her body was slowly ebbing away.

The surreal feeling was more like a trance she was entering, as she slumped to the ground, she closed her eyes and passed into darkness.

Chapter 40

▲▼▲▲▼▼

By now, he should have been totally lost. All right, he was lost. Bo had been driving for the better part of four hours and seen nothing but scrub bushes and vipers. Once or twice, he dozed and drove off the poorly marked gravel sand pit they called a highway. After one of these episodes, he was forced to get out and dig the rear wheels from where they had lodged into the sand. To say he was lost was to admit the obvious, but lost he felt he was. He knew he was in Spain, somewhere north of Almeria, and from what he could tell, he was about five miles from the Filabres. It had been dark for two hours, so he probably should find a suitable place to pitch some kind of camp, even if it only meant he'd sleep in the car until daylight.

    The headlights were in his windshield for several minutes before he realized their significance. They were growing considerably brighter when he finally awoke to the fact they were coming straight at him. It was the first sign of any civilization he had seen since he began the journey from the rental agency near the hotel. Slowly they grew in significance and after what seemed an eternity, they raced by him without as much as blinking their recognition. Bo could see there were at least four men in the first vehicle and now he realized there were two SUVs. The second one a few hundred meters to the rear and pacing the lead one, swept past startling him with their horn. The haunting image of a man in the back seat with a neatly trimmed mustache and coal black hair stared out inquisitively. Even though it was for only a brief moment, the impression on the face of the stranger stayed with him as the tail lights raced away into the dark of the desert.

    Suddenly conscious, he was alone again with nothing but the radio to accompany him on his passage into the blackest night. Instinctively, he reached for the dial and tuned it manually as he studied the stranger's face in his mind; the music assailed him with a combination of Spanish salsa and hip-hop. What a strange mixture, what had the world come to, he asked himself. Flipping on the interior lights, Bo smoothed his map with one hand while keeping an eye on the road with the other. Even though the vehicle was equipped with a navigation system, there was nothing on the highway he could use for navigational purposes. The rental agent told him the drive was at least a hundred and fifty miles of desert. He had accepted the additional gas cans in the trunk graciously, even if the charge of four dollars American per liter seemed excessive. Running out of gas in the desert was not an option.

    Well, if the map and the odometer were right, he was getting close. Of course, the porch light would not be on the way his mom always left it. He would just have to stop at any old campfire he saw to ask directions. A nagging thought in the back of his mind told him he could go right by and miss them. After all, they had pack animals and planned to explore areas not on the beaten path, even if it was a gravel super highway.

Might as well call Drew, perhaps he had a line on the exact location. He had meant to check in when he landed, but he got in a rush and he didn't know much anyway.

Raising the satellite phone, he pressed speed dial and waited for the metallic clicks indicating the transmission was in progress.

He was not as young as he used to be and his health was deteriorating faster than he could believe. Yes, the sentence of death his doctor had given him was actually going to happen he realized. Short of breath, he stopped on two occasions to breathe deeply and restore his weakened condition. As he lay there, he laughed silently at he thought of how his doctor would feel deprived if he actually died of suffocation in this hole in the ground.

A hacking cough ensued and he spit up phlegm with a small amount of blood. Not the first time, this had been a persistent problem for the last two weeks. Doctor McLaughlin might be right, he might not last another three months. If it were up to the physician, he would be in some hospital undergoing chemotherapy to drag out his sentence. No, he was in control and he would end his life on his own terms. Enough feeling sorry for himself, time to get back to work.

Sliding the trowel in front of him, he hacked at the corridor and widened it just enough to ease himself along. He had been at this for the better part of an hour and had traveled only sixty feet along the passage. However, he could not know this, only that he was exerting a lot of energy for little in return. Still, the flickering light at the end of the tunnel was encouraging.

Good thing he was not claustrophobic, if he were he would have given up. The confines of the opening were so tight his back rubbed the ceiling of the hellhole on every other push.

At that precise moment, something near his face flushed and ran across his hand scampering along the path with him. The suddenness of the action startled him and he almost cried out in fear. Flashing his light, he saw two small green eyes staring back.

A rat, a small gray rat was staring him down and daring him to proceed. Stringfellow chuckled and doused the light. With a Herculean effort, he again began his assault on the small passage with all his strength.

The rat stood his ground for a moment, but when he saw the large creature moving, he gave in and ran away towards the light at the end of the tunnel.

Venting her anger would do no good and she knew it, but there was at least an emotional release in anger that gave her satisfaction.

The two on duty guards stood there with their heads hanging afraid to return the stare of the small woman who was their employer. She might be petite in stature, but she was a giant in character. Waving them out of her tent, she proceeded to get dressed while they awoke the third guard and the guide she had hired in Almeria.

When she exited the tent, she was dressed in hiking boots and tight fitting jeans. Her hair was pulled back and the men realized that under that façade of toughness was a beautiful woman. Nevertheless, beauty was wasted on Marie Louise; she cared only for power and riches. She knew that beauty was a fleeting thing; tomorrow she would be a middle-aged gray haired woman trying to hide her wrinkles.

"All right show me where you have looked and where you think she may have gone."

The group moved away from the camp and headed on a path towards the face of the mountains. The lead man, the guard that made the discovery, quickly pointed out the obvious tracks near the tent. As they progressed, the ground grew firmer and the tracks were harder to see and eventually disappeared all together.

Bending to one knee the woman stared at the fleeting steps and shined her light off towards the mountains.

"She could not have gotten far, she must know we will track her and find her. You go with me and the two of you go along the edge of the rock face. If you find anything, call or fire a shot to alert us. Now hurry, she is probably close by, don't miss anything," she demanded.

The group split up as she had instructed and made off in separate directions. Within a few minutes, they were out of sight of each other.

Meanwhile in the cavern below the ridge Marie Louise's group was scouring, a lone figure stirred and opened her eyes.

Bonnie was exhausted and her encounter with the giant stone statue, had caused her to faint from fear and fatigue. Lying on the ground, she raised her head and slowly tried to sit up.

It was at that moment her memory jarred her and she remembered the terrifying moment when the statue appeared to be looking at her.

Drawing back, she gazed up at the giant above her. It was dark and free of any emotion or life. She almost laughed to help her gather her confidence, but could not wrestle the emotion from her throat. Rising, she dusted herself off and looked for the torch she had dropped. It was lying on the ground a few feet away but had burned itself out. Retracing her steps to the ledge where the instrument was attached, she found the flints where she left them.

Carefully she placed the torch on the ground and repeated her procedure to light the instrument. No luck as the sparks rained down, no fire burst forth to greet her.

"There must be something combustible in this place," she thought.

Her eyes became adjusted to the reduced light, as she began to search the area for something, anything to burn. As she approached the pit in front of the altar, she noticed steps leading down the side into the hole. Boldly she stepped on the first one and moved down the side of the opening into the pit. A large pile of something was at the bottom and she hoped it might be her salvation. The steps were few and when she reached her destination; she leaned over to pick up something she thought was another torch. Pulling it close to her face she gasped as she realized it was a human bone. Startled, she dropped it immediately and pulled back from where it fell.

"I must get a hold of myself," she said aloud. After a moment to gather her thoughts, she kicked at the pile in front of her and reached down to retrieve a piece of material of some kind. She discovered more combustible scraps in the pile as she rummaged around like a homeless person. She praised her luck as she found wood chips from a fire that must have been started eons ago.

Gathering everything she could find, she climbed up the stairs and retrieved the flint. With a new source of combustible material, she easily started the fire. Carefully she fed it the material and scraps of wood until it was blazing.

There it was again, he thought he must be imagining things when it disappeared, but now it was back. The light was closer and it appeared to dance as he crawled along the tiny corridor. Now he had hope again and this time he would discover the source of the mystical dancing light.

When it disappeared, he was crestfallen, thinking he must have been dreaming it all, but now he knew he was not imagining the light he saw in the distance. Pulling himself along with all his strength, he now swore the end of this tunnel was at hand. It could only be another twenty feet of agony. His fingers had torn the skin from three of his knuckles. One fingernail was bleeding, and he knew he would lose it from the pain he was feeling.

Almost there, the light now glowed like a spotlight in the abyss. Still it danced and he deduced it must be a fire of some kind. Just as he thought he could reach out and touch it, he found himself stuck tight at the waist.

It was no use; he could not pull free with his remaining strength. So close, what could he do? When he realized there was no alternative, he cried out, "Help me, please help me!"

Bonnie whirled around and stared over her shoulder at the pit. She could taste the fear in her throat at the sound of the voice coming up from below. Cautiously she moved over to the edge and peered into the hole. She swore she could hear breathing or gasping, she could not be sure.

"Is someone there?" she asked timidly.

"Yes, help me; I'm here in this tunnel."

Bonnie pushed the makeshift torch in front of her and lit the empty pit again. Scouring the entire area, she noticed a small opening near the far side. From the darkness, a light pierced the side of the barrier dancing on the wall of the ancient sacrificial cavity.

Now her curiosity was getting the better of her and she scampered down into the blackness. Thrusting her torch in front of her, she got down on one knee and stared into the crack in the wall. Not three feet away the exhausted countenance of Professor Stringfellow returned her stare.

Chapter 41

▼▲▼▲▼

Bo was only mildly upset at his inability to connect with his partner Drew Wells. These things happened sometimes when you travel the world, so he'd just have to make the best of it.

Turning off the main highway of gravel and asphalt, he slowed his pace as he traversed the little used mountain trail. The Filabres loomed up ahead and he felt alert and confident, even though he had been at this for over ten hours. His plan was to follow this trail as long as it held out, then walk if necessary. He knew it was a large piece of geography, but he was confident in his ability to find Bonnie and Stringfellow's camp.

As the rocky path wound along its way, he was reminded of his wanderings through the Mayan Jungle in Southern Mexico and Northern Belize. He was on his own for three days there with no partner, food, or supplies. He was able to manage then and he knew he would now. Much better prepared this time, he thought, as he patted the knap sack full of food and water next to him on the front seat.

The desert for all practical purposes had ended and a mountainous terrain with scrub bushes, dwarf pine, and small creatures scurrying in front of his headlights now greeted him.

"Whoa, what's this?" Bo almost shouted, as he applied the brakes.

Hopping out of the vehicle, he left the door open as he moved to the front of the car and bent to one knee. Tire tracks, and they were fresh he was sure, cleanly outlined in the mixture of sand, gravel, and dirt.

Now who was out here in a car or truck? His first thought was Drew, of course. His partner had beaten him here and this was a sure sign he was on the right track.

Staring ahead of his SUV, he noted the tracks continued clearly into the distance. Good, as long as he followed them he could make it through this terrain without being stuck again. Returning to the cab, he climbed in, shifted back into 4WD mode, and returned to his pursuit. The scenery changed little as he progressed and he was cursing his bad luck when he pulled around a large boulder and entered a clearing.

Just as he was about to give up, he found it, a campsite, with a small fire burning and four tents where the explorers must be sleeping. He hated to wake them, but it seemed like the proper thing to do. The vehicle he had been following was parked next to a boulder. For all appearances, the camp was peaceful and sleeping. Funny, he did not see a guard posted for protection in this wilderness. If the rumors he heard were true, there might be some Spanish bandits in the neighborhood.

Pulling in next to the jeep, he killed the engine and stepped out. Stretching, he ambled over to the first tent, not sure what the proper protocol was with a tent, he decided to lift the flap and peer inside the canvas.

The interior was dark, but he could see an empty cot and a woman's personal belongings stacked on a chest. Still, no one was home.

That seemed strange, two Americans and three bearers, surely all four tents were necessary for sleeping. That is, unless he was in the wrong encampment. Well, he'd find out soon enough he reasoned. Dropping the flap, he approached the second tent. Following the same procedure, he lifted the flap and peered into the dark. Again, no occupant, but he reasoned this tent was probably Stringfellow's. It contained a spare pair of hiking boots and a man's bush jacket lying across the cot.

Confused, but undeterred, he approached the third tent. This one was much larger and probably contained supplies and the sleeping laborers.

Lifting the flap, he peeked in and sure enough, there were two laborers, propped against one another sleeping blissfully.

Wait a minute, their feet were tied and so were their hands. "Now why would that be?" He asked himself quietly.

One of the two men moved and groaned, and rising up in his cramped position, he stared at Bo. Immediately, he began grunting and trying to speak, but the gag in his mouth kept him from forming the words in his native language.

Now, more curious than confused, Bo pulled his Glock and made his way to where the two men were tied. The man making all the commotion finally caused his partner to come out of his slumber and stare in wonderment at the new stranger.

When Bo reached the two men, he grasped the tape from the nearest one and ripped it from the man's mouth.

The bearer immediately spit out a cloth and began jabbering away in Spanish.

Bo raised his hand as he said, *"No hablo Espanol, muy poco."*

The frightened man stopped his babbling and composed himself. Finally, he was able to tell Bo the story. A woman and four men came up while Bonnie and the professor were exploring a deep well. They had guns and tied him and his partner up while they proceeded to haul Bonnie out of the hole.

He finished his story by telling Bo that Bonnie had escaped from the tent, but he did not know where she had gone.

Bo took it all in and decided the man was probably telling the truth. Moving around to the man's back, he proceeded to cut the bindings from the first man. Finishing him, he quickly completed the second and watched as the two men fled the tent. Bo followed them out as they clambered upon two of the tethered horses and raced away into the night.

Staring in silence, he could not blame them. Now it was Bo against the five intruders. From the description, he deduced the woman had to be Marie Louise and some of her henchmen. Rechecking his handgun, he removed, inspected, and reinserted the magazine. Checking the pocket in his bush jacket for the three spare magazines, he felt a little more secure, but where and how to start. The smart thing to do would be to hide his vehicle. Hustling back to the SUV, he hopped in, started the engine, and without using the headlights, backed it away from the camp. After a half mile, he stopped, pulled over and parked near some scrub bushes. He would hide the car there and make his way back to the camp on foot.

"Professor, I can't believe it's you!" she shouted excitedly.

"Please help me, I think I'm stuck."

Getting down on both knees, she reached into the small tunnel and tried to grasp his outstretched hands. After sliding partially into the tunnel herself, she was able to grab his fingertips and pull. He was stuck firmly, but after a few minutes of pulling and pushing, she took the trowel from his outstretched hand and proceeded to widen the exit. With one final pull, his six foot four frame popped forward like a cork from a champagne bottle.

"Oh, thank you, Bonnie, I was afraid I was going to end my days in that hole. Are you all right? Where are we? What happened to you?"

"Whoa, one question at a time! Are you all right and what were you doing in that tunnel? I left you on a ledge in another part of this desert at least six hours ago."

"After you went up top, I checked out this tunnel. I thought it was nothing of significance and then tried to have the laborers pull me up. That's when I got the shock of my life and found my rope loose as it fell in on me. I yelled for an hour with no response. I finally decided to try the tunnel and that's where I've been for the last several hours. I discovered several more that connect, but as luck would have it, I came out here following a light at the end of this exit."

"That must have been my torch. My story is a little more bizarre than yours. I was pulled out of the sinkhole, drugged, and then interrogated. I was lucky enough to escape, but they're after me and I found this cavern to hide."

"Lucky for me you picked this spot. I never would have escaped if you hadn't pulled me out," he said.

"Professor, I've found some interesting wall paintings I want you to look at. I think we may have to adjust our thinking a little bit. I'm not sure now this is a Hittite city. Nevertheless, I'd like your opinion."

As the two ascended the stairs out of the sacrificial pit, Stringfellow looked up at the statue staring down at the two of them.

"My god, what a find," he gasped, as he ran to the base of the towering figure.

Bonnie trailed close behind and stood in his shadow as he closely inspected the statue. Paying attention to detail, he circled the being and twirled his mustache as he went. Unconsciously pulling loose sand and grit from the facial hair, he mumbled to himself.

After three complete revolutions, he stopped and stared at his associate. "I think you're right, this is not Hittite, much too recent. This cannot be more than a thousand years old. I think it is Viking or 'Sea People', as some called them."

"Vikings? I would never have guessed they came here, there is no record of any in this part of Europe."

"True, but they were an unusual lot. Show me the pictographs you found. They may shed some light on this giant."

Bonnie with her makeshift torch, led the way towards the exit. Retracing her steps up the incline, she went twenty yards and then stopped.

"I think this is the end. It seemed to me to start further up and progress as a story as it came down the inclined walkway."

Stringfellow passed her without comment and continued up the walkway. Traversing a hundred yards, he stopped and began to trace the paintings as he walked back towards Bonnie. From time to time he stopped and studied a particular section closely before moving on. It took him a half hour before he was again standing next to her.

"I'm no expert on the Vikings. I actually know very little, but this story seems to enforce the belief that Vikings circled the globe and put down roots in many places. Of course, you have heard the story of them discovering America four hundred years before Columbus, which is certainly feasible; however, this find baffles me. Still, it would seem that 'Thor,' that's who the statue is by the way, if you haven't made that connection, and his gang arrived here and set up a community that lasted only a few years. The Egyptians, who fought with them anywhere they could, drove them off. Vikings were nothing like the Hittite or Macedonians, or any of the civilized nations of Europe. Only in their homeland of Scandinavia did they erect cities. In most instances, they were Mercenaries."

"Mercenaries, you mean hired guns? I think I heard that once, but would never have associated it with this discovery."

"Yes," he said and then paused for effect, "they would fight for almost anyone if the pay was right."

Chapter 42

▲▼▲▼▲▼

"If that's all, Agent Eyes, I'll be getting back to my Office now. Tell Agent Boggs I appreciate his kind words and would consider it an honor to assist your team any time I can," the lanky bespectacled Information Technology expert said, as he rose from the terminal and turned to leave.

Alan Taylor was no ordinary Computer Geek employed by this country's Federal Bureau of Investigation. His skills at manipulating databases and hacking into government and private sector computers around the world had become legendary after he helped bring down Winston Bartholomew, mastermind of the 'Marsupial Virus.'

Today had been a simple task, Doe had asked him to assist her by cracking the firewall at the Deutsche Bank of the Caymans. Prior to Alan's effort, she had repeatedly requested information from the bank through normal legal channels. However, cooperation was not in the bank's vocabulary. If she were to have access to Randy Edwards' account, she'd have to find another method. After two days effort with no success, she relented and called in Alan, her ace in the hole.

In a matter of minutes, the techno nerd broke into the bank's computer network and accessed Edward's account as if he were standing in the vault. Fulfilling Doe's request to the smallest detail, he finished the job by printing a complete dossier of the Edwards file. The balance was accumulating interest daily for the deceased assassin and would remain locked up tight until withdrawn by its proper owner. Of course, if the account were dormant for fifteen years with no beneficiary named, the bank would set in motion legal proceedings and return all of the money to their coffers. Therefore, it was in their best interest not to cooperate with American authorities. By rules established for their benefit, they played the game and stonewalled any effort by the US government to gain access. This was not the first time the Bureau had been forced to use any method at their disposal. Although the Director did not want to know the details, he gave his approval when all else failed.

Doe scanned the last page with a certain smirk of satisfaction, before placing the files in her manila folder. The record showed Edwards had amassed eight hundred fifty seven thousand dollars in the short period of six years. All but one of the deposits came from Girard Enterprises. The other deposit of twenty five thousand dollars came from a company in Nevada that was associated with a large casino chain.

"Probably freelancing in his spare time," she thought. "I'll track that one down later."

Realizing the evidence she acquired could not be used in a court of law due to the method of acquisition, she nevertheless patted herself on the back for confirming Edwards on the payroll of Marie Louise and Jean Paul Girard.

Now if she could place him at the scene of the crime at Sacred Heart Hospital in Destin, she would have fulfilled her commitments to Bo and cemented her position as a full-fledged member of the 'Odd Couple,' as the other agents referred to them.

The jangling of her desk phone startled her before she reached to pick it up.

"Agent Doe Eys, may I help you?"

"Agent Eys, this is Mac McLaughlin, the harbor master for Okaloosa County, Florida. I'm returning your call about the yacht 'NO Pain, No Gain.'"

Sitting up straight, Doe's dark eyes flashed as she began her interrogation of the harbormaster. If he could confirm Girard's yacht in the Destin neighborhood the week of July 2, she'd be a step closer to pinning Eckenstadt's murder on Edwards. Yes, it was all coming together nicely now, she thought.

"Mr. McLaughlin, thank you for returning my call so promptly. I hope you have good news for me."

The harbormaster was a clever old salt that had made a career of the U.S. Coast Guard for thirty years. After retirement, he went to work for the City of Destin in the time-honored position of harbormaster. Having been in the service, he was well versed in boats and boat people. As the harbormaster, he had responsibility for the city's small marina where boats were secured for a day or longer. This was official and what he was paid for each month. However, the city commission really used him as a bridge between them and the thousands of boat owners in the area. McLaughlin had resolved many a complaint to the commission and proved himself a worthy politician in his own right. Dealing with the FBI wasn't new to him, and he treated it with the respect he felt it deserved.

"Yes, Ms. Eys, my pleasure, I assure you. I only wish I had better news for you about the yacht."

"I take it that means you have no record of it during that week in July then?"

"That's right, course I only have the actual records for the city's marina and the state's down near Henderson Park. You're looking for a needle in a haystack, Agent. Why, by my last count there were three hundred and twelve private marinas with space for anywhere from six to seven thousand slips. I don't envy you your task in running them all down."

"I'm sorry to hear that. Are all of the private marinas required to keep records on their customers? I mean, is there a common data base they all share?"

"Why no, they're the only ones that can access their accounts. You may have to call each one and ask them to search their records for you. I don't envy your task. I know all of them personally and they are apt to push back if they feel the government is prying around the edges of their business."

"I'm not prying, just trying to gather evidence for a crime that took place in your community. Do you remember the Eckenstadt Murder a few months ago?"

"Eckenstadt, now where do I know that name from? Oh yeah, why I remember, the fellow that was fished out of the Gulf around Blue Mountain and transported to Sacred Heart. Murder, I thought he died of undetermined causes, I think the newspaper said."

"Just keep that to yourself. I think someone came into the area on that yacht from Miami and did a number on him. I need proof it was here, and all I've got for now are two witnesses who say they saw the boat in the area."

"Tell you what; let me proceed on your behalf, Agent Eys. I'll have more luck than you. I'm not promising anything, you understand, still I may be able to get the information you're seeking."

"Thank you, Mr. McLaughlin, please get back to me with anything you think can help me in my investigation."

"Should take at least three days, maybe a week, but I'll find out if the boat was here. You have my word." McLaughlin hung up the phone and leaned back in his creaky rocker.

"Where to start?" he asked himself.

After making his way back to the campsite, Bo cautiously examined the fourth tent before deciding to explore the area. If he could believe the two laborers, Bonnie and Stringfellow might be being held captive by a number of characters, the most likely being Marie Louise and her gang of hired thugs.

The moon was rising and cast a bright light on the campsite as it progressed across the evening sky. Clouds glided across the beam occasionally and Bo was thankful for the darkness. He left the campsite and followed a trail up towards the base of the mountains. Using skills he had acquired as an Eagle Scout, he followed the path for nearly a quarter of a mile before stopping to take stock of his situation.

The road narrowed and the large vehicle rumbled along bumping from boulder to boulder. Drew was now driving and Carlos was keeping an eye out for signs of a camp. They had left the main road and were nearly five miles from their entry point. The dirt road, which looked so promising, was beginning to run out of hardpan. In a few more hundred yards, they'd be on sand, dirt, and nothing more.

"*Senor* Drew, I think the tracks we saw have disappeared. If we don't pick up more soon I think we should turn back. Are you sure this is the way?"

"No, I'm positively sure I don't know the exact way to their camp. If I could just get Bonnie on the phone, it would be a lot simpler. I'm sure we must be close. My last conversation from her detailed their camp and this fits that description to a tee. How far do you think we've come from the main road?"

No sooner had he asked the question than the Escalade's lights spied a vehicle off the side of the trail partially hidden in some scrub bushes.

"Whoa, now what have we here?"

Stopping, the two men exited the SUV and approached the car. It was new and dusty like their own transportation, with a sticker on the rear window from National Car Rental.

"Another stranger out here in the desert, I wonder if it could be a friend of mine."

Trying the door handle, they discovered the owner had locked it and further investigation was impossible without breaking the glass. Drew peered inside, but nothing he could see told him about the missing occupant.

"*Senor* Drew, here are some tracks leading off to the east. Do you think we should follow them?"

Drew scratched his chin as he considered the suggestion.

"Why not, what have we got to lose?"

Climbing back into the vehicle, Drew doused the lights and said to Carlos, "Keep a sharp eye out. I don't want to advertise our approach."

"*Si, senor.*"

The Escalade moved off to the east as Carlos peered into the darkness for anyone on foot.

She grabbed him by the arm and whispered, "Professor, I think someone is coming."

The two turned to stare up the passage and saw a faint light in the distance bobbing up and down. Bonnie pulled on her partner's coat and urged him back down the passage towards the sacrificial pit.

"It must be Louise and her hired help; I don't know where we can hide."

"Why not the pit, we can crawl back in the tunnel and push some rocks in front of us. I doubt they'd find us there."

"Hurry then, follow me!"

The couple made a hasty retreat down the slope and into the open area. Quickly they retraced their steps into the pit beneath the statue.

"Professor, you go first. Back in and I'll follow. If they find the hole, I'll come out. They won't expect you to be in there too."

"Bonnie, I can't let you give yourself up to them again."

"Don't worry about me!" Then as an afterthought, she said, "Wait, do you still have your handgun?"

"Why yes, I always keep it for snakes and such. It's only twenty two caliber, I guess it could stop a man, but I've never tried."

"Give it to me and hurry! They're closer, get in the hole!"

Chapter 43

▲ ▼ ▲ ▼ ▲ ▼

Stringfellow slid backwards into the opening he had exited only a few minutes before. Bonnie helped him as he inched his way back into the blackness. When he was out of sight, she dropped to her knees and followed him into the narrow space. It took only a few moments before both of them were swallowed up in the shadows. Stringfellow passed several large rocks up to Bonnie and she carefully placed them in the entrance. With some luck, they'd look as though they'd been there for decades.

    The pit was as dark as the inside of a coffin and Bonnie wondered if this would be her final resting place. A few muffled voices were all that could be heard as she tried to make herself invisible. After several agonizing minutes, a stream of light played around the bottom of the pit, and she could imagine the group staring into the cavity where she and the professor were hiding. The voices continued and she tried to make out the words, but only garbled sounds reached her ears.

Suddenly, the light disappeared and as the darkness enveloped them, she heard a terrifying scream. Then, more frightened voices and another scream, only this time it was cut short. Next came two short explosions and another confused shout. More popping sounds and an agonizing wail pierced the darkness. Then, all was quiet.

"Bonnie, what is it, can you tell?"

"No, shh, listen!" she demanded.

The minutes ticked off and still, no more sound from beyond the pit. Bonnie shivered as she contemplated what could have happened.

"I'm going out."

"I don't think that's a good idea, they may be bluffing to get you to expose yourself."

"No, I don't think so. That woman's scream sounded too real. Trust me, I know."

"Well, I'm coming with you then."

"All right, but be quiet, wait until I signal you."

"Very well, only be careful."

She was already pushing the small boulders out of her way as she poked her head into the opening. It was black everywhere with no light appearing above the rim of the pit. An unusual smell assailed her nostrils and she breathed it in deeply to determine its meaning.

Dragging her legs out, she began to crawl to the small set of steps they had descended. Crouching, in case someone was waiting, she nevertheless inched her way up the stone passage and peered into the vast opening. Only silence greeted her with no sign of the intruders.

From below, she heard him ask, "Anything?"

Still not sure if she should speak, she waved her arm and placed her finger to her lips. He nodded and sat down on the bottom step.

As her eyes adjusted to the dark, she looked around for some sign of the intruders. Staring around the vast clearing, nothing appeared out of the ordinary. The smell again caused her to stop and stare, like rusted iron she thought. Carefully she inched her way along the edge of the pit and stopped when she saw something white near the foot of the statue. Little by little, she made her way in that direction, stopping abruptly and placing her hand over her mouth when she realized it was a woman lying face down in the dirt. Her torso was turned at an unnatural angle and her head twisted to one side. There were bloodstains all over her white blouse and the entire side of her skull was crushed. Reaching down, she turned the head toward her and gasped as she recognized Marie Louise.

Bonnie bit down on her hand stifling a cry. Blood had pooled around Louise's head and her beautiful face was only a memory. Turning away, she had a sudden urge to vomit and she did everything in her power to overcome the sensation.

At that moment, Stringfellow exited the pit and rushed to where she was standing.

"My God!" he proclaimed. "Who did this?"

"I, I, don't know, but it looks as if she were struck with some kind of blunt object."

"What about her associates? I thought she was traveling with bodyguards. What about the shooting, did you hear that too?"

Bonnie reached down and retrieved Marie's flashlight from where it had fallen to the ground. Flicking the switch, she illuminated the immediate area with the instrument. Playing the light around, she noticed what appeared to be another body near the ramp. They approached the form and again a gruesome sight greeted them. One of the bodyguards lay twisted; the back of his head was caved in, and in his eyes, the look of terror leaped out at the two spectators. Once more Bonnie turned her head and stepped away from Stringfellow. This time she could not contain herself as she wretched on the ground. The old man placed his arm around her and dabbed at her face with a handkerchief he removed from his jacket.

"There, there, you'll be all right. Just calm yourself."

"I'm so sorry. I just couldn't help it, what has happened? Who did this? Do you think there are more?"

Shining the light up the ramp, another body no more than thirty meters away lay in a similar pose.

"I'm afraid so, don't look at this one. I'll check the exit and see if there're any more."

"Please be careful, you don't know what's out there. Here, you better take the gun," she said as she handed him the small caliber weapon.

Bonnie held the handkerchief and dabbed her face as the professor disappeared up the incline. She watched him stop again and inspect the next victim. After a few moments, he continued his search and she saw him stop once more after a short trek.

The fourth victim was lying face down and blood was spattered all over the wall behind him. Stringfellow didn't need to turn him over to determine the cause of death. It was the same as all of the others. The total was three men and one woman. According to Bonnie, that accounted for all of her captors. Now he retraced his steps down the ramp and approached Bonnie who had moved closer to the statue. As he came along side, he noticed she was staring up at the huge stone figure.

"What is it? Have you found something else?"

Without uttering a word, she pointed towards the statue's upraised arm. Turning, he stared at Thor and then blanched as he saw what had caught her attention. There, in the god's hand, he held aloft his hammer, now covered with blood.

Stringfellow reached out and grabbed Bonnie as she began to slip to the ground. The terror had finally caused her to consciously leave reality and slide into a peaceful trance.

Holding her gently he eased her to the ground where he placed her head on his folded jacket. As he stood, he heard the unmistakable sound of someone coming down the ramp behind him. What to do? He must turn and face his adversary, no matter what it was. Grasping the flashlight firmly in his left hand, he raised the handgun and stared into the distance.

"Someone there?" I said, "Is anyone down here?" The voice from the dark inquired, as the form and the light approached. Stringfellow thought the voice familiar, but struggled to place it.

"Just keep coming, I have a weapon and I'll use it if I have to."

"No need to shoot, I'm looking for Bonnie Lane. Is she with you?"

Stringfellow felt some of the tension ease at the mention of Bonnie's name.

"Like I said, just keep coming until I can see you."

The stranger continued his approach and within moments, he stepped into the light beam held by Stringfellow. Stopping, he stared at the professor.

"Professor Stringfellow, you must remember me, I'm Bo Boggs, I met you at Mr. Eckenstadt's memorial service."

Lowering his weapon, Stringfellow relaxed for the first time in twenty-four hours.

"My God, Mr. Boggs, you certainly have impeccable timing. I can't tell you how glad I am to see you."

Looking around the opening, Bo appeared perplexed as he asked, "Did you do all this?" How, I mean, why in the world?"

"No, no, I didn't kill them. Did you see anyone when you came in?"

"No, it was quite dark, though someone could have slipped by me. The trail was dark and I was just stumbling along looking for Bonnie."

Bending to one knee, Boggs inspected the closest bodyguard and then stared at the ground around the body. Rising, he approached the woman's body and again bent down flashing a light all around the perimeter. After a few moments, he rose and strode back up the ramp and methodically inspected the bodies of the remaining two men. After several minutes, he returned to where Stringfellow was standing.

"Well?" the taller man said.

"Scratching his thinning hair, Bo began slowly, "I'm not the best at forensic work, just picked up some of it from the lab boys as I've gone along. However, it appears as if the three men were all killed and dragged to their present location. If you look close, you can see traces of where the marks are. Someone tried to cover them, but apparently was rushed and didn't finish the job. I would guess they were all killed here near Marie Louise and then separated to make it look as though they were running away. Why, I can't tell you."

"Too bad, I was hoping someone would explain all this to me." The voice from the top of the ramp filtered down on the two men.

Bo instinctively removed his weapon from the small holster that resided behind his back. Stringfellow, who had not replaced his weapon, raised it and pointed it into the dark.

The man attached to the voice ambled slowly down the ramp stopping to inspect the two men lying face down on the ground.

"You know, that voice can only be one person. Drew, how in the hell Drew did you walk into this cavern ten minutes behind me?"

Rising from the last body, Drew stepped into the light, "I see they got Marie Louise as well. From what little I heard, I take it you think the bodies were dragged from the killing spot to their present location."

"I'd almost bet you a beer on it. Wish we had some of our technical helpers to clean up this mess and give us a better guess."

"How long would you say they've been dead, professor?" Drew asked, as he replaced his Glock in the shoulder holster.

"Not more than thirty minutes. We were hiding in the pit and heard the shooting and commotion that sounded like a couple of screams. We waited for ten minutes or so and then came out to investigate. This is how we found them."

"Is Bonnie all right?"

"Yes, she fainted at the sight of all the gore. I can't blame her, felt a little queasy myself."

"You heard gunshots, but all of them appear to have been bludgeoned and then drug to their location?"

"Yes, they must have used their weapons and then were beaten to death. Oh, there's more, come look at this." Stringfellow said, as he turned and approached the statue.

Drew and Bo stared up at the cold relic of the god from the north.

"What's this fellow all about?"

"Can't explain everything yet, working on a hypothesis that I think will explain him being here. But that'll have to wait, look at the instrument in his hand."

Flashing the light along the base of the cold slab of stone, Drew traced it out and locked on the upraised arm.

"Jesus, I don't believe what I'm seeing! Is that blood?"

Chapter 44

▲ ▼ ▲ ▼ ▲ ▼

It was after ten PM and the two agents sat around a fire in the middle of the campsite discussing the events of the evening. Bo was cleaning his Glock while listening to Drew try to piece together the mystery that confronted both of them. Occasionally the Greek would interject a thought of his own and then go back to listening to his partner elaborate on the murders.

The flap on the nearest tent flew back and the familiar frame of Professor Stringfellow straightened as he exited.

"Here comes the Professor, let's see if he can shed some light on our ideas," Drew said. "Professor, please join us, how's Bonnie doing?"

"She is resting quietly; I think she'll be all right in the morning. She asked you to stop by before you went to bed. The fire looks inviting to these old bones, there's a nip in the air this evening, and I wouldn't be surprised if there isn't snow in the highlands before sunrise."

"Make yourself at home; we've been discussing the murders and the blood on the statue. I'd be interested in anything you could contribute on that subject. In the meantime, I made a call to the local authorities and they are sending a team out in the morning. I had my guide Carlos cover the bodies with blankets and left them in place. I'm sure their forensic people will want to see it untouched. Oh, buy the way, the statue hasn't moved any. But all joking aside, Bo and I'll take turns tonight standing guard. Whoever killed those people is somewhere near by and may be watching us right now."

"You really think someone is watching us?"

"I'd bet my reputation on it. They may try something tonight, but if they do, we'll be prepared."

Stringfellow laid his hat on a nearby rock and produced his well-worn pipe. Pulling an old Zippo from his cargo pants, he lit the pipe and savored the aroma.

Bo inhaled deeply as the smoke curled past his nostrils, remembering his younger days and how much he enjoyed tobacco.

"Wish I could be of more help to you with the murders, but I've told you all I know. Of course, I knew the statue couldn't have done it, but someone was trying to frighten us. I'm sure Bonnie will corroborate my story in the morning. We saw pretty much the same thing. Her fainting happened only a few moments before your arrival, Mr. Boggs. I've been spending all of my time trying to figure out how the statue got down in that cavern. I will share that with you if you're interested. I don't think it will help you with your investigation, but I'm not a law enforcement officer. I believe I may have pieced together the mystery of all this mixed up history."

Shaking his head in the affirmative, Drew said, "Yes, those people were murdered for something, and your missing City of Gold is the best reason I can come up with. Please share your thoughts with us."

"Very well!" he agreed, as he puffed on the old pipe.

"I have been perplexed with the confusing different cultures we have discovered here. Before you arrived, Bonnie and I unearthed an equestrian in the dessert near here that was from another civilization. He was Macedonian, and alone except for two servants. That mystery was puzzling enough, but then after I found the cuneiform writing and the statue of Thor in the cavern, well; it seems to fit together in a strange sort of way."

Bo finished cleaning his handgun and placed it back in the small waist holster. Reaching across the fire, he retrieved the coffee pot and poured himself a cup.

Smoothing his handlebar mustache, Stringfellow stared at the foothills of the Filabres that ran on endlessly behind them before continuing.

"A long time ago, perhaps three thousand years, the Hittites made their home somewhere in those mountains," he said, as he waved his hand in that direction.

I believe they lived here peacefully and alone for at least a thousand years. They were a puzzling culture and all of the experts place them near the Golan Heights in Syria as I've mentioned before. However, I am confident they were here first. This location suited their needs perfectly and the Hammurabi stone is as good as a map pointing to this very spot. I'm sure when I find the remains they will predate the site in Syria."

"If that's so, what happened to them, why haven't you found a sign of their culture here?" Drew asked.

"That's a good question and the answer I trust is the one I've held all along. The Egyptians, the perennial tough guys and bully of their day, are to blame. The two cultures were at war for over a thousand years. The Egyptians tell about it in their writings and on the walls of their tombs. I'm firmly convinced the Hittites were eventually crushed by Egypt's superior numbers and driven from this valley. Forced to leave, what was left of them split up and moved on to safer places where the Egyptians wouldn't bother them. I'm sure the Syrian city was one of their last splintered locations. As for this location, I believe the remains lay in ruins and unoccupied. Then, maybe as long as a thousand or fifteen hundred years later, the Sea People, who I think were the Vikings, discovered this site and built their home over the Hittite's ruins. They were able to reside here for several hundred years until those meddling Egyptians returned. Another battle like the one we saw depicted on the walls of the cave ensued and the Vikings were driven out."

Returning the pipe to his lips, he paused to gather his thoughts. It was obvious Bo was intrigued and listening with rapt attention.

"That's it?"

"No, not exactly all of it, but yes that is the timeline I'm working with. I'm convinced we have found a common ground used by both cultures. If I were a young man and had ten years to devote to my theory, I'd spend it right here. In due course I would prove they both resided at this juncture at different times in history."

"Seems to make sense, Professor. The Hittites got here first and were eventually driven out by the Egyptians. A thousand or more years later the Sea People, as you called them, showed up, liked what they saw, and settled. Then along came those annoying Egyptians again and drove them out. The one common denominator seems to be Egypt."

Stringfellow tapped the ashes from the pipe's bowl and looked off into the distance as if pondering Drew's assertions carefully.

"What happened to the Hittite gold? Do you think it's still around here somewhere or did it get carried off by the Egyptians?" Bo asked.

"Ah the gold, yes I'm sure the Egyptians took what they found on both occasions. Still I'm sure there is more somewhere, I would bet my soul on it. The cuneiform writing in the cave has a story to tell and we haven't had time to decipher it all. I plan to get back to it at first light."

Drew poked at the dying flames and tossed another few branches into the fire. Leaning back you could see the gears change in his mind as he asked, "How well did you know Marie Louise, Professor?"

Stringfellow's head snapped around and his silvery gray eyes flashed before he spoke, "Not well, she was another one of the many who purchase objects for a price without asking questions on the legality of the transaction. I've crossed paths with her over the years."

Drew was now looking directly at Stringfellow and the two of them engaged in a silent match of wits until Bo interrupted.

"Wait a minute, Professor. You knew this Marie Louise and did business with her? You never mentioned that."

"I don't remember you actually asking, but as I said, from time to time, I must admit our paths crossed."

Drew leaned back on a boulder behind him and said, "If you only knew her casually, why did you ask her to fund this dig?"

"That's preposterous, I did no such thing!"

"I'm afraid I have proof you did. We were able to determine from your bank accounts you've deposited a large check from Girard Enterprises within the last three weeks. Marie Louise is not prone to charity; you asked her for help and promised her great riches. If that wasn't enough, your phone record is an open book. You called her twice from this location. That's damning evidence, and I can only assume you wanted to give her a report on what was happening. It must have surprised you when she showed up and left you dangling in that hole in the ground."

The last comment seemed to take all of the air out of Stringfellow's bluster. Realizing he was beaten, he held his head high before replying, "All right, you win, she funded the project, and I promised her forty percent of the find. But I didn't kill her and I don't know who did."

"No, I know you couldn't have killed her, but I suspected you were in this for more than glory. The find would be worth millions, although I don't understand how you thought you would keep it quiet from the Spanish government. I wonder if you even have permission from their agency to dig here in the desert."

"How dare you, I've secured all of the documents from the agency in Madrid and they've granted me exclusive rights to this dig," Stringfellow shouted, as he stood to stare down at his accuser.

"Glad to hear that. However, the government in Madrid would not grant you exclusive rights without some legitimate backing. Is that where you used your friend from the Louvre's influence, Mr. Marchant?"

Stringfellow felt the noose closing around his neck and he lowered his gaze again from the penetrating stare of the Federal Agent as he slumped back to his seat.

"What have you found besides that statue and the hole in the ground where the bodies are lying?"

"Nothing of any value yet, I assure you. Still, I believe that cavern we discovered is the key. I plan to inspect it closer before the police arrive and get in the way."

For a few moments, the three men were silent and the popping of the fire was all that could be heard. Then a soft shuffling sound was discernible coming from the south and growing louder by the moment. Bo removed his recently cleaned handgun and prepared for whatever was making the noise. Gradually the resonance grew louder and it could be identified as horse's hooves. From out of the darkness, a lone rider appeared and reigned in his steed. Stringfellow stood and along with Bo, held his weapon on the stranger. Only Drew remained seated with his back to the intruder and apparently disinterested. The horseman dismounted before Drew spoke, "Been waiting for you, Rafe. What took you so long?"

Chapter 45

▲ ▼ ▲ ▼ ▲ ▼

"You know this guy, Drew?" Bo asked, as he deliberately lowered his Glock.

Rising, Drew turned and smiled at the new arrival to the camp.

"Let me introduce you to Eduardo Rafael Castillo, but you may call him Rafe, all his friends do," Drew said, repeating the joke.

The stranger smiled broadly, as he began to beat the trail dust from his clothes.

"Mr. Castillo is with the CNI, that's the FBI of Spain. He's out here hunting bad guys in the Basque organization. Did I get that right?"

"Perfectly, I was alerted this afternoon about your call and request for assistance. Naturally, I was asked to participate since I am already in the area. May I have some of your coffee? It was a chilly ride this evening, I think it may snow."

"Yeah, the Professor gave us the weather report earlier. Let me introduce my partner, Bo Boggs, he's the one with the heavy artillery pointed at your midsection. The tall distinguished looking gentleman is Professor Stringfellow, the leader of this archaeological expedition. The Professor is attached to Harvard University in Boston."

Bo holstered his weapon and handed Rafe a cup in which he poured a thick black liquid.

"Sorry, we ain't got anything to put in it; you'll have to drink it black."

"I like it that way," He said, accepting the offering and raising the cup to his lips.

Drew stirred the fire again, "I thought you might be here sooner, what with all the murders."

"Yes the hammer murders, I was informed by my contact in Madrid and was asked to join the team that is coming out in the morning. Where exactly did all this happen?"

Drew pointed over the Spanish Agent's shoulder, "Over there, about five hundred meters from here in a cavern with a mystery it's unwilling to give up."

"May I see it?"

"Now?"

"Yes, I would like to get a head start on the team that will be here tomorrow."

"Very well, follow me, Bo will you join us. Professor, I think it would be best if you stayed here in case Bonnie needs you. If anybody shows up unexpected, just fire a couple of shots in the air."

"Very well, as you wish."

Striding off to the west, Drew, followed by Bo and Rafe, headed back to the cavern entrance. The flashlights played their bright lights off the rocks and the three men moved along in silence.

Reaching the entrance, Drew slowed, "Better pay attention, there're a couple of drop offs to either side of this ledge, would hate for you to lose your balance and fall."

"I will not fall, lead on."

The three men eased their way down the passage past the wall paintings until they reached the first body. Bending down, Rafe pulled the blanket from the man's head and shoulders.

"Gruesome, I should have been prepared for the crushed skull."

Drew watched as the agent took a closer look at the damage.

"I wonder how he got behind them to do this."

"If you look very closely, you can see the bullet entry right at the base of the skull. It is nearly obliterated by the massive damage. Whoever did this made it look like they were all killed with a blow to the head. Actually, they were all murdered execution style. Each of them has a similar wound, if you know where to look," Drew said, as he placed his finger on the base of the man's skull.

"If you check the knees of his pants, you'll see the ground in dirt and sand from the cavern. He was on his knees for a short time before he was shot. All of the bodies are the same."

"Execution style, I would never have guessed. I'm surprised you found the entry, Drew. Good work." Placing the blanket over the body, the three men continued down the ramp until they reached the opening where the statue of the God of Thunder stood.

"I see the dried blood, why would someone go to all that trouble?"

"You don't know?" I would have thought that would be obvious to you."

Rafe stared at Drew and Bo watched, as the two men appeared to size each other up for the first time. It reminded Bo of two prizefighters as they circled the statue, all the while not taking their eyes off each other. Bo had that funny feeling he was the only one in the room that didn't know what was coming next.

Then in a surprise move, Castillo drew his 38 Smith and Wesson and leveled it at Wells.

Shocked at the action Bo was slow to go for his Glock.

"I wouldn't do that, Mr. Boggs, please to step over here next to your friend. Now, both of you toss your weapons on the ground."

The American Agents slowly removed their guns and complied with the request.

Bo hesitated before moving, trying to evaluate the situation, but quickly realized his futile attempt would only get him killed sooner rather than later. Extending his hands in front of him, He took three steps and stood beside Drew, both men staring the CNI agent down.

"How did you know, Drew? I thought I was so clever and smart. But you saw right through it."

"It wasn't that difficult, especially since you announced after your arrival you were here to see the corpses with their skulls smashed in."

Castillo turned his head slightly in a puzzled manor.

"I'm afraid I don't understand, you called our headquarters and told them about the murders. You knew of course that they would contact me. How did that play into your hands?"

"Yes, I did call your people and told them about the murders. However, I didn't mention they had their skulls crushed. In fact, I had already concluded they were shot in the head. As soon as you mentioned the method, I knew you were involved. Oh, I had my suspicions before now, the attempt on my life by removing the roadblock sign told me someone with knowledge of the area and my travel plans would be the only one that could arrange such an accident. When you showed up at our camp, I was suspicious you were the one, tonight only confirmed my theory."

Castillo shook his head and frowned, "You're a clever bastard, Wells. I should have known back at your camp, but I was a fool who underestimated you again."

"Why did you kill Marie Louise? Did she plan to cut you out of your share?"

"No, I decided she was expendable, she was an unnecessary middleman. With Stringfellow working for me, I could arrange to sell the artifacts to the highest bidder. Why did I need Marie Louise? She hired me to keep a close watch on the old man and the woman. I decided from the start that I wouldn't need her. When she showed up here unannounced, it seemed like the perfect time to eliminate her. I would strike my own deal with the Professor and the museum in Paris, or eliminate them if they tried to cross me."

Bo was closely observing the two men whose eyes were locked during the conversation. Very slowly, the Greek shuffled his feet sideways and moved casually to Castillo's right. Shifting his feet as if he were uncomfortable, he continued to move farther from Castillo's line of sight.

Bo wasn't the fastest on his feet, but when he made his move, all five foot nine, two hundred twenty pounds hit like a hockey player. The attack was swift and accurate, Bo's lunge crashed into Castillo driving him back against the cavern wall. The CNI agents' immediate reaction was to fire a round as they fell to the ground. The bullet struck the side of the cavern harmlessly as the two men hit the earth. In an instant, Drew retrieved his weapon from where he tossed it and swung it around towards Castillo.

As the two men rolled on the floor, Castillo lashed out at Bo with his weapon and struck the smaller man across the temple with the barrel. The blow stunned Bo, and he momentarily released his grip. That was all Castillo needed, rolling to his left, he freed himself from Bo and came to his knees.

"Drop it or I'll shoot!" Drew shouted.

Castillo did not intend to surrender his weapon. Trying to steady himself before he fired, he adjusted his line of sight and squeezed off two rounds.

Drew felt the breeze from the first shot as it passed close to his ear. Instinctively he returned fire striking Castillo in the chest right above the heart. The Spaniard looked confused as he stared down at the gaping hole in his chest. Then with a twisted smile, he pitched forward and fell face down in the dirt.

The ringing of the three shots was still echoing off the walls as Bo regained his feet.

"How in hell, I mean, how could you?"

"At ease, Bo, you all right? That cut on your forehead looks nasty, we better have it looked at."

Bonnie tenderly wiped the dried blood from Bo's forehead as Drew and the Professor observed the proceedings.

"Professor, I need you to fill me in on a couple of the loose ends. I can understand how you might think you could trust, or even fool Marie Louise, but Castillo and Marchant are a strange couple. I assume Louise made contact with Castillo and asked him to watch over your operation and keep an eye on me when I showed up. Would you please go back and tell me your story from the beginning. This whole episode is still somewhat confusing.

What you say and your cooperation will go a long way in how you're dealt with by the authorities."

Stringfellow was now quite ready to cooperate. The weight of all his deception had finally been lifted from his shoulders and he was more than willing to tell his part of the tale.

Absentmindedly he tapped the pipe in his hand, before placing it back in his pocket.

"It all started about six months ago. Funny, it somehow seems a lot longer than that now. I got a call from Aaron and he was so excited he could hardly talk coherently. He informed me that he was about to take possession of the Code of Hammurabi statue. Aaron was convinced the stone held the key to the lost Hittite civilization. Both of us had worked together on a project to unearth the city over forty years ago. Since that time, we continued to believe the city was in this area and planned to return at some future date. The stone was the missing piece, and when Aaron said he had acquired it, I was immediately excited. The two of us were naturally competitive and the thought of him finding the site and getting all the credit enraged me. After the call, I contacted Marie Louise and told her the story hoping to get her interested and willing to fund my expedition. I led her to believe I could get the stone from Aaron never thinking she would try to do it herself. In my haste, I misjudged Louise and when I heard Aaron had been murdered, I knew immediately the person responsible."

Pausing to gather his thoughts, he continued, "I have to give Aaron credit, he never told them. He was a stronger man than I was, and yes, a better person too. After his death, all of the clues to the stone vanished with him. Then unexpectedly, Bonnie called and said she had it and would I work with her to find the city. You can imagine my excitement at this good fortune. Now I would find the Lost City and get all the credit. I would still have to use Marie Louise's money to fund the dig because she would not ask any questions. I also brought Louis Marchant into the picture so I would have the prestige of his museum in Paris backing my find and displaying the artifacts. It all seemed so simple to me when I planned the operation. I had worked with Marie in the past and she had been easy to manipulate. This time, however, she wanted control of the entire business. I was able to hold her off at first, but she became increasingly difficult to manage. I never expected her to show up here at the site.

When I was cut off down in the hole, I suspected immediately who was responsible. You must believe me, I was genuinely afraid for Bonnie; she was completely innocent and didn't deserve this fate."

Finishing her bandaging of Bo's wound, Bonnie stared at her mentor before speaking, "Professor, how could you? I trusted you; Aaron never had anything but kind words about your generosity and intelligence. I shudder to think you caused his death, for that I can never forgive you."

Dropping his head in shame, Stringfellow nodded his understanding.

"Bonnie, I have had a lot of time to think in that hole and I want you to know if you will give me another chance I will do all in my power to help you with your search. Please let me assist you, I'm sure we are very close."

"Lest you forget, Professor, you're an accomplice to murder," Drew said.

"Oh, Drew, he didn't know Marie Louise would kill, he surely can't be considered a murderer, a fool maybe, but not a murderer."

"Yeah, Drew, if I were on a jury, I couldn't find him guilty of anything but stupidity, like Bonnie said," Bo added, as he stood steadying himself against a chair.

Drew stared at Bo and realized he was right; the Professor may have unintentionally set everything in motion, but no one would believe the old man had murder as his objective. He only wanted to grab the glory for his legacy. Besides, according to Bonnie, he only a few months left to live and a trial would accomplish nothing. They had identified the real culprit in Marie Louise; she killed Eckenstadt and was in turn murdered by Castillo. Ironically, she was the person responsible for the Director's death as well. Drew realized he had a case that was neatly tied up the way Director Riley liked it. Why rock the boat.

Epilogue

▲ ▼ ▲ ▼ ▲ ▼

Six weeks later Filabres Mountains

He lay the trowel aside and removed his broad brimmed hat, wiping the perspiration from his forehead, as he squinted into the distance. The season was changing and the days were getting longer, but the Professor knew his time was growing shorter. Each morning, he had to push harder to get out of his cot and begin the search anew. The pain in his lower abdomen had intensified, and he was aware the cancer was spreading rapidly throughout his body. If he were at home, they'd have him strapped into a hospital bed and filling him with the chemo he so despised. However, he knew when he was diagnosed that was not the way he wanted to go out. Here in the wild with the thrill of adventure at his feet was where he wanted to be, and that is where he was.

It seemed like years since Aaron's death and the murders in the cavern, but it had only been a few months. Agent Wells had done what he promised, to free him from any association with

Marie Louise and the murders. Somehow, the FBI agent had convinced all of the authorities in his report that Stringfellow was a hero, not a villain. He didn't need to be called a hero, he knew the part he played in his friend's death and he would take it to his grave. If he could just find the missing link to the city, he swore Aaron would share equally in the credit for the discovery.

Bonnie was back at their base camp and for the first time in several days, he was alone with his digging and thoughts. The laborers were providing most of the effort and he was only participating in the areas that showed promise. There were now fifteen men all bending to the task. This valley was the last best place to explore. It had to be here; he was running out of time and promising real estate. His studies had shown the seismic activity over the last three thousand years would have buried a city on this spot below their feet. His calculations were meticulously drawn and he was positive they would have to dig at least fifteen to twenty feet before finding any sign of their goal. The hole was now twenty by fifty across and close to the magic depth he had calculated. If they did not reach something man-made in the next twenty-four hours, he would have to reassess this decision. For now, he held a positive attitude they would find something today.

"Professor, professor come quick!" the excited voice from behind him screamed and he twisted around to see who was calling. It was Achmed, his trusted friend.

"What is it?"

"We have found something, I think you will want to see, please come quickly!"

The two men climbed down from Stringfellow's perch and headed back to the massive hole. As they approached, the laborers ceased their activity and watched as the old man peered at the find. Achmed was already on his knees and pointing at the smooth surface that ran along the edge of their dig. Stringfellow joined him and got down on one knee. Placing his forefinger on the surface, he traced it along for a few feet. It was smooth and precise. No doubt about it, the level flat surface was man-made.

"What do you think, Professor?"

Staring at the object, he did not reply for several agonizing minutes. Achmed had seen him like this before and knew better than to interrupt his thought process. Finally, he spoke in a hushed tone, "It appears to be an entrance to a tomb or some such place, I can't be sure, but here is what I want you to do. First, let's find the exact outline of the horizontal surface you have uncovered, and then remove all of the rock and stone covering it. I think it goes the entire length of our dig and then disappears under this ledge," he said, as he walked along the span of their excavation.

"See, here is where it disappears. Start here first, I want to see how big it is before we try to force any entrance."

Achmed was beside him and sprang instantly into action, shouting commands to the laborers and urging them to move quickly. Whatever he said worked as all of the men grabbed their digging apparatus and began working in earnest.

Meanwhile, Stringfellow sat down on a boulder near the dig and watched in wide-eyed anticipation like a child at a birthday party. Minute by agonizing minute, the ground was shifted and the area began to give up its secret. Still, the depth of the find was causing them problems and he wondered how much success they would have today. How long would it take to uncover the entire surface area?

As the sun moved slowly across the sky, the object became more visible to all of them and they seemed to gain enthusiasm from it. From time to time, they would stop and Stringfellow would cautiously clean the surface with a soft brush. A message in cuneiform was scrawled across the entire area and told a mysterious story. As the day slipped away, the sun danced between the mountaintops, finally Stringfellow stepped down into the hole again and raised his hand.

"Stop, enough, I think we may have it!"

She had come to find him since he was late returning to camp for his dinner. As she grew closer to the dig, she noticed all of the men standing around and peering into the hole. When she reached their location, she stopped next to Achmed.

"What is it, what are you looking at?"

Stringfellow heard her voice and wheeled around.

"Bonnie, come quickly I must show you what we have discovered! Please hurry and watch your step! Achmed, help her."

"I'm fine, I don't need help Achmed," she said, as she made her way carefully down into the hole.

"Now what have you found?"

The entire surface lay spread out before them. It was a smooth stone slab approximately ten meters by twenty-five meters. Etched into the stone were markings and hieroglyphs from a bygone era.

It had gotten so dark, Bonnie could not begin to read it completely without more light.

"Tell me Professor, what have you deciphered?"

He stared into her eyes and she could tell he was nearly delirious with excitement.

"Bonnie, this is it, we have found it! The hieroglyphs are Hittite and tell a wondrous story. If I can believe what I have read once we open this stone entrance, I believe we will find the remains of the Hittite civilization. They must have buried everything of importance they could not carry with them, then they hid this from the Egyptians. I don't know if they planned to return or not, but once we get inside we should be able to tell. Oh, Aaron would be so excited, I truly wish he were here."

Three months later Destin, Florida

"Drew, this is truly a beautiful place you have. I'm sorry I didn't see it on my last visit."

"That was the time of Aaron's death and you were quite upset, besides you hardly knew me. I only purchased it last year and have just finished decorating. I was living on the golf course until the big recession hit. So many of these beach units came available at ridiculous prices, I said I might as well take the plunge. If President Mitchell makes good on all her promises about restoring the economy, I should make a tidy profit on the transaction. However, I can't imagine I'd ever want to sell. Come check out the view from the balcony."

"A penthouse on the top of the Destin Yacht Club twelve stories up, I'm impressed."

Stepping through the curtains, Bonnie followed Drew to the rail and stared out at the Destin Harbor and beyond Holiday Isle to the Gulf of Mexico.

Leaning over the balcony with a drink in his hand, Drew said, "I must apologize again for not making Stringfellow's funeral. The President had Bo and me in Argentina and well, I was a little tied up at the time. Even though it was expected, I know it was hard on you."

"That's all right, I understand. It was a lot like Aaron's and I know he would have been honored. It was attended by nearly a thousand academics. I had no idea he was so well respected in his community. He was a brilliant man, Drew."

"I'm glad it turned out that way."

"Oh, Drew, I only wish you could have been with us when we opened the entrance to the Lost City. It defies imagination and I can only begin to describe the treasures hidden there. The gold, jewels, and incredible opulence, all boggles the mind. We spent the first two weeks just sorting and cataloging the find. Even then, that didn't do it justice; Marchant's people from the Louvre took over for us when Professor Stringfellow became too ill, and are still sorting it all out. The Department of Antiquities in Madrid sent a team to secure the area and insure nothing was mishandled or misplaced, if you get my drift. The find is worth more than anyone could imagine. It is truly priceless."

"I read the report and I saw the press conference Stringfellow held that first week. I was pleased to see he gave Eckenstadt his due credit for finding the key to the location. Down deep inside I know he was a good man. I'm sure his health and the rush to find the city caused him to bend his morals. I was sure the commitment he gave me in Spain would be honored.

"Yes, he was a good person. I truly looked up to him my whole life. I was with him when he died and he treated me as the daughter he never had."

"You see, I was a good judge of character after all. Well, now that this little adventure is over what will you be doing?"

"Over? Oh, it's not over, my phone has been ringing off the hook for speaking engagements around the globe the last two weeks. I've had to hire a personal secretary just to manage my calendar. Who would have ever believed I'd be so popular and sought after?"

"Well, you've earned it Bonnie. Say, speaking of popular and sought after, how about the two of us having dinner tonight? I know this great seafood restaurant just down the road."

"Oh, Drew, I'm so sorry, I promised Bo I'd have dinner with him tonight. He's been acting all mysterious and strange. He wanted to insure we were alone, perhaps some other time."

"Bo, I should have known, he's had this thing for you from the beginning."

At that moment, Bo entered the room following his gentle tapping on the entrance.

"Hey, ran those errands I mentioned. Well Bonnie, what do you think of my partner's new pad? A lot plusher than that stuffy golf course townhouse he had. I'm thinking of moving in and taking up permanent residence."

Bo laid a paper on the coffee table and stepped alongside Bonnie at the rail looking over the harbor.

"Where's the Absolut?"

"Over on the bar where you left it, I understand you and the lady have dinner plans for this evening. Was hoping I might join you."

"Sorry Drew, the restaurant is sold out and only could fit the two of us in, maybe some other time."

"Gotcha, okay, guess I'll just stay home and read the report the White House sent over this morning. It's our next assignment, so don't make any plans for the next few weeks without consulting me."

"Assignment, what assignment? You didn't mention any assignment on the phone."

"I haven't sorted it all out yet. From what I've read so far, it seems some nuclear weapons are missing from a military arsenal."

"Nuclear weapons, where are we going, Iran, Pakistan? Come on Drew, let me in on it, will ya?"

"Very well, we're off to Colombia."

About the Author:

C. T. Dowling resides in the small community of Niceville, Florida, located in the panhandle of the sunshine state.
Retired from the IBM Corporation after 31 years in Sales and Marketing, his numerous management positions and assignments, afforded him an opportunity to meet and observe many unique and unusual individuals. With a background in computers and software, he manages to create intricate and absorbing scenarios that most of us would never grasp. Using this talent Dowling has created a series of Drew Wells novels that will be released over the next few years. The series shows the maturing of the characters as their personalities and attitude change. The following is the list of these novels:

Murder on the Country Club Plaza
Terror in Paradise
Secret of the Maya
The Marsupial Virus
The Medallion of the Gods
The Valley of the Geysers
The Lost City of Gold
The Methuselah Caper